Norwich ◉

Ranworth ○

Wicklewood ○

Buckenham ○

Burgh Castle ○

Gorle...

Calster by Norwich ○

Reedham ○

F O L K

Hopton ○

Herringfleet ○

Corton ○

Lowestoft ○

Bungay

Carlton ○
Colville ○

Kirkley ○

Beccles

Pakefield ○

Harleston ○

Sotterly ○

Kessingland ○

Shaddingfield ○

Mendham

Ilketshall ○

Diss ○

South Elmham ○

Covehithe ○

Brome

Rumburgh ○

Brampton ○

Hoxne

Fressingfield ○

Spexhall ○

Wangford ○

Eye ○

Stradbroke ○

Cookley ○

Halesworth ○

Easton Bavents ○

Huntingfield ○

Blyford ○

Bulcamp ○

Southwold ○

Laxfield ○

Wenhaston ○

m ○

Keveningham ○

Blythburgh ○

Walberswick ○

Bramfield

Dingle ○

Darsham ○

DUNWICH

Badingham ○

Yoxford ○

Dennington ○

Brulsyard ○

Sibton ○

Westlern ○

Minsmere

Middleton ○

Kelsale ○

Theberton ○

Framlingham ○

Saxmundham ○

Knodishall ○

Benhall ○

Leiston ○

Sizewell ○

Stowmarket ○

Hacheston ○

Thorpeness ○

Wickham Market ○

Snape ○

Aldeburgh ○

y ○

Tunstall ○

Coddenham ○

Utford ○

Rendlesham ○

Butley ○

Orford ○

K

Woodbridge ○ ○ Sutton Hoo

◉ Ipswich

Bawdsey ○

Chelmondiston ○

Goseford ○

Felixstowe ○

Walton Castle ○

Harwich

NORTH

SEA

C000198168

THE LOST CITY
OF DUNWICH

i

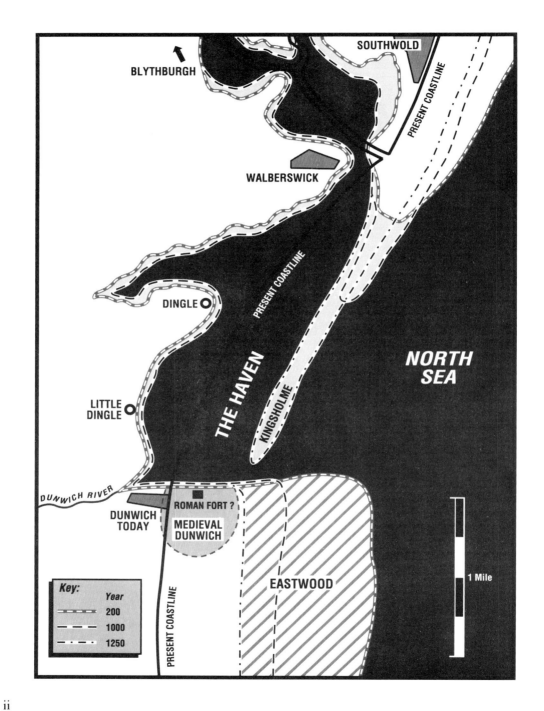

THE LOST CITY
OF DUNWICH

NICHOLAS COMFORT

The Ruins of Carthage, of the Great City of Jerusalem, or of ancient
Rome, are not at all wonderful to me; the Ruins of Nineveh, which are so
entirely sunk, as 'tis doubtful where the City stood; the Ruins of Babylon,
or the great Persepolis, and many Capital Cities, which Time and the
Change of Monarchies have overthrown, the Capital Cities necessarily fell
with them; But for a Private Town, a Sea-Port, and a Town of Commerce,
to Decay, as it were of itself (for we never read of Dunwich being
Plundered, or Ruin'd, by any Disaster, at least not of late years); this I must
confess, seems owing to nothing but the Fate of Things, by which we see
that Towns, Kings, Countries, Families and Persons all have their
Elevations, their Medium, their Declination, and even their Destruction in
the Womb of Time, and the Course of Nature. It is true, this Town is
manifestly decayed by the invasion of the Waters, and as other towns seem
sufferers by the Sea, or the Tide withdrawing from their Ports, such as
Orford, just now named; Winchelsea in Kent, and the like; so this Town is,
as it were, eaten up by the Sea, as above, and the still encroaching Ocean
seems to threaten it with a fatal immersion in a few years more.
Daniel Defoe, A Tour through Great Britain. 1724–26

TERENCE DALTON LIMITED
LAVENHAM, SUFFOLK 1994

Published by
TERENCE DALTON LIMITED

ISBN 0 86138 086 X

Text photoset in 10/11pt Baskerville

Printed in Great Britain at
The Lavenham Press Limited, Lavenham, Suffolk

Contents

Preface

The Fascination of Dunwich

FROM Atlantis to Lyonesse, tales of lands lost to the sea have enthralled peoples of every degree of sophistication. Yet round the coast of Britain many areas once inhabited by man lie submerged. Since the last Ice Age the sea has been rising, with up to six thousand square miles lost since Anglo-Saxon times alone. Hunters once roamed the Dogger Bank, the Scillies have turned from a single island into an archipelago and the Goodwin Sands were swamped in Norman times. Villages and even towns have gone: Saxon Selsey, Old Winchelsea and Hayling; Ravenspur, Aldbrough and Easington in Yorkshire; and in East Anglia, Shipden and Goseford.

By far the greatest was the port of Dunwich, on the Suffolk coast between Aldeburgh and Southwold, which in the early thirteenth century was the sixth greatest town of England. John Stow wrote in 1573:

> The common fame and report of a great number of credable persons is, and hath been for a long time paste; that there hath been in the town of Dunwiche, before any decay came to it, 70 pryshe churches, howses of religion, hospitalls, and chapelles, and other such lyke, and as many wynde milles, and as many toppe scheppes, etc.

Aware that proof was lacking, he added: "Therefore, in this behalf, use yower discretion." A slice of the town remained then, and even today the ruins of a friary and a Norman chapel still stand.

Dunwich's port was doomed from Norman times by a spit that first narrowed the haven, then blocked it, forcing the waters to seek a new outlet. A sliver of woodland still lay between the town and cliffs that had been yielding for centuries. But on the night of New Year's Day, 1287, a fearsome storm blew up and the sea tore into those cliffs, sweeping away houses, shops, churches, orchards, livestock—and people. Dunwich struggled to recover, but in 1328 a second storm swept more of the town away and blocked the haven for good, giving its neighbours better access to the sea. Further blows followed: losses of ships and men in the Hundred Years' War, the Black Death and several disastrous fires. The wealthy began to leave and decline set in, the town shrinking faster than the sea advanced.

Some prosperity returned around 1500, but then the elements struck again, reducing Dunwich to a crumbling anomaly. The legend of a city beneath the waves, where churches stood intact and their bells tolled, grew until a poet could write:

> Oft 'tis said
> The affrighted fisherman a steeple spies
> Below the waves; and oft the mariner,
> Driven by the whirlwind, feels his vessel strike
> Upon the mingled mass.

Local fishermen have never credited the legend of the bells; but they have their own superstitions, a few still claiming to hold the belief that on dying they become seagulls. But visitors' credulity prompted the Victorian bargee John Day to say that a bell from the depths told him when he was off Dunwich. The travel writer Mark Wallington has a less charitable explanation involving the local brew: "If you have had enough Adnams, you can hear them off Southwold as well"[1].

Visitors who gather at low tide in the hope of seeing ruins are not totally misguided: All Saints', the last medieval parish church, succumbed only in 1922; a freak tide to the south can reveal long-submerged tree stumps; and fishermen have brought up masonry from lost churches. In the eighteenth century the sea uncovered foundations of houses and chapels, banks of old watercourses and part of the quay overwhelmed in 1328. The sudden stripping away of lengths of cliff in 1739 and 1904 left groups of brick-lined wells standing on the beach like factory chimneys.

The loss of Dunwich's graveyards has exposed human bones, in the cliff face or fallen to the beach. After the cliff fall of 1904 a journalist wrote[2]:

> From the black earth and yellow sand gaunt bones protruded—not one but dozens . . . I counted a score of fragments of human limbs, there a thigh bone, there a part of a pelvis, and there, perched on a mound of earth and masonry, a broken, toothless skull, the sockets where the eyes had been staring out on the restless waters.

Indeed Alfred Scott Thompson, vicar of Dunwich 1903–33, would inspect the foreshore with his verger after each cliff fall and load the skulls and bones they found into a coffin for interment in St. James' churchyard[3]. Geoffrey Grigson wrote more recently[4]:

> Once I looked down from the graveyard at Dunwich . . . and saw flakes of snow settling on two skulls—husband and wife, do you think? —which had come to a temporary rest halfway down the dribbling clay and sands of the cliff.

The wreckage of medieval brick well shafts scoured from the retreating cliff, 1913. Dunwich Museum

Bones on the beach, though, may equally be from prehistoric oxen that roamed the lands to the east.

Since 1971 divers have been searching offshore for traces of old Dunwich. They did not expect to find buildings intact—most of the town slid over the cliff in ruins—but their enterprise has paid off. Most finds have been mundane: Second World War defences, skulls, and anonymous lumps of stone and masonry from All Saints' Church. But some way out they have recovered a piece of stone of *c*1300 that once bore a brass; part of a fourteenth-century knight's tomb; twelfth-century stonework and a mason's plumb; and parts of a church window. Their leader reckons to have found the debris of St Peter's, where he experienced an "odd feeling"; he also saw what looked like a font, but it vanished before he could bring it ashore.

There is much about Dunwich that we will never know, and much else we may suspect but can never prove. We are thrown back on fragmentary records, historical writings of alarmingly variable accuracy from Bede to the present day, the occasional contemporary description and coins, stonework and pottery. Between them they confirm Dunwich's greatness, though Stow's caution is justified. There were no gates of burnished brass:

Gildengate was named after the Dunwich merchants' guild. Nor could tailors have seen ships in Yarmouth Roads from their windows; they would have had to be several miles out to sea to do that. Nor were there seventy churches. But there was a town, large for its day, that struck its own coins, traded with many nations and had a rich and varied life, boasting up to ten churches and as many other religious foundations. Its first church was probably founded by St Felix around 630 on his arrival to convert the Angles, though its continuity may have been broken by the Vikings.

The Angles' kingdom, first ruled from Rendlesham, near Woodbridge, gave rise to the legend of the holy crowns, retold by M. R. James in *Ghost Stories of an Antiquary*. Three precious crowns were buried then, at Rendlesham, Dunwich and a place still unknown; as long as they were undisturbed, England would be safe from invasion. The Dunwich crown, the story goes, was long ago washed away; the second was identified with a sixty-ounce silver crown dug up at Rendlesham in 1687 but melted down before it could be examined. The third was said by James's characters to have prevented invasion in the First World War.

Beyond the legends lies a true story of a proud community with its roots in antiquity that goes full circle in a way that is almost unequalled. Romans, Angles, saints, barons, corrupt burghers and devious politicians have a place in it, with priests, lepers, fishermen, lords of the manor, pirates, smugglers, the thousands who made Dunwich and the hundred who watch over its shadows. It is to them that its story is dedicated.

Acknowledgements

MANY people over 20 years have helped to prepare this book. On the ground, thanks are due to Mr Stuart Bacon, Dr Ormonde Pickard, the Right Reverend Kenneth Riches, Dunwich Museum, the Dunwich Town Trust and Mr J. D. E. Hollingworth of Southwold who sadly did not live to see it in print. Mrs Katharine Chant, Roger Nicholson, Marion Archibald of the British Museum and Dr W. S. Bevan shared the results of their research and the History of Parliament Trust traced Dunwich's MPs. Gail Lynch typed my first attempt at a manuscript, and many friends and colleagues gave me valuable help and encouragement.

Above all, I am grateful to my wife, Corinne Reed Comfort, for helping me see through a project which at times seemed fated never to come to fruition.

The past revealed: a skull and accompanying bones from All Saints' graveyard revealed in a cliff fall, early 20th century.

EARLY TIMES

Before St Felix   1

THE SITE of Dunwich is based on rock known as Norwich Crag, covered by London Clay. First it lay under the sea; a fossil whale vertebra has been found at Dunwich. Elephant molars discovered near Southwold show that it next became land. Ice Age glaciers deposited sand and gravel known as the Westleton Beds and scoured out the valleys of small rivers feeding a giant waterway combining the Thames and the Rhine. Just before England was separated from the Continent, around 5000 BC, forest-dwellers crossed from Scandinavia; they passed on, leaving no trace in the area.

The Neolithic peoples who followed by sea found more to detain them. Rising waters created a fine sheltered harbour, and around 3000 BC these folk began clearing the surrounding forest. The soil, though easy to dig, was not very fertile and they soon moved on to fresh clearings. This process, continued into the Middle Ages, created the heathland known as the Sandlings, more recently the domain of sheep. The farmers were active until around 1800 BC, leaving the earliest evidence of settlement at Dunwich: flint flakes, scrapers, choppers and a polished axe.

From the time they moved on or merged with later arrivals with bronze implements, the trail runs cold. East Anglia is rich in pre-Roman finds, but not this part. In the late seventh and early sixth centuries BC the coast was raided by warriors with iron weapons from Belgium, but if they vanquished a Bronze Age community at Dunwich we know nothing of it. Around 550 BC the area was settled by the Trinovantes, peasant farmers from southern Holland and central Belgium who may have created the round barrow beside King John's Road, still traceable after centuries of ploughing. The forests inland shielded these people and the Iceni, a sister tribe to the north, from the Marnians, who arrived from the south and the Wash soon after 200 BC. But the Trinovantes were finally matched by the warlike Catuvellauni, a Belgic tribe who arrived around 100 BC, pushing up the coast from the south.

When Julius Caesar landed in 55 BC to intervene on their side, the Trinovantes were still the dominant tribe in the south-east. But when Claudius came in AD 43 he had to oust the Catuvellauni from Colchester, former capital of the Trinovantes, whom the Catuvellauni had reduced to vassals. Claudius took tribute himself from the Trinovantes and from the Iceni, who kept some autonomy. This arrangement lasted eighteen years, until Roman taxmen arrived at the camp of Prasutagas, late King of the Iceni, to collect the Emperor's share of his estate. Met with hostility, they flogged Queen Boudicca and raped her two daughters. The Iceni and the Trinovantes rebelled, and when they were finally crushed, the Romans imposed direct rule; it was to last almost four centuries.

There were almost certainly Romans at Dunwich, on evidence found over the centuries. At Scotts Hall, Minsmere, a coarse earthenware pot over eight inches high was found, containing brass and silver coins too decayed to be identified but apparently Roman; and at Blyford Bridge a statuette of Venus was found. Parts of a Roman scabbard, needles, keys and figurines have come to light at Dunwich, and also tiles, bricks and many fragments of pottery, notably in the friary grounds. In 1858 the Reverend Granville Chester found, five feet from the cliff top:

> numerous pieces of coarse blue, black and brown pottery, some of which were manifestly of Roman manufacture, while other fragments were perhaps Saxon. Of one variety I found fragments lying together, almost enough to form an entire urn. Animal bones with teeth of the ox, sheep and deer were also numerous. In one place I discovered a rounded seam of black earth full of bones, ashes, charred wood, cockle, oyster and whelk shells, with broken fragments of Roman pottery. This apparently was an ancient rubbish pit. I saw an imperfect small brass coin of the Lower Empire which was picked up near this spot.

Dunwich Museum has a fragment from a pair of Roman tweezers, a T-shaped brooch from the first century and a red and blue enamelled disc brooch from the second, a small scale beam and the bottoms of a vase and dish. There are coins of Domitian (AD 81–96), Tetricius II (270–73), Constantine the Great (306–38) and Valens (364–78).

The Romans' road pattern suggests that Dunwich was not just a tribal centre, and may have been known as Sitomagus. They set up a regional centre at Venta Icenorum (Caistor by Norwich), connecting it first to Colchester and London, then to other towns and forts, by straight, well-made roads—three of which peter out pointing towards Dunwich. One, running south-east from Bungay to Blyford, is on a direct line from Caistor. The others divided eight miles inland, one running north-west, the other south-west, to join the direct Caistor–Colchester road at Coddenham, a major Roman settlement. Dunwich is the one obvious destination for

Romano-British brooch in red and blue enamel from the 2nd century, now in Dunwich Museum.
Russell Edwards

these roads; archaeologists cannot explain why they come to a dead stop but guess that as the final miles to the coast lay over sandy heath there was no need for a roadbed.

Sitomagus appears in the Antonine Itinerary, a list, produced between the late second and early fourth centuries, of the Empire's major roads and some 110 settlements along them. Route IX in the British section, from Caistor to London, includes the entry "From Venta Icenorum, to Sitomagus 32 miles. To Combretovium 22 miles. To Ansa 15. To Camuldonum 6." A medieval copy gives the name as Sinomagus, more plausible maybe given the roots "sinus" (bay or inlet) and "magus" (camp). The distance from Caistor to Colchester was given as seventy-five miles (the Roman mile was slightly shorter than ours), but as the crow flies they are only fifty-five miles apart. The thirty-two-mile distance from Caistor accords with a detour via Dunwich; whether the other distances tally depends on where Combretovium was: Coddenham (a little far) or a settlement near Woodbridge (about right). From Combretovium it was fifteen miles to Ansa (Stratford St Mary), then six to

3

Colchester. Sitomagus could also have been well inland, but this possibility has to balance the fact that three Roman roads point straight at Dunwich. Rowland Parker put Sitomagus at Hacheston near Wickham Market, a Roman settlement also thirty-two miles from Caistor. Sitomagus has also been claimed as home of the Sitones, a Belgic tribe, and as a capital of the Trinovantes.

Sitomagus or not, there was some kind of settlement at Dunwich by early Roman times, possibly to seaward of the medieval town. Its relative prosperity came in the second century, owing much to good roads and its anchorage for grain ships from the Continent. There would have been a market, with a limited range of local produce, some imported goods and plenty of fish. The Roman presence might have warranted a pagan temple: Parker, from Thomas Gardner's account of the strange foundations of St Francis' Chapel, suggested it was there.

In the late third century Saxon pirates appeared, a few at first but later in organized packs. The Roman admiral Carasicus let them sack coastal towns, then pounced and kept their loot. Summoned to Rome in 287, he declared himself emperor and stayed to put the coast from the Wash to the Isle of Wight under a "Count of the Saxon Shore", who shared responsibility with the military headquarters at York. A chain of forts was set up, including Burgh Castle, up river from Yarmouth, and the now-lost Walton Castle near Felixstowe. The Saxons were deterred until 342 when they returned in force, bringing the Emperor Constans hurriedly to Britain. A further raid in 367 by Saxons, Picts and Scots killed the Count himself; Rome sent a new commander, Theodosius, with reinforcements. Between fortresses, he added smaller "signal stations", one at Corton, north of Lowestoft. If there was a town at Dunwich, there was almost certainly a fort, either established with the Saxon Shore or later, to fill the gap between Corton and Walton Castle and manned first by Roman legionaries and later by continental *foederati*, barbarians recruited into the imperial army as the supply of Roman troops declined. The Saxons would hardly have ignored such an anchorage for long.

Life became less secure as the raiders grew in numbers and boldness, and Roman forces were ordered back to the Continent to repel barbarians. Coastal forces were withdrawn in 401 to fight Alaric and his Visigoths, and while Constantine III's British army was away in Gaul the Saxons launched a devastating attack. In 417, when the Romans apparently returned for a brief campaign, East Anglia was not reconquered.

Angles and Saxons who had come to plunder were now staying, peasants joining the warriors; we know this from pottery found at Burgh Castle and Caister-on-Sea. The tribesmen brought from the Continent to repel the Angles, among them fellow-Celts to the Britons, were also settling. Some refused to go home; others never had the option. Those at Burgh Castle, from Egypt, Macedonia and Spain, moved south in 407 in a vain attempt to stop Alaric sacking Rome, leaving their British wives and children behind.

Dunwich after the troops left might have housed a few Roman civilians of mixed blood, rather more Britons, some *foederati* who had stayed or dependants of those who had left and a few Angles. If there were a fort, they would have moved into it for safety. Bede described Dunwich as *civitas*, a word he used elsewhere for a former Roman town occupied by squatters—which is just the sort of place Mr Chester's probing of the rubbish-pit in 1858, and pieces of Romano-British pottery found in the town ditch in 1970, suggest it became.

The first recorded name for Dunwich (if not Sitomagus) is Domnoc. It probably derives from the Celtic *dubno* (the Welsh *dwfn*) meaning deep—a port with deep water; in time this was compressed and the old English *wic*, or town, added Domnoc first appears in the Anglo-Saxon Chronicle for 636; in Bede's text *c*730 it was Domnoc or Dommoc; in a charter of 803, Dummucae ("of Dummuca") and in an edition of Bede around 890, Dommocceaster. In Domesday Book it was Doneuuic.

Romano-British pottery found at Dunwich and now in its Museum.
Russell Edwards

The name's likely origin links Dunwich to the legend of King Arthur. Welsh ballads name the birthplace of Medraut or Mordred, a central character, as Dyfnauc—and according to John Morris's authoritative *The Age of Arthur*[5], the only such place in post-Roman Britain was Dunwich. No one can prove that Medraut existed, let alone where he came from, yet the names Medraut and Dyfnauc were passed down together for centuries.

The basic legend is that in the late 530s Arthur and Medraut fell at the Battle of Camlann, which was either the end of organized resistance to the Anglo-Saxon advance, halted at Badon Hill in 499, or the climax of a feud that reopened the way. Welsh triads only written down in the twelfth century make it the result of a quarrel in which Gwenhwyfach (Medraut's wife?) struck Queen Gwenhwyfar (Guinevere), with Medraut and Arthur—nephew and uncle or natural son and father— fighting on opposite sides. In the most elaborate tales Medraut seduced Queen Gwenhwyfar and rebelled against Arthur. He arrived at Arthur's court at Celliwig (which the bards placed in Cornwall), consumed all the food and drink there, and dragged Gwenhwyfar from her throne and struck her. Arthur paid a return visit to Medraut and devoured all put before him.

It is conceivable that once the Romans left, Dunwich became the base of a British chief, who fled before the tide of Anglo-Saxon immigration. Whether his people retreated westward with their fellow-Celts would depend on how far the Angles had been assimilated and whether Dunwich had been fought over. More Romano-British communities were destroyed in East Anglia than anywhere else; maybe that at Dunwich was one.

The eruption of peoples from eastern Europe as Rome lost its grip was due to a population explosion just as other tribes were pressing out of Asia. The Franks had taken Gaul, so the Germanic tribes who followed looked further north. Legend has the Angles and Saxons being invited to Britain before 450 by the Celtic king Vortigern, who later realized he had made a mistake. The Angles, from Schleswig on the German/Danish border, poured in up Fenland rivers and via the Suffolk coast; by 500 they had settled in strength. At the time of Camlann the push westward resumed, prompted by a new wave of settlers who arrived in Kent, then sailed to the estuaries of Suffolk. Their rulers, from the royal house of Uppsala, became known as the Wuffingas after Wuffa (or Uffa), the son of Wehha, who apparently brought them to Britain. Wuffa, who reigned about 550, took control over the whole region, and under Redwald—who was ruling by the turn of the century— the East Anglian kingdom reached its zenith.

Redwald, who claimed to be eighth in line of descent from Odin, was acknowledged as Bretwalda—the pre-eminent English king—after defeating the Northumbrians in 616. Yet his kingdom's power was primarily economic, stemming from its high population and trade with the Continent, Byzantium and Egypt—much of it probably through Dunwich, which is known to have prospered through the Rhineland wool trade at this time. It may also have benefited from the trade in slaves—Celts and Angles—that had prompted Pope Gregory to send St Augustine on his mission. And Dunwich fishermen must have been exploiting the rich seasonal herring shoals and the ever-present flat-fish, cod and sprats.

The discovery of the Sutton Hoo ship burial in 1939 near Redwald's hall at Rendlesham vividly confirmed the Wuffingas' influence. The treasure was interred before 650 to honour an exceptional leader—very probably Redwald, who died in 627. By a large dish with the mark of the Emperor Anastasius (491–518) was a pair of silver spoons inscribed "Saulos" and "Paulos", maybe a baptismal gift from a pope. Redwald was baptized in Kent during Augustine's mission and went home intending to practise Christianity. But, according to Bede, his wife objected, so he compromised, building one altar to his new-found Saviour and another to offer "blot" to the spirits. Aldwulf, King of East Anglia from 664, remembered seeing the pagan altar as a boy.

Edwin of Northumbria, who had been blessed by the Italian bishop Paulinus while an exile at Redwald's court, converted his own kingdom and then persuaded Redwald's son and successor Eorpwald to convert the East Angles; before Eorpwald could do so he was assassinated. In 630 Redwald's stepson Sigebert returned from France to claim the throne; according to the Lives of the Saints[6], he had fled there "to secure himself from the insidious practices of his relations". While in exile Sigebert, too, had been converted, by a monk named Felix.

A Bishop's Seat   2

THE DUNWICH story really begins with St Felix's arrival in 630 or the year after[7]. A Frank born in Burgundy who followed the regime of the Irish ascetic St Columban, he was invited over by Sigebert, took papal advice on how to conduct his mission and was ordained bishop at Canterbury by Archbishop Honorius. Bede says that Felix[8]

> did not fail in his purpose for, like a good farmer, he reaped a rich harvest of believers. His episcopal see was established at Domnoc, and after ruling the province as its bishop for 17 years, he ended his days there in peace.

It was long assumed that Domnoc was Dunwich, but in 1961 the archaeologist Stuart Rigold published a paper arguing that it was probably Walton Castle. His case was that the Roman fort was already there, that Felixstowe later honoured Felix and that the earliest linking of Domnoc with Dunwich dates only from the fifteenth century. Some writers now asume Walton was the seat; Dr Nikolaus Pevsner wrote that the theory "accords both with early records and with archaeological probability"[9]. Anyone writing about Dunwich clearly has an interest in disputing Rigold's theory, but it must be said that his case is thin. If no one associated Domnoc with Dunwich until much later, there may well have been no need to state the obvious; no documentation exists equating it with Walton or anywhere else. Experts agree that Felixstowe takes its name from the Anglo-Saxon Fylthestow, and there is no record of its existence until 1254. Nor was Walton Castle revered prior to its loss. By contrast it is a small step from Bede's Domnoc to the Duneuuic of the Domesday Book . . . which certainly was Dunwich. The strongest argument against Dunwich is its later indifference to Felix, while a medieval church and priory at Walton—founded c1105 by the notorious Roger Bigod—were dedicated to him.

Felix's first church would have been little more than a shed unless, as Gardner suggested, it was adapted from a pagan temple. The diocese lasted long enough to gain a minster of flint, but there is no word of one. We know more about the school, one of England's first, founded by Felix at Sigebert's behest to emulate those the "most learned and Christian King" saw in France, with teachers from Canterbury. Bede described the school as one where "boys should be instructed in letters"; it probably taught them reading and Latin, and to study the Bible, master the Gregorian

Opposite page:
St Felix: from the north chantry window of Blythburgh Church. From Hamlet Watling's sketch book. Dunwich Museum

chant and work out the date of Easter, an essential with the Church split on the issue. We cannot be sure the school was at Dunwich, though Bede did not imply otherwise. It might have been at Bedrichsworth (Bury St Edmunds) where Sigebert set up his monastery; at Burgh Castle; at Beccles, where some local traditions place it, or at one of Felix's own foundations like Soham Abbey in Cambridgeshire. Some Victorian writers claimed it as the forerunner of Cambridge University—but that was founded by scholars from Oxford 650 years later.

Felix was soon joined by Fursa (or Fursey), son of the Irish King Fintan, former Abbot of Tuam and founder of a monastery at Rathmat. Fursa was famed as a sensational preacher and purveyor of phenomena: Bede told how he had visions of the fires of hell, and how a friend found him in midwinter wearing a thin garment but miraculously sweating, as if it were summer. Oriental holy men today can vary their skin temperature; doctors might suspect a thyroid disorder. Sigebert gave Fursa and his brothers Foillan and Ultan Burgh Castle as a monastery, and there they prayed and fasted while Felix built up the diocese. Felix was a bridge-builder between the Roman and Celtic traditions at a time of strain, while Fursa's head was hallowed in the crypt of Canterbury's Saxon cathedral. If ever a church at Dunwich were dedicated to St Patrick, this would have been a tribute, maybe from Felix, to Fursa's tradition.

In 633 Fursa persuaded Sigebert to become a Benedictine monk, probably at Bury; his cousin Egric became king. Penda, pagan, king of expanding Mercia, looked on in cynical amusement and in 637 launched a devastating attack from the Midlands. The people, chary of Egric's leadership, dragged Sigebert from the monastery, but after four years in the cloister he would carry only a white staff. The East Anglians were routed and Sigebert and Egric slain; Fursa, by now a hermit, had prudently fled to France.

The saintly and practical King Anna now took over. He brought Felix Mercian refugees as converts, among them Penda's grandson Coenwalch, whom he baptized in 643. This baptism, taken as an insult by Penda, is one of the few recorded events in Felix's career. He left no writings and his church had no chronicler; Bede had to rely on his friend Albinus, abbot of St Peter's, Canterbury. Yet one article said to have belonged to Felix, the Red Book of Eye, did survive into recent time. This leather-bound copy of the Gospels with silver fittings was reputedly taken to Eye by monks when their cell at Dunwich, by their tradition the site of Felix's episcopate, was washed away in the early Middle Ages. The book could indeed have been there since Felix's time if Dunwich escaped the attentions of the Vikings, or if it had been well hidden. John Leland, who saw the Red Book soon after commissioners dissolving the monasteries valued it at 20 pence, described it[10] as being in "large Lombardic script". It was used at Eye for the taking of oaths until the early nineteenth century, then vanished. M. R. James probed in vain a rumour that it had been cut up at nearby Brome Hall for game labels.

Another remarkable book has been linked with Felix: a manuscript in the Archbishop Parker collection at Corpus Christi College, Cambridge, of parts of Luke's and John's Gospels. The churches today accept the book as one of several St Gregory sent to St Augustine of Canterbury; in 1982 Pope John Paul II and Archbishop Runcie venerated it in Canterbury Cathedral. Yet some authorities assert that it was of Irish origin and belonged to Felix. If so, it could have come from Fursa, who probably studied with him under Columban in Burgundy.

Felix died at Dunwich, by tradition on 8th March[11] (which became his feast day) in 647. He was buried there too, but monks from Soham dug him up for reinterment there. The twelfth-century *Historia Ramesiensis* implies that they acted soon afterward, but Blomefield's *History of Norfolk* has them doing so two hundred years later for fear of the Danes. They certainly moved him before 869, when the Vikings sacked their abbey, Felix's remains being lost in the rubble. They were rediscovered in the reign of Canute, who approved their removal to Ramsey Abbey, across the Fens to the west. Abbot Athelstan, Alfaric the prior and a party of monks took a boat to Soham, got Felix's remains on board and set off for home. But, wrote Ramsey's chronicler, the monks of Ely, "envying the possession of so great a treasure, took ships with a strong company to strive by superiority of numbers to take away from the weaker the dust they carried off". A miracle rescued the monks of Ramsey; as the boats converged and unmonklike cries rent the air, a dense fog arose and they got their cargo home.

When M. R. James wrote that Felix "failed to impress himself on the imaginations of later generations", he was not being unkind. Of 325 saints with English churches dedicated to them, Felix ranks seventy-seventh with six, including Walton Church and Priory—hence the theory that Walton had been his seat. Felix's evangelism was one of the few successes of the Kentish mission, but no relic of his was kept at Canterbury. Suffolk lore only has him persuading the people to build their churches of flint. A few works of art depicting him are thought to have survived: stained glass at Blythburgh; a painting on a screen at Ranworth, Norfolk, of a bishop giving blessing; and a wall painting at Soham. Medieval Dunwich was a centre for pilgrims, but they were bound for Bury St Edmunds or Walsingham, or over the sea to Compostella; not until 1927 was there a pilgrimage to Dunwich. Yet despite the lack of miracles or colourful tales, Felix is known to this day as the bringer of Christianity to East Anglia. That he was a man of *gravitas* and did not suffer a martyr's death can hardly be held against him.

The Dunwich story for two centuries after Felix's death relies on church records, which suggest a cloistered community surrounded by the happy faithful. Yet the town was far more likely mean and worldly. It lay, assuming it was on its medieval site, on the estuary's sheltered flank with maybe a mile of woodland between it and the sea. Tradition gives it a royal palace, a bishop's palace and a mint—a mint there indeed was later, but any "palaces" will have been simple wood-framed buildings, and the king's home was in any case now at Blythburgh. Dunwich was certainly a commercial centre: trade with the Continent and Scandinavia flourished from the time the Angles secured the coast, and internal trade too was picking up. In Gardner's time three silver coins from this period, one bearing the name Anna, were washed up at Dunwich; more were found along the coast after a freak tide in 1911.

Felix's successor, Thomas of Jarrow, was only the second English-born bishop. Born near Ely, he was trained by Paulinus, now Archbishop of York, and ordained deacon; when Paulinus was expelled from Northumbria on Edwin's death, Thomas returned south to join Felix. He served for five years as bishop, not long enough to groom a successor; on his death in 652 or 653, a Kentish man named Bertgils (Boniface) was consecrated at Canterbury by Archbishop Deusdedit to succeed him.

An earthwork contained the Mercians until 654, when they overran it near Newmarket after what the Anglo-Saxon Chronicle deems treachery by Penda. They swept eastward to engage Anna's forces at Bulcamp, near Blythburgh. Anna was slain, leaving five children, all destined for sainthood, and a weak brother, Aethelhere, who became Panda's vassal. Aethelhere may have fought beside Penda at Bulcamp; certainly they bore arms— and died— together a year later when the Northumbrians defeated him at Winwaed in Yorkshire. East Anglia now passed under the influence of Oswiu of Northumbria.

By 667 the province of Canterbury was in poor shape—partly because of an outbreak of plague—with only one bishop in place out of five, and when the 65-year-old St Theodore became Archbishop he set out to revive it. Bishop Bertgils, whose fate is unknown, proved hard to replace; it was two years before Theodore chose the elderly Bisi and two assistants, Acci (apparently based at Dunwich) and Etta. Bisi attended the Synod of Hertford in 672 which consolidated the English Church under Roman influence, but in Bede's words he was "gravely vexed with sickness". Theodore soon retired him and split the diocese of the East Angles in two.

Dunwich now had a bishop of its own in Acci. He may not have stayed long; there is a tradition that after two years he retired to St Osyth Abbey. Etta, or Baldwin, became Bishop of Elmham—either North Elmham in Norfolk, as logic would suggest, or South Elmham, just in Suffolk, where there are the otherwise inexplicable remains of a peculiar ancient church. The bishops of Dunwich who followed Acci were shadowy figures until Cuthwine (716–31). Bede knew Cuthwine as a collector of manuscripts who had brought from Rome a book depicting the flogging of St Paul, maybe a copy of Arator's History of the Apostles. Cuthwine also owned an Italian manuscript of Sedulius' *Carmen Paschale*; a copy he probably sent to St Boniface, who had left England to become a missionary in Germany, is preserved at Antwerp.

During the eighth century Dunwich thrived as a backwater. The Wuffingas died out and power reverted to Mercia; Offa, who reigned from 757, had such influence that in 787 he persuaded the Pope to found an archbishopric at Lichfield to which Dunwich and five other dioceses were subject for sixteen years. The Bishop from 790 to 798, reckoned the eighth from Acci, was Aelfhun; he attested several of Offa's charters, died at Sudbury and was buried at Dunwich. An anonymous Victorian manuscript in Dunwich Museum says that a stone coffin which split in two when washed from the ruins of St Francis' Chapel in 1740 and was later used in turn as stepping-stones and a pig trough was Aelfhun's. Yet the writer's claim that a chalice lay at the dead man's breast contradicts Gardner's contemporary statement that only old tiles were found.

Aelfhun's successor, Tidferth, is Dunwich's best-documented bishop. Over twenty years he attested a series of charters and regularly attended synods at Chelsea and Clovesho, whose location is unknown. At that of 803, Lichfield lost its archbishop and the Dunwich diocese returned to Canterbury; Tidferth's oath of obedience to Archbishop Ethelheard survives. He also signed a statute from Ethelheard on the liberties of the Church: "Ego Tidfrid, Dummucae civitas episcopus signum crucis subscripsi" ("I, Tidferth, bishop of the town of Dunwich, have ratified this with the sign of the Cross"). Abbots Wulfheard and Lull and the priests Ceolhelm, Cynwulf, Tilberht and Eadberht, no doubt the Dunwich delegates to Clovesho, also signed. Lull was in touch with Alcuin, who as Charlemagne's tutor had exported from York a brief but important cultural revival. Now Abbot of Tours, Alcuin heard from Lull that Tidferth and Alheard, Bishop of Elmham, were men of "good conversation" and "Godly conduct". He wrote wishing them well and asking to be remembered in their churches; he urged them to be active in preaching, and not to join in secular sports.

After Tidferth, last heard of at the Council of Chelsea in 816, came Weremund and, in 825, Wibred. Dunwich's last diocesan bishop was probably Aethilwald, installed in the 860s. His profession of faith to Archbishop Coelnoth survives, as does his conical bronze seal, found two hundred yards from the site of Eye priory by a labourer digging his garden. It was almost lost when his small child threw it on the fire, but a local gentleman, a Mr Fenner, identified it and in 1822 gave it to the British Museum. It is 2¼ inches high, with two tiers of pierced arches, each containing an animal's head, one still with an eye of garnet. The imprint is of a star, the eight points alternatively leaf and flower shaped, and inscribed "+ SIR EDILVVALDI: EP". The best explanation for its discovery at Eye is that monks brought it from Dunwich with the Red Book.

By now East Anglia had thrown off the Mercian yoke for good. Its king, whose name amazingly is not known, made overtures to

Replica of Bishop Aethilwald's seal. Dunwich Museum

14

*The seal of Aethiwald,
Bishop of Dunwich in the
860's which was dug up
in a garden at Eye
almost a thousand years
later. It is now in the
British Museum.*
British Museum

Wessex and in 825 Beornwulf of Mercia launched a pre-emptive attack; he was slain and his army routed. Two years later an avenging force headed by Beornwulf's successor, Ludeca, swept eastwards, only to share his fate.

In 793 a fearsome horde poured from long ships to sack the monastery of Lindisfarne, ending three centuries of peace on the east coast. Regular raids on East Anglia began in 838; at first the Vikings pillaged coastal towns then went home for the winter, but in 865 a great army stayed under Halfdan and Ivar the Boneless. If the Danes sacked Dunwich, as is generally assumed, they must have struck after 866 when it was still the centre of a diocese. It is hard to imagine so tempting a target escaping notice, the more so as Dunwich offered a safe anchorage with only one disadvantage: its river did not lead inland to plunderable cities, as did the Orwell and the Wensum.

In 866 the Nuremberg-born King Edmund bought off the attackers with horses; they rode north to sack York, returning in 869 to devastate monasteries at Ramsey, Soham and Thorney and crush the forces Edmund had assembled. By tradition Edmund held out at Framlingham but was taken prisoner and put to death on 20th November, 869, at Hagelisdun (either Hoxne, Hellesdon near Norwich or Halgeston near Sutton Hoo; one story has him

15

buried in a mound not yet excavated). He was tied to a tree and shot at by archers until his body resembled a pin-cushion, then beheaded. Edmund was immediately hailed as a martyr, as was Bishop Humbert of Elmham, who died with him.

In the ensuing anarchy the Dunwich diocese expired, perhaps being governed from Elmham for a couple of years more. For a time the Church in East Anglia was beset by the Danes and also by a lack of priests, as there was no one to ordain them. But the Vikings' enmity to Christianity was short-lived, even though the conversion of their leader Guthrum in 878 was a condition of his being freed after his defeat by King Alfred. Soon men of Danish descent were helping to rebuild the Church.

Those who think Roman Dunwich may have been downstream of the medieval port see this period as the latest when it could have moved. Devastation could have been so great as to compel rebuilding from scratch; but unless the town was also at risk from the sea, its people would always have settled for the most sheltered point of the estuary. Anyway, Dunwich seems to have done well out of the Danes once the anarchy was over, with trade reviving, in some cases under new management.

Strife between Wessex and the Vikings continued. The nearest sea battle, the rout of a hundred Northumbrian and East Anglian longships in 885, took place thirty miles to the south; maybe Dunwich men and ships took part. On land the action was distant; the decisive battles in 917 were at Colchester and Tempsford, near Huntingdon. When East Anglia's Danes made peace, Wessex imposed its own system of government under an ealdorman with viceregal powers. Dunwich became part of the county of Suffolk and of Blything hundred, based on Blythburgh, which was to last almost a thousand years.

When the Church began to rebuild, East Anglia was without a bishop of its own, being supervised from Hoxne by the bishop of London. In 956 the bishopric of Elmham was revived, but not that of Dunwich; resources were limited, and the town was not centrally sited and may have been devastated by Danish raids. Yet Dunwich may have had special treatment: Blomefield wrote that Theodred, Bishop of Elmham c962, had a palace there as well, but that it was given up before the move to Norwich in 1094. Theodred's "palace" could have been Felix's base and have passed to the monks of Eye when the bishops gave it up.

In 980 fresh waves of Vikings appeared. Their first serious attempt at invasion, in 993, ended in defeat for their fleet at Maldon. They returned victorious in 1004, but had to go home because they had so pillaged East Anglia that they feared they would starve. Ethelred the Unready reacted by expanding Alfred's navy, ordering groups of three hundreds to provide a ship of sixty oars or pay for one. Dunwich must have helped fit out one such ship in 1008, the first of many. Even this fleet, however, could not prevent Thorkell the Tall sailing up the Orwell two years later to rout the English at Thetford in a battle so fierce that Alwyn, Bishop of Elmham, had St Edmund's body taken from Bury to London for safety. In 1012 the Danes under Sweyn were paid £48,000 to go away, but returned the next year; they were still rampaging in 1016 when Edmund Ironside, who was barely holding the kingdom together, died and Sweyn's son succeeded him. Canute turned out to be a man of peace and religion, who approved the reburial of St Felix's remains at Ramsey and made a pilgrimage to St Edmund's reinstated shrine. He also followed Wessex practice by putting a strong man, with the rank of earl, in charge of East Anglia.

By the time Edward the Confessor became king in 1042, Dunwich was showing new signs of prosperity. Yet the town had already had a foretaste of its fate. In 1014 a freak tide struck the Suffolk coast, sweeping inland to drown hundreds. It is a near certainty that Dunwich harbour and low-lying areas round it were overwhelmed, and the storm may also have eaten further into the belt of woodland between the town and the open sea.

Detail of stained glass window in Long Melford Church, depicting St Edmund.

17

COMING OF AGE

Domesday, Prosperity and Siege   3

THE DOMESDAY Book gives a first clear view of Dunwich and also shows that it grew rapidly in the twenty years from the Conquest to the book's compilation in 1086. The Dunwich entry in the "little Domesday Book", which dealt only with East Anglia, reads:

> Edric of Laxfield held Duneuuic T.R.E. [at the time of King Edward] as a manor, and now Robert Malet holds it. Then 2 carucates of land, now one; the sea carried away the other. Then as now one plough on the demesne. Then 12 bordars, now 2. And 24 Franci with 40 acres of land, and they render all customs to this manor. And then 120 burgesses, now 236. And 178 poor men. Then 1 church, now 3; and they render £4 and 10s. And altogether it is worth £50 and 60,000 herrings by way of gift. And T.R.E. it rendered £10. Moreover Robert de Vallibus holds 1 acre of land, worth 8d. And Norman holds 1 acre, worth 2s and 8d. And Godric one acre, worth 8d. And this they hold of Robert Malet. And Gilbert Blund holds of the same Robert four score men [who] render £4 and 6,000 herrings.

In addition Ely Abbey held two carucates of land at Alnet'ne (Parker suggested this was a detached community linked to Westleton and later washed away): "To this manor belong 80 burgesses in Dunwich, and they dwell upon 14 acres."

Under Edward, Dunwich belonged to Edric of Laxfield, who had fallen out with him and for a time been outlawed, forfeiting then regaining all his possessions. At the Conquest, Edric was drawing £10 a year from Dunwich, by far the largest of his 221 Suffolk manors. Not a full borough, it enjoyed a mixture of autonomy, deference to Edric and subservience to the King. Thus thieves caught at Dunwich were tried there but taken to Blythburgh, a royal manor, to be flogged. Their property was forfeit to Edric, but any man who failed to attend the hundred court which passed sentence had to pay a fine to the King.

Dunwich in 1066 probably had just over one thousand inhabitants; Domesday mentions a dozen smallholders (bordars) and 120 burgesses or tax-paying householders. It also had one

Opposite page: *The ruins of St James' chapel, circa 1800. Even today they have a decidedly Continental feel and could well be even earlier than the overall Norman style which predates the leper hospital the chapel served.* Dunwich Museum

19

church; some claim that it was established by St Felix (conceivable) or was dedicated to him (most unlikely)—the truth is that we do not know its identity or origins. Several churches of medieval Dunwich can be ruled out; they were built in a later style (All Saints'), do not appear in diocesan lists until much later (St Peter's) or were dedicated to a saint who had yet to come into favour (St Nicholas'). If Dunwich's pre-Conquest church did survive into the Middle Ages, albeit heavily rebuilt, the favourite would be the centrally sited St John's.

William the Conqueror replaced Edric as lord of Dunwich with William Malet, a comrade from Normandy. He granted all Edric's Suffolk manors to Malet, who built a castle (and founded a market) at Eye, which was central to his lands and easier to fortify than Dunwich. The Normans were reminded of the coast's vulnerability in 1069 when the Danes launched a final attack on it; they were defeated in the Orwell and sailed north, past Dunwich, to besiege Norwich. Also threatened were the people of Dunwich, who soon after threw up the Palesdyke—a town wall of earth topped by a palisade that provided a rudimentary, but at times successful, line of defence.

The Conquest gave a powerful stimulus to Dunwich's commerce, not least through the arrival of twenty-four "Franci" who probably traded with the Continent; up to 1066 Dunwich merchants had been hampered by the need to go to Blythburgh to change money. The Franci—also recorded in Hereford, Shrewsbury, Southampton, Stanstead Abbots, Wallingford and York—need not have been Normans; half of William's five thousand knights were French, Breton, Aquitainian or Flemish, and as many nationalities followed as settlers. Whoever they were, they could have included the forebears of the great trading families of medieval Dunwich. Domesday says nothing more of Dunwich as a trading centre beyond mentioning properties held by other manors, probably as lodgings for visits to market, for sea travellers or for storage. Nor does it mention its market, or its seagoing trade. Yet the strength of its fishing industry is underlined: Dunwich's tribute to its lord exceeded Beccles's sixty thousand herrings and Southwold's twenty-five thousand. One can also deduce that Dunwich's hinterland was, as now, heathy and ill-suited to agriculture; some corn must have grown nearby as there was a watermill close to the town, but sheep and pigs were few.

William Malet had little time to get to know Dunwich. Captured by fighting rebels in the North, he was freed but died soon after, probably in a campaign against Hereward the Wake in 1071. His son Robert came of age in 1076 to become England's sixth greatest manorial lord. Between then and 1083 he endowed the Benedictine priory at Eye, granting it all churches in Dunwich built or under construction, with their tithes and "the schools also of the same town". It is tempting to imagine Felix's school surviving into the eleventh century, but far more likely that a newish foundation existed which Dunwich's Norman lord entrusted to politically "safe" clerics. The priory's charter also ordained a three-day fair at Dunwich; at first linked to St Lawrence's Day in August, it came to be held in November on the feast of St Leonard, to whom a church was dedicated.

By 1086 there were three churches in Dunwich, two newly built; Domesday says they were worth £4 10s a year. St John's, St Martin's, St Bartholomew's or St Michael's could have been standing then. Another contender is St James', whose shell still stands beside its nineteenth-century namesake. It has every appearance of being Norman, and was almost certainly there before the leper hospital whose chapel it became. Sited by the old Leet Hill and possibly a parish church early on, it was left stranded outside the town by the erection of the Palesdyke. Its saint's day came to be marked by a fair; the people must have felt a strong attachment to it.

The building of two new churches in twenty years is one of many signs that Dunwich's growth accelerated under Norman rule. With a population in 1086 estimated between a precise 1,596 and over three thousand depending on household size, it was one of England's ten largest towns or cities, after London (around fifteen thousand inhabitants), Winchester (maybe six thousand), York, Norwich and Lincoln (five thousand), Thetford and Oxford. Dunwich was much the same size as Bristol, Bury St Edmunds, Canterbury, Colchester, Exeter, Wallingford, Gloucester, Chester, Huntingdon, Cambridge and maybe Bedford and Salisbury. It was also paying five times more in taxes and rents than in 1066; the £50 it yielded for Robert Malet (plus sixty-six thousand herrings) put it in tenth place nationally. It was rare for so wealthy a town to have its own lord, or for the King to draw no rent from it. Nor could William control it through royal officers; Robert Malet (like his father before him) was Sheriff of Norfolk and those parts of Suffolk, including Dunwich, outside the authority of the Abbot of Bury St Edmunds.

Since the Conquest the number of burgesses had risen sharply, from 120 to 236 plus eighty attached to the manor of Alnet(er)ne, apparently to ensure the monks of Ely a supply of fish; eighty "men" were also listed, presumably without property. But the number of smallholding cottagers was down from twelve to two. They could have been squeezed out by new building; we know that the town eventually crowded up against the Palesdyke, and eleventh-century pottery found in its ditch suggests there was already pressure. But a more likely culprit is the sea.

Domesday gives the first mention of the erosion of the coast and the sea's rate of advance, stating that two carucates of manorial land in Edward's day had been reduced to one. A carucate was the area a team of oxen could plough, between a hundred and 240 acres; the loss of this much in twenty years, even if well away from the town, must have cast a shadow. Taking a carucate as a hundred acres and assuming that the land lost covered three miles of coast, more than a yard must have gone each year, about the same as today; to remove a carucate of 240 acres along one mile of coast, the sea would have had to advance almost ten yards a year. The eleventh-century coastline seems to have been a mile east of today's cliffs, half a mile beyond the edge of the town. Between lay the last of the Eastwood, the great oak forest, which reputedly still covered twelve square miles; Gardner wrote that William the Conqueror allowed the Rouses of Badingham and other gentry to hunt and hawk in it. According to seventeenth-century antiquaries, Dunwich petitioned William for aid to offset the loss of the forest; it is unlikely that he gave it.

Dunwich's association with the Malets ended abruptly in 1101 on the accession of Henry I. Robert Malet, who had risen to be Great Chamberlain, had backed Henry's brother Robert, Duke of Normandy, and was banished. Dunwich, with its high yield in taxes, was taken by the Crown while the strategic centre of Framlingham went to Roger Bigod, Earl of Norfolk.

The Bigods, until humbled by Edward I, betrayed almost every occupant of the throne. Roger Bigod, who had ranked second to Robert Malet in Suffolk with 117 manors, was now unchallenged and began turning Framlingham into an impregnable fortress. He died in 1107 and his heir, William, was lost with the White Ship in 1120. The next son, Hugh, swore fealty to Stephen in 1135, falsely declaring that Henry I had disowned Matilda, his heir presumptive. Soon after being made Earl of Norfolk in 1140 (the title had not hitherto been hereditary) he deserted Stephen for Matilda, only to switch back and be pardoned. In 1148 Bigod mediated between the King and Theobald, Archbishop of Canterbury, entertaining the prelate, three bishops and a party of knights at Framlingham, which now bristled with fortifications. By Stephen's death in 1154 he had again broken ranks to support Matilda's son, the future Henry II. On his accession, Henry confirmed Hugh's title; he would regret it.

Dunwich, meanwhile, had prospered until it was England's sixth commercial centre after London, York, Norwich, Lincoln and Northampton. During the anarchy, at least, it had a mint. And by 1154, wrote William of Newbury, it was a "town of good note, abounding with much riches and sundry merchandises". This was reflected in the rise of a merchant class who financed several new churches including St Nicholas', its parish superimposed to cover the most opulent quarter. Wealth had its drawbacks—in 1168 Dunwich had to find £138 6s 8d toward the dowry of Henry's daughter Maud on her marriage to Henry the Lion of Saxony, against Ipswich's £50 6s 8d. By this time the fee-farm, the yearly rent paid by the town, had reached its highest: £120 13s 4d and twenty-four thousand herrings, against £10 in 1066 and £50 (though sixty-six thousand herrings) in 1086. When Dunwich passed to Henry I in 1101, he appointed a collector—at first the Bishop of Ely—to make sure the fee-farm reached the Exchequer.

Hugh Bigod coveted this wealth that had eluded his family on Robert Malet's banishment, and his chance came with a revolt capitalizing on disgust at the murder of Thomas a Becket and championing Henry II's second son Henry; its leaders included the King's other sons Richard and John, his wife and the Kings of France and Scotland. Henry's Norman vassals rose, but even with him away quelling them, most barons stayed loyal. On 29th September, 1173, three thousand Flemings under Robert Beaumont, Earl of Leicester, landed at the port of Orwell *en route* to join rebels in the Midlands; Blomefield stated that they first tried to put into Dunwich but were driven off. Once ashore, they looted their way to Framlingham and joined forces with Bigod.

The stage was now set for the first documented siege of Dunwich. The order of events is disputed, but by that most widely accepted, Bigod invested Norwich on his own, taking the town but not the castle, then besieged Dunwich with Leicester in October or November, 1173. Remarkably, we have a full and possibly eye-witness account of the siege, written by Jordan Fantosme, a monk on the secretariat of the Bishop of Winchester. However partisan and embroidered it may be, it is a tale worth telling:

Do you know what news we have heard?
The Earl of Leicester has betrayed us all
He landed in Orwell, no doubt about it,
And has fleeced the land as though it were his.
From there to Dunwich he collected money by force;
All is at his command.
Many a Flemish knight follows him this day
Which later gave the King of England joy.
Earl Hugh Bigod has sent his messengers
And proclaimed to the men of Dunwich that he is their friend
Let them side with the Earl if they want sports and mirth
Or they will all lose their heads.
They answered that they would be fools to take his advice;
Better to sell themselves to their enemies dearly.
Indeed look to the proverbs, wherein it is told:
"He who is guilty of treachery to his lawful lord

Or any offence whereby his lord may suffer wrong
Is certain to reap his just deserts,
But he who loyally serves is held in high repute."
Thus spoke the people of Dunwich of whom you hear me tell.
The Earl of Leicester wished to besiege them,
And swore his customary oath
If the burghers and notables should not surrender to him
Not a man would escape death or injury.
And those who were the chief people answer him:
"Woe be to him with a pennyworth of fear for you,
The good rightful King still lives
Who will full soon bring your campaign to nothing
As long as we live and can stand on our feet
We will not surrender the town for fear of attack."
The Earl of Leicester began to grow angry
And had gallows erected to frighten them,
Then he bids sergeants and squires to arm in haste
He resolves to make every effort to attack the town in strength.
That day saw the burghers, right valiant knights
Issue forth to their ramparts; each knows his business
Some to shoot with bows, others to hurl darts
The strong to help the weak rest frequently;
Within the town there was neither maid nor wife
Who did not carry a stone to the palisade for throwing.
Thus did the people of Dunwich defend themselves
As these verses tell which are here written
And so brave were great and small
That Earl Robert retired completely mocked.
He felt no love for the people of Dunwich—
Neither threats nor trickery had been of use.

So, to the jeers of the townspeople, Leicester, Bigod and their men abandoned the siege. At dawn next day they struck camp and moved off.

Fantosme's narrative is the only record of the siege to survive (in two copies, at Durham Cathedral and the University of Nottingham). It shows a force of some professionalism taken aback at the spirit of a community it thought it could easily cow. Even at short notice, however, Dunwich could offer more than the desperate resistance of civilians, being one of the few towns that still had a general levy, a militia that in most places had fallen out of use. The Dunwich levy, abolished by the Assize of Arms of 1181, must have been called to the ramparts during the siege. It was joined by knights who lived in Dunwich or were there when the gates were bolted, and maybe by Crusaders of the Knights Templar, who were soon to set up a house in the town—the battle would have been meat and drink to them. Yet it must have been touch and go, with men and women hurling missiles and worse from the Palesdyke at the Flemings swarming into the ditch twenty

24

feet below and up the rampart towards them. The Palesdyke did not completely encircle the town, but besiegers were deterred by spiked mounds from scaling the slope from the river. Gardner wrote that the barons built earthworks for the siege at Westleton, but there is no proof that tumuli there date from this period. He also suggested that they broke off the siege because of the impregnability of the town rather than the ferocity of the resistance; yet elsewhere they overcame sturdier fortifications than this earthwork topped by wooden spikes, and the wealth of Dunwich was too tempting to pass up. The Flemings would certainly have welcomed the chance to loot; though their slogan was

> Hop, Hop Wilkyne, Hop Wilkyne,
> England is myn and thyn

their cry in Suffolk was: "We haven't come into this land to stay here but to destroy King Henry, the old warrior, and to have his wool."

The rebels marched west, levelling Haughley Castle near Stowmarket, but justiciar Richard de Lucy caught them near Bury St Edmunds. Incensed by the Flemings' atrocities, his peasant army routed them, inflicting horrible deaths on those they could catch. Leicester was captured but Bigod escaped; he made peace with the King, but Henry felt it wise to demolish the fortifications at Framlingham anyway. After Hugh Bigod's death in 1178, his son Roger rebuilt them in even more threatening form.

Dunwich went on from strength to strength. It soon boasted at least seven churches, a preceptory of the Knights Templars, a Benedictine cell and a hospital, the Maison Dieu. And close by was one of the earliest windmills in England. Traditionally the first recorded was that mentioned in Carlyle's *Past and Present*; it was destroyed in 1191 by an abbot who saw it as a threat to his watermill, but there was one on land owned by the Dunwich Templars. That was mentioned in a document written before 1200, possibly in the late 1180s, and was clearly a novelty then.

The people of Dunwich now began to press for a degree of autonomy, petitioning for the right for the town itself, rather than the sheriff, to collect taxes. Richard I refused, and in 1197 Dunwich's merchants returned the compliment by exporting corn to Flanders, then enemy territory, without a licence. Their punishment was severe: a fine of 1,060 marks (£706 13s 4d), almost six times the fee-farm and comparing with just 200 marks each for Ipswich and Yarmouth and 15 marks for Orford. It must have looked crippling to civic leaders who had only just paid off five years' back rent; however it was quietly written off after twelve years[12].

Good King John 4

EVERY schoolboy knows that King John was weak, stupid, vain, evil and incompetent, the worst monarch to sit on the throne of England. He has even been branded a psychopath. But Dunwich revered him. From the moment he succeeded his brother, a hero throughout Christendom but not here, John favoured the town and its people, who suffered for their loyalty when the baronial wars resumed. The main road north from Dunwich became known as King John's Road though it probably dates back to Roman times; he was credited with founding St James' Hospital before he became King; and as late as 1692 the freedom of the borough was bestowed under the charter of "our late Sovereigne Lord John, long since of happy memory".

John immediately granted Dunwich some of the liberties Richard I had withheld, signing its first charter in Normandy on 29th June, 1199. He may well have visited Dunwich first; he went to Bury St Edmunds in the first month of his reign and could easily have gone on by the road that bears his name. Ipswich celebrated the grant of its first charter at the same time with a week of pageantry and rejoicing; Dunwich too must have had a party to remember. John was not acting out of generosity; because funds were needed for the losing battle for Normandy, towns could buy their freedom by instalments. For its first liberties Dunwich paid 200 marks (£133 6s 8d or slightly more than the fee-farm) plus ten falcons and five hunting horses (gyrfalcons were sent instead). It may also have promised to fit out ships for the King's fleet.

The charter established a borough governed by port-reeves and bailiffs, with the right to collect the fee-farm for the Exchequer. John gave the men of Dunwich the rights to pick twelve of their number to represent it before his justices and to choose a panel of six to fine tax evaders. Freeing the townspeople from a feudal duty to him, he gave them the right to marry whom they wished. And to cut red tape and stimulate trade, they were given the rights to build, buy and sell freely and to try certain minor offences up to and including hamsoken (forcible entry to a house or injury to those inside).

The new borough chose a seal whose square design is worn today as an ornament by women who know nothing of its origins. The motif is a ship of the period with a man aboard holding on to the rigging, steered by an oar near the stern; in the water are four fishes. Around the edge is the inscription: "SIGILL: BURGI: DE: DONEWIZ."—"Seal of the Borough of Dunwich."

Opposite page:
Dunwich's first borough seal, under King John's charter of 1199 and (below) the bailiffs' seal.
Russell Edwards

27

Although Dunwich found the money to buy its first liberties, it was no longer booming. It had fallen behind with the fee-farm in the mid-1190s, implying a slump in trade which the corn exports to Flanders may have been a desperate attempt to remedy. Returns after John introduced a new customs system showed Dunwich's foreign trade for seventeen months from mid-1203 at just £78 11s 3d, barely one thousandth of the total for eastern and south-western ports. In 1206 John cut its fee-farm by £40 to £80 13s 4d, waiving the rental in herrings. Most likely Dunwich was by now experiencing problems with its harbour, with the spit known as Kingsholme, which had for centuries sheltered it, encroaching to obstruct the haven. Dunwich may also have been suffering from a particularly bad outbreak of piracy; this, together with the town's proven loyalty, might explain John's ordering three of his galleys to join the two already stationed there, giving it as many royal ships as London. Problems with the harbour must have been seen as temporary; there was no point in stationing warships where they could not put to sea.

John confirmed Dunwich's privileges when he cut its fee-farm, and on 6th July, 1215, he extended them. His second charter replaced the unwieldy system created in 1199 with a mayor, four bailiffs and a sheriff; the first mayor was John de Valeyns, a merchant venturer and no doubt the town's pre-eminent figure. The charter also speeded justice, authorizing the bailiffs to hear less serious cases. Men could end their obligations to a lord by spending a year and a day in Dunwich, and the townspeople were freed from most of their remaining feudal duties. Crucially, Dunwich merchants gained the right to form a guild, with a hall of its own, and trading rights that they were zealously to defend. Moreover, Dunwich ships were exempted from a wide range of tolls and taxes imposed in other ports; the bailiffs were already collecting a tax of one fifteenth on goods passing through, imposed nationally in 1203; they were overseen in this task by a committee headed by a knight and a priest to ensure fair play.

Just a month before, the barons had forced John to accept Magna Carta. And among the magnates who had their privileges confirmed at Runnymede was Roger Bigod. With Framlingham refortified and the barons restive, he followed form and rebelled. John sent for a force of Flemish mercenaries, put by tradition at forty thousand men with their families but surely not that many, under Hugh of Boves; their fleet sailed from Calais in September, 1215, but a sudden storm tore into it and not a soul survived. The bodies of men, women and even babies in cradles were washed ashore north of Dunwich; those of Hugh and several knights were found near Yarmouth. "The very air was tainted by the stench", wrote a chronicler. "They were left to be devoured by the birds and

beasts of the ocean." John was left at his most exposed, with the Dauphin Louis on his way with seven thousand Frenchmen to join the barons and claim the throne.

John was now in East Anglia; he probably went to Bury; he was due to visit Dunwich and indeed may have done. Such a visit might not have been entirely welcome, the reassuring presence of his army being offset by the need to feed it, the risk of freelance looting and the likelihood of baronial reprisals. The barons, free of the threat of the Flemings, were reducing loyalist strongholds one by one . . . and eventually threatened Dunwich with a second siege. Bigod arrived at the gates with a powerful force and threatened to reduce the town to rubble. The people decided that they stood little

King John's 1215 charter to Dunwich extending the borough's powers of self government and granting it a mayor. Lost for centuries, it came to light in the 1920's in the papers of Sir Kenneth Kemp. Eventually acquired by the Town Trust, it is now in safe keeping at Ipswich. Suffolk County Record Office.

chance, probably on the advice of their new mayor, who may in his youth have helped repel the first siege, and bought Bigod off.

Defiantly, Dunwich backed John during the campaigns of 1216 which culminated in his death at the nadir of his fortunes and the tailing-off of the rebellion as Henry III exerted his authority. John asked twenty-one towns including Dunwich to send ships to the Thames estuary to repel Louis' invasion force, and when he believed it was about to sail from Calais, sent them to engage it. A squall off Dover sank some ships and scattered the rest, and Louis dashed over two days later. John could only watch; his troops were Frenchmen (few Englishmen would rally to him), who would fight the barons but not the dauphin. Louis was greeted wildly in London, and pushed on into East Anglia. The barons embarked on an orgy of pillage, aided by Robert Fitzwalter and William Huntingfield, a justice and former sheriff who had deserted John the year before. At one point Fitzwalter, "laden with inestimable booty and spoils", was ravaging East Anglia; then Huntingfield and his former lord were playing cat-and-mouse through Suffolk and Norfolk, each seeking out the other's property to destroy. Roger Bigod tried to keep his hold on Framlingham, but John's mercenaries, unable to fight Louis, marched straight there and sacked it.

Amid this anarchy, Dunwich came under attack a third time. Rival traditions have Fitzwalter inflicting serious damage in a hit-and-run attack, as he did at Yarmouth, Ipswich and King's Lynn or a baronial force augmented by Frenchmen besieging the town. Whether Dunwich resisted or not, Mayor John de Valeyns, who had already paid off Bigod with money the town could ill afford, now had to find a second ransom. If resistance was even contemplated, he may have had help from Nicholas FitzRobert, recently granted the manor of Westhall for paying the wages of the Dunwich galley crews. The next year Nicholas became keeper of the coast for Norfolk, Suffolk and Essex, a combined judicial, martial and naval office; a well-planned defence of Dunwich, even if not executed, would have advanced his claims to the post.

Matthew Paris wrote that the barons' exactions from Dunwich, Yarmouth and Ipswich "provoked God to anger . . . in that people became ever more troublesome to people, servant against servant, subject against master, low-born against noble, laymen against the religious"[13]. Dunwich men were indeed taking advantage of a breakdown in law and order: during a truce with the French, the galley skippers Robert Woodcock and Vincent of Dunwich seized a cargo of wool and hides from a French merchant, Stephen de Croy, at sea and landed it at Scarborough, also making off with the goods of Roger FitzMichael of Rouen. The King of France protested, but the merchandise was not returned.

Henry III's sixty-year reign marked the final period of Dunwich's greatness. With peace on land and sea once Henry had dispersed the rump of the rebellion against his father, the town attracted wealth, trade and patronage. Yet other centres were beginning to catch up. At the start of the reign Dunwich was assessed at 100 marks (£66 13s 4d) on top of the fee-farm, against £100 for Norwich, 60 marks for Yarmouth, 30 for Ipswich and 15 for Orford; Henry cannot have known how the two ransoms had depleted its coffers. Failure to meet the fee-farm despite the cut made by John was ascribed to bad housekeeping; it was not unusual for towns to fall behind and even for a receiver to be called in. But throughout Henry's reign into that of Edward I, Dunwich was genuinely hard pressed to pay; a decline in trade would have made every target harder to meet. By 1220 Dunwich was more than two years behind, owing £168 15s. Henry ordered Hubert de Burgh, his justiciar, to chase up the debt, making him personally responsible for 100 marks of it. In 1230 Henry confirmed the charter of 1215 and cut the fee-farm payment by a further £20 to £60 13s 4d, also deducting £15 from the Easter's fee-farm payment (the sum was paid in two instalments) in belated recognition of Dunwich's loyalty to his father.

Blockages of the harbour, highly damaging to trade, were now critical as Kingsholme encroached on the haven. Parker deduced that by 1216 inhabitants of low-lying, poorer areas were moving to Blythburgh and Walberswick because of regular floods. In May 1222 Henry granted £200 toward building a dyke; in a begging letter to the wealthy of Suffolk he wrote:

> The tide of the sea has occupied, and occupies from day to day, a great part of our town of Dunwich and the adjacent land, whereby a great loss will result to us and you unless preventive measures are quickly taken.

It seems the town had started work as a matter of urgency and run out of money, and that but for the dyke parts of it would have been lost for good. When Henry confirmed Dunwich's charter, he gave a further £47 10s to "repair the port".

Relief was temporary, as within thirty years Kingsholme blocked the haven altogether. The waters built up in the estuary, bringing further floods, then burst through Kingsholme a couple of miles to the north. The Blyth now flowed straight into the sea and Dunwich's sheltered harbour was at the head of a creek. At first this appeared—to Dunwich at least—an aberration of nature that could be reversed: a new channel was cut close to the town and in 1250 Henry remitted £67 10s in taxes to help pay for the "moving and remaking of the harbour".

Erosion, however, was not yet seen as a threat, as Henry's

charter of 1230 granted a plot on the seaward side of town to the newly formed Friars Minor. As Francis of Assisi had died only four years before and his order had only just spread to England, this was a feather in Dunwich's cap. The town had fewer monastic houses than others of its size, so the friars would also face less competition when they sought alms. The Franciscans duly built their friary, yet were to have to move after the storm of 1287; the king would hardly have granted them a site in obvious danger from the sea, nor would they have built on one.

Henry granted Dunwich further privileges in 1256, empowering it to appoint a coroner and making the bailiffs responsible to the Crown for civil debts and for executing summonses, with the sheriff to act only if they failed to. More important, his charter stipulated that:

> all merchandise and wares both of fish and of other things coming into the port of Dunwich, whether found in ships or without, shall be freely and openly sold and bought by the hands of merchants dealing in this sort of wares without hindrance from any.

Brokers were thus excluded, to protect Dunwich merchants and the monopoly of their guild. Times were getting hard: Dunwich's port and markets were under challenge from Blythburgh, Walberswick and Southwold, a feud with the seamen of Yarmouth led to both towns ignoring a royal call for ships, and a general slump in the fishing industry brought the waiving of the "fortieth" duty on catches landed at Suffolk ports.

Not surprisingly, Dunwich was again falling behind with its taxes. In 1267 the bailiffs failed to answer for the fee-farm and the sheriff seized the town for the King. Three years later, the debt still unpaid, the townspeople set upon two royal tax collectors. It was 1279 before Dunwich made its peace, the newly enthroned Edward I clearing the slate in return for £65 (a little more than the fee-farm) to cover his gifts to local charities. Dunwich also became embroiled in a struggle between Church and Crown over taxation of the clergy. The Norwich diocese was a centre of clerical resistance, and collectors sent by Bishop Middleton harrassed the laity as well. When they tried this in Dunwich late in 1280, the people appealed to the King to stop this "extortion and vexation", and Middleton was ordered to call them off.

Dunwich was now to gain representation in Parliament. The barons, angry at their exclusion from royal councils, rebelled in 1258 under Simon de Montfort; inevitably Roger Bigod, Earl Marshal and fourth Earl of Norfolk, was among them. By his death at Evesham in 1265, de Montfort had sown the seeds of constitutional change by associating the boroughs and shires with his aims. Dunwich was not represented at the initial meeting of what became the House of Commons, but it was one of twenty-seven boroughs invited to a second session in 1268. Sadly, the names of Dunwich's first two MPs are not known.

The Bigods still posed a threat to Dunwich. There are doubts over even the decade in which their final assault took place—it may have come thirty years later—but Parker put it between 1266 and 1270. Roger Bigod with a "multitude of armed men, knights and foot soldiers" blockaded the town while men in ships and barges seized the harbour. They halted trade for six days, carried off "certain of the townsmen" to captivity at Kelsale and took all the jewellery and merchandise they could carry. The people appealed to the King, who ordered Bigod to return what he had taken: not surprisingly he took no notice.

The people of Dunwich later looked back to 1279, when Edward I commuted the fee-farm, as their time of greatest prosperity. Tolls from the "commodious port" enabled them to live almost tax-free. Steps taken to reopen the haven and curb flooding seemed to be succeeding and Dunwich could boast eleven warships, sixteen merchant vessels, twenty Iceland barks and twenty-four fishing boats. Stagnation may have set in; the great benefactions by the wealthy to found churches and religious houses in Dunwich were nearly all made by the early thirteenth century. Yet there was no sign that disaster was imminent and that within a century Dunwich's days of power, wealth and influence would be over—none, that is, save a phenomenon noted by the chronicler of Bury St Edmunds and no doubt looked back on as an omen. In his entry for 1284 he wrote: "At Dunwich on 27th November, from the third hour of the day until the sixth hour, the sea seemed to burn with a flame of a lurid yellow light rather than a clear one." It was soon to do far more than that.

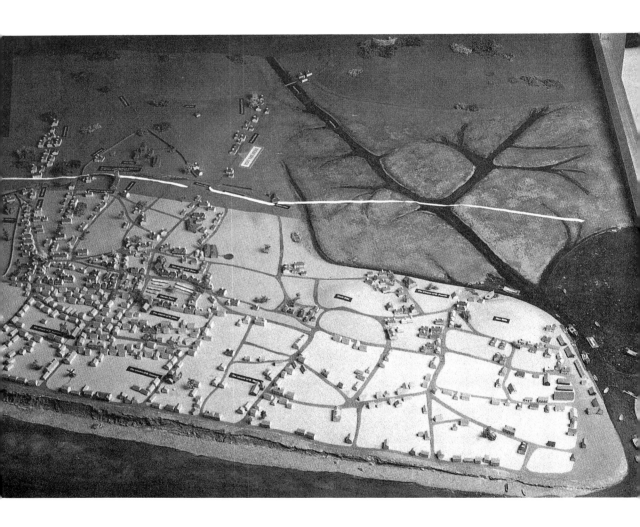

The Town   5

DUNWICH in its thirteenth-century heyday must have been an impressive sight. Travellers approaching by sea picked out first the tallest landmarks—its church towers, the beacon atop Cock Hill and the sails of numerous windmills—next low cliffs topped by a few trees and, beyond, the jumble of the town. Inside the haven, on the lowest ground hard to the left, lay hovels abandoned after persistent flooding; a dyke had been thrown up to protect them but few families had returned. From All Saints' churchyard and Cock Hill, Dunwich sloped unevenly down to the water's edge, with a gap in the Palesdyke where the slope was steepest. Ahead lay the low coast of Dingle, with a beacon on the mound known as the Great Hill. And hard to the right, closer every year, lay Kingsholme, the spit of shingle and pasture between the estuary and the sea joined to the mainland near Southwold, four miles to the north.

Within the port—a term used varyingly for the whole estuary or just the southern half—Dunwich quay, known as the Daine, was the most sheltered point. Ships could tie up there, anchor in the haven or lie at a pier jutting from the opposite bank. To cross the port, Dunwich and Blythburgh each operated a ferry charging ½d for a man and a horse. It is unclear whether the Dunwich ferry plied to Kingsholme or to Walberswick, but the service changed after 1328 when Dunwich was left at the end of an inlet rather than on one side of a lagoon; before long just one boat was crossing the shrinking estuary, usually just south of the latest cut through Kingsholme. The ferry remained lucrative: in 1490 Henry VII granted it to Clement Plumstede, one of the grooms of his chamber. By 1634 travellers from Dunwich to Walberswick had to take two ferries across separate inlets; eventually only that across the Blyth between Walberswick and Southwold was left.

Ships threaded their way to the Daine through a throng of fishing smacks, Iceland barks, merchant ships and naval galleys. Having got ashore past piles of merchandise and huddles of men seeking work or arguing over the price of fish, travellers could look up the narrow, twisting streets toward the market-place. The lower town was looked down on in more ways than one by better-off folk at the top; the resentment (also found in Ipswich) was mutual and seafaring folk at times used force to demand a say in the running of the town, as in 1287 when they prevented the bailiffs' court from sitting.

Opposite page:
Dunwich Museum's model of the town as it must have appeared in its prime. The light area nearest the camera, was lost between 1257 and Agas' map of three centuries later. The portis is on the right. The town is seen from the east. Bridge Gate is at the top of the picture and the main churches and market square to left of centre.

35

Travellers by land first saw the town as they came down King John's Road to cross the Dunwich river at Deering Bridge, until the Second World War a ford with a footbridge. Ahead was St James's Street and beyond it Bridgegate, probably left open most of the time as carts, flocks and travellers passed through. To the left, just before the Palesdyke, lay the Maison Dieu, half-timbered and E-shaped, and beyond it first a creek whose bank sloped steeply up to the town, then the shipyards and finally the Daine. To the right lay the lepers' gate to St James's Hospital and beyond it Leet Hill, where the people met in Anglo-Saxon times. Ahead, on eight small hills, was the town: again the view was of timbered buildings, churches (the front of St Peter's ahead, All Saints' higher up and to the right), windmills and the occasional tree.

Middlegate, a little to the south, was less busy; though Middlegate Street later became a main road into the town, traffic from the south then curved round by Sandy Lane to join St James's Street by the hospital. The approach to Middlegate was less panoramic, with only a glimpse of the port below and to the left; before long the perimeter wall of the rebuilt Greyfriars would almost hide it. All Saints' Church, a little to the left just beyond the Palesdyke, loomed large. Duck Street lay ahead, and to the right stood the Temple, Blackfriars and, behind them, St Nicholas' Church tower. Hard to the right outside the Palesdyke as it curved southward lay the Sea Fields and Co(n)vent Garden.

How many people lived in Dunwich and how large was it? A precise estimate of its population is impossible, but given a likely 1,500 to 3,500 in 1086, a further doubling in two centuries, probably to a little over five thousand, is plausible. Tax records when Dunwich was already in decline list some eight hundred houses, and not all would have been taxed; Stow put Dunwich's area at six hundred to eight hundred acres, and there was clearly more than one house per acre. The town stretched a mile from north to south, and on best estimates was a little over half a mile across. Dunwich should thus have had over five thousand inhabitants even if it contained sizeable open spaces—as it did, sites of up to four acres owned by the wealthy remaining unbuilt-on despite pressure on space. Some buildings, such as the leper hospital (obviously) and the Maison Dieu, lay outside the Pales-dyke, but Dunwich never extended far beyond it, even after 1287 when the western extremity was levelled to link the new Greyfriars with the town.

Within the Palesdyke lay the storehouses, schools, churches, guildhall, mills, gardens, backyards, shops, workshops, alehouses and prison of Dunwich—and the fish smokeries that added a kippery pall to the dank autumn air. The rampart flanked Dunwich to the west and south and to be secure should have skirted the east side as well, though only a sliver of the Eastwood stood between the town and the cliff edge. The circle was certainly broken to the north west; where Hen Hill fell steeply to the port, mounds topped by spikes awaited intruders. There were at least four gates in the Palesdyke. Though a far cry from the mythical portals of burnished brass, they were solid enough; Stow wrote that "all the gatte spaces were howssed over, and stronglye gatted". Apart from Bridgegate and Middlegate, we know of Gildengate (Guilding Gate) and Southgate. The former, built around 1142[14] and later named after the guild established in 1215, lay at the town's south-west corner and led out to the Covent Garden; it fell into disuse in the late Middle Ages. Southgate, washed away in 1570, straddled a lane through woodland toward Minsmere. If the Palesdyke skirted the east of town, there would have been a gate leading out to the Eastwood. After 1287, as the Palesdyke lost its defensive function, a gap was opened north of Middlegate, near All Saints' Church, to let in traffic from King Street which came from Deering Bridge by way of the Leet Hill. This was probably a main route into Dunwich until Norman times, blocked when the Palesdyke was thrown up to keep the number of gates to a minimum.

A visitor in 1590 wrote that "ye chiefest buildings is about the market place". This was the heart of the town, but amazingly no one writing of Dunwich before the square was washed away in the late seventeenth century noted its location; even Agas' map of 1589 does not identify it. We assume that it lay to the east of Duck Street, with St Peter's Church at its south-west corner and to seaward the front of St John's, the town's best-loved church if not its wealthiest. At its centre was the roofed market cross, its sides open so that stalls could be set up; twenty-one regular stallholders paid an annual rent to the borough. In the late fifteenth century traders from Blythburgh and Walberswick objected because mercers and butchers were being asked for 12d a year, drapers 6d and other craftsmen and vendors 4d. The square must have been crowded with townspeople from wealthy merchants to beggars, together with shoppers from nearby villages, traders from all over Suffolk, foreign traders and seamen, buskers in strange attire and mendicant friars. The people's language had evolved into something recognizable as English, and the nobility who rode into town were ceasing to speak French; in the late thirteenth and early fourteenth centuries townsfolk of French origin took English names.

By the mid-thirteenth century the market faced competition from traders who sold imports and fresh fish direct from ships in the harbour in an effort to evade taxes; stallholders later lost business also to markets and fairs staged by religious foundations and manors. Some took the law into their own hands; in 1294 twelve Dunwich men were among a gang that attacked a fair staged at Benhall by Sir Guy Ferre. Dunwich market remained a daily event, Sunday sales attracting a special church tax, possibly as late as the early sixteenth century; by Queen Elizabeth's time it was held only on Saturdays. The market cross was pulled down in 1677 as the sea closed in.

Dunwich had two great fairs. St Leonard's was held from 5th to 7th November in the parish of that name. One of the first recorded in England, it went back at least to Robert Malet's grant of 1075 to the Prior of Eye, who took a percentage and gave 5s to the fee-farm; at the very beginning it was held at St Lawrencetide in August. Disrupted in 1270 and 1285, it apparently lapsed soon after 1334, its site being washed away. The two-day St James' Fair, which may even have been started to replace it, was held in St James' Street, latterly near the hospital, at the end of July. The high point of Dunwich's summer and a chance for games and merrymaking, it degenerated by the early nineteenth century into a drunken romp and an excuse for vandalism. By contrast, the Dunwich herring fair was simply the fish sale conducted from Michaelmas (29th September) to Martinmas (11th November). But given its timing just before the end of the fishery, St Leonard's Fair would have been all the merrier had catches been good.

Medieval Dunwich boasted all manner of shops—tailors, bakers, saddlers, drapers, cobblers, fishmongers, dyers, tanners, ship's chandlers and many more. Even in 1334 there were forty-seven shops in and around the market-place and others throughout the town. By then shopkeepers whose windows faced east could look out over the cliff edge and wonder how long it would be before they had to move—or went out of business as trade declined. There must also have been many inns (at least three in 1334 after the devastation of the quayside area), but none of their names survives.

Radiating from the market-place was a maze of narrow streets, some leading to the Daine or out of town. We know the layout in Tudor times, but little of streets lost before. Duck Street ran eastward from Middlegate, then curved north to seaward of St Peter's. King Street ran due east, crossing Duck Street where it changed course, then seaward across the south of the town. From the King Street/Duck Street junction the High Road crossed St James's Street, passed to landward of St Peter's, then fell to the Daine by St Francis' Chapel. Midway between St Peter's and the quay it crossed Maison Dieu Lane, which, having run round from Bridgegate below Maison Dieu Hill, struck seaward across the town. St James' Street continued eastward inside Bridgegate to a junction with the High Road at the west end of St Peter's. Scotts

Lane ran from the Palesdyke parallel to King Street on the north flank of All Saints' to join the High Road near its junction with King Street and Duck Street. In the north of the town, Dam Street, down to the port from the original Greyfriars. One street lost early on probably led from the Duck Street/King Street junction to Gildengate, and another from Southgate to the market-place and into the town's north-eastern corner.

The churches and religious houses of medieval Dunwich were built of flint or stone, but most other buildings would have been half-timbered. Brick was not much used until the late fifteenth century, by which time there was little new building. The main secular building, the Town Hall, may well have doubled in Dunwich's great days as the headquarters of its merchants' guild. The borough was governed by an élite of traders, not necessarily the richest, with most burgesses enjoying only an occasional say. The guild, whose aim was to further the interests of its members and protect their monopoly against outsiders, had an effective life of less than two hundred years; after the wealthiest merchants left in the fourteenth century the promotion of trade was left to the corporation, on which the second rank of traders had assumed power. If the Guildhall of 1215 became the Town Hall of later days, the change of name probably dated from then; either way, there must have been a civic building before John established the guild.

At the Town Hall, known for this purpose as the Tollhouse, taxes, dues and market fees were collected, mainly by a "keeper of the town" paid 6s 8d a week. It was at the Town Hall, too, that MPs were elected. On the landward side of the market-place, the building (maybe not the original) was damaged in a riot over a disputed election in 1695, washed into the sea in 1702 and replaced by a "town house" outside Bridgegate, which still stands. The courts, including the assizes held by the king's justices, sat in the Guildhall, which must have resembled its half-timbered counterparts at Aldeburgh and Laxfield.

It would have suited merchants in continental ports to have agents in Dunwich. And to help Dunwich merchants finance their operations, there may well have been Jews in the town, lending for interest as Christians were forbidden to do. Stow hinted at this in citing the existence of the Temple Church "in the Jews' time"; he may just have been noting that it was there in 1290, when Edward I expelled all Jews from England, but it would have been simpler to say that it survived the storm of 1287. Royal records of the Jews mention communities at Bury and Sudbury, but not at Dunwich. After their expulsion, Italian bankers stepped in to provide finance; they, too, could have settled in Dunwich.

The merchants, concentrated in St Nicholas' parish, had the

largest and most ornate houses, each storey overhanging the one below and shutting out sunlight from the narrow, often rubbish-strewn streets. Other fine houses were kept by lords of outlying manors for their visits to town. Next in size and quality came the homes of better-off artisans, often doubling as workplaces. Tucked behind them would have been yards with a few beasts, or tiny gardens. Down the scale were the wood-framed homes of fishermen, seamen and labourers, and the hovels of the poor, little changed from Anglo-Saxon times and huddled on the least appealing sites such as the flood-prone quarter by the harbour. Everyday articles dug up or washed ashore over the centuries give us some idea of how the people lived: an iron latch lifter, bronze and iron keys, jugs and cooking pots, personal seals, lead tokens for the cloth trade, purse frames, buckles, brooches, ear and finger rings, spurs, heraldic pennants and bronze weights for scales, pilgrim badges and English and foreign coins.

Until 1989 there was no proof for the tradition that Dunwich had a mint. Then a hoard of 482 twelfth-century silver coins was

Fine 13th-century Bellarmine jug found at Dunwich and now in Ipswich Museum.
Russell Edwards

dug up at Wicklewood in Norfolk, twenty-seven of them minted at Dunwich in Stephen's reign. Examples inscribed "DUN" or "DUNE" are now in the British Museum; they were struck by moneyers named Hinri, Rogier, Turstein and Walter—men of standing, who were trusted to mint coins when they were needed and when bullion was available. Previously, Stow had come closest to finding proof, writing:

> It is comenly said by credable persons that hath sene dyvers coynes that were coyned in Donwyche, as Mr Hallydaye for one, who once, as he hymself toulde me that he had a grote that had the superscription of the one side of the same grote was Civitas Donwic, and I myself ded ons see a grote about 30 years past that had the like superscripcion; and in lyke case divers other psons have sayd that they have seen the lyke.

The only other coin Dunwich definitely gave rise to is a token issued in 1656.

Dunwich also had schools. The first was set up by Felix, then Robert Malet's grant to Eye Priory mentions the "schools" of the town. A century later, schoolmaster Ralph of Dunwich "was delivered of a swelling of the throat by calling on the name of St Etheldreda". Ralph was not a cleric, though his school may have been attached to a monastic house; joining a religious order was the best chance a child then had of an education, though it did not follow that it got one. By the time lay education caught on, Dunwich could not afford to endow a grammar school, as Ipswich did in the 1460s. Education continued on an *ad hoc* basis; in 1596 a master was hired for inmates of the Maison Dieu and in 1754 Gardner wrote that a gentleman had financed a school for the poor, but it had ceased some time before. The Barne family eventually endowed a village school, but it sadly closed in 1964.

There were also windmills to grind grain brought to the town and to drain the marshes. One of England's first was erected nearby, and others followed, some inside the Palesdyke. Built on mounds for their sails to catch the sea breezes, they were vulnerable to strong winds, the storms of 1287 and 1328 turning several on their backs. All were post mills, the entire structure over a wooden base revolving into the wind and held there by first a rudder and later a fantail; the tower and smock mills now common in East Anglia came later. In 1589 there was still one mill just outside the rampart to the south east of the town and another within it, close to the cliff edge. Most of the drainage mills were on Minsmere Level; one of four smock windpumps erected in the late nineteenth century at Eastbridge is now in the Museum of East Anglian Life at Stowmarket. On the marshes to the north, windpumps gave way to a Victorian pumping engine; the engine house was gutted by fire in 1960.

Coins minted at Dunwich during the reign of Stephen by the moneyers Torstein and Walter. Found at Wicklewood, Norfolk by metal detectors in 1989, they were the first proof of an ancient legend that medieval Dunwich had a mint. British Museum

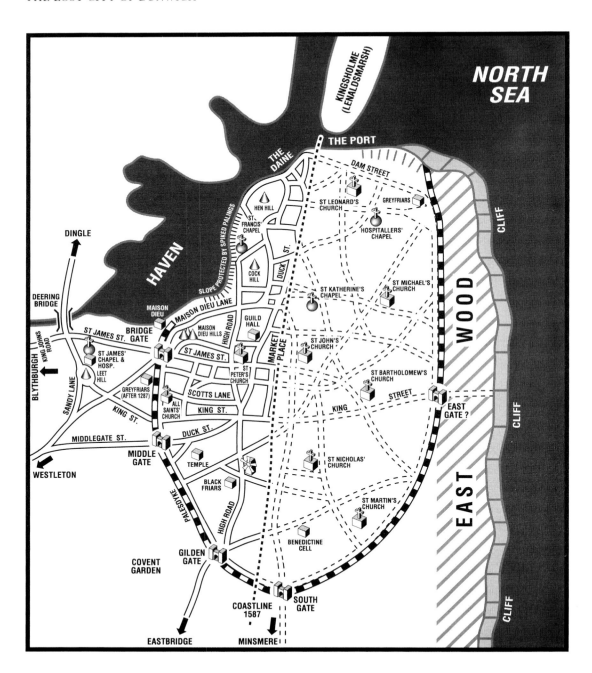

Its People   6

THE FIRST known list of Dunwich folk just predates the Norman Conquest and shows an Anglo-Saxon base, with a touch of Dane. Thirty-two Dunwich men and women were among the benefactors of Blythburgh Priory—including Brictrih, Godwin Oxefoot, Huntman, Arnold the Priest, Safuli, Ulf the Rich, Walter Leadenpenny (a moneyer?), Ulf Canun, Snotyng the Rich, Alwin Blunt, Adwin Kenewald, Godeseald, Dice, Lenene Tod, Godenard, Thiedri and Brithmar son of Gotha[15].

Medieval records often mention ———— of Dunwich. Locally such a person may have been from a particular family that as yet lacked a surname. Robert of Dunwich was fined 5 marks in 1177 for some offence and later moved to Sussex. His son William lost a trial by battle in 1182 against an alleged forger, forfeiting houses in Dunwich with a rent of 6s 10d; he fell foul of the law again in 1197, when his brother Reginald was in trouble too, being fined for "wine sold contrary to assize". In 1202 Reginald was involved in a lawsuit at Ipswich over land at Heveningham; his son Robert FitzReginald was claimed in 1243 to have plundered the Maison Dieu. In 1199 Albert de Dunewic was fined 1 mark for some misdemeanour, the galley skipper Vincent of Dunwich angered the King of France in 1216 by stealing the cargo of a ship from Rouen, John de Donewic was a Dunwich shipowner in the 1220s, Edmund challenged five men to a duel in 1237 and in 1245 Geoffrey de Dunewic helped ferry the King's army to Ireland. John of Dunwich was suspected of murder in 1254 but apparently acquitted.

Peter of Dunwich, maybe son of that John, was sued in 1273 by Roger Cristepeny over land in the town; two years on, he was defending a similar suit from Robert de Pirlon. By 1295 he had charge of Dunwich's coastal defence, with two neighbouring constables under him. The next year, apparently after taking part in the siege of Berwick, Edward I installed him at nearby Yester Castle as escheator for lands north of the Forth, lucratively handling possessions forfeited by "traitors". In 1302 he was empowered to punish south coast towns that failed to send ships to the Scottish war. Nearer home, Peter gathered taxes in Suffolk and became lord of Westleton; he had rights there by 1298 and four years later sued Thomas of Bavent and others for impeding his efforts to revive the manorial court. Knighted by 1303, he also became a king's clerk and prebendary of Old Roxburgh. In 1305

Opposite page: *The churches, streets and rampart of Dunwich at the close of its greatest days in the mid-13th century. The street pattern to the west is confirmed by Agas' map of 1587; east of the then coastline the layout and siting of main buildings is conjectural. Whether the Palesdyke stretched right round to the east of the town is not known, but there was almost certainly an eastern gate.*
Adam Green

43

his brother Richard was aboard a ship (possibly his own) attacked by pirates. Alexander of Dunwich, instituted in 1310, was the first recorded vicar of Walberswick, and another Peter was a Dunwich parish priest from 1331 to 1334.

Away from Dunwich, the tag explained a person's origin. As papal delegate, William of Dunwich judged a dispute involving the monks of Butley Priory in 1205. Another William of Dunwich, a Norwich burgess, and his wife Catherine gave a garden in 1271 to the Dominicans at Dunwich. He was one of four Norwich bailiffs who in 1249 attested the foundation of the Franciscan church of St Helen's, to which he left a meadow by the Wensum; Roger of Dunwich and his wife Alice also gave a plot. Robert de Donewic, also from Norwich and maybe a relative, traded regularly at St Ives Fair in the 1270s. John of Dunwich became Master of Clare Hall, Cambridge, in 1317 and Chancellor of Cambridge University the next year. And Thomas of Dunwich, ordained deacon in 1353, was a Franciscan friar in Cambridge.

Dunwich's premier family were the Valeyns. They probably came over with the Conqueror; Peter de Valeins held six Suffolk manors by Domesday. Others may have been among the "Franci" who settled in Dunwich. James Bird's poem "Dunwich, the Tale of the Splendid City", gives a Walter de Valeins a major part in resisting the siege of 1173, but this is not corroborated. John de Valeyns, as the town's pre-eminent figure, became its first mayor at the end of John's reign when it bought off Roger Bigod only to come under attack from French mercenaries. He was followed by Andreas de Valeyns in 1230–31, Roger (1242 and 1247) and Walter (1260). Augustine de Valeyns, mayor in 1292, was captain of the *Rodeship*, lost in the disastrous Gascon campaign of 1296, reputedly with all hands; in fact he survived to sit in the Lincoln Parliament of 1300 and be buried in Blackfriars. The Valeyns also had links with the Franciscans, helping to find them a new site after the storm of 1287 put their first house at risk[16]. They kept some influence for a century into the town's decline. In 1334 the heirs of Augustine de Valeyns held two plots of land worth 14d in St Martin's parish. Walter, who sat in Parliament in 1338, had land and a shop in St John's worth 3s and a plot in St Peter's assessed at 6d; an Augustine still living paid 40d on property in St Martin's. After this mentions of the Valeyns are few—the Black Death or removal could explain this. Walter de Valence was an MP in 1377, and Sir Robert Valence was buried at Greyfriars. The name lived on in Dunwich for a while; a plot of land in St Martin's parish was known as "Valenes" when sold in 1430.

Not to be confused with them were the Falaises, also merchants of French origin. None was ever mayor, but in the thirteenth century several served as bailiffs. Their influence was

greatest as Dunwich's decline set in, the family providing three MPs: Augustine in 1300, 1310 and 1317; Robert in 1307; and John five times between 1326 and 1333. Augustine received the manor of Westleton from Edward II and John anglicized his surname to Cliff. One son, Augustine, a priest, stayed a Falaise; the other, Peter Cliff, owned the fifty-ton cog *Margaret*, whose travels Parker chronicled from its launch in 1326. John, his wife Beatrice and son Augustine were buried at Greyfriars. Another Robert Cliff sat in Parliament in 1339 and 1341; after that the trail runs cold.

Ruins of the second Greyfriars, from the north. Roger Nicholson

Many Dunwich folk bore the prefix "Fitz" (son of), first as individuals—Robert FitzReginald was the son of Reginald of Dunwich—and then as a surname. The FitzJohns, FitzRoberts and FitzWilliams had most influence, and the FitzRichards were substantial merchants early on.

The FitzJohns spent two centuries as merchants, acquiring houses, land and mills in the town; Richard FitzJohn and his wife Alice were founders of Greyfriars. But they are remembered for their later inability to keep out of trouble; maybe they were as much sinned against as sinning, but Parker, on his study of the records, indicted them for "arrogance and cupidity". In 1258 William (junior) and Augustine FitzJohn killed Edmund and John Brun, successfully pleading self-defence. And in 1266 Roger FitzJohn was accused of murder, but Henry III ordered his release on bail—too late, as he had escaped and been caught and beheaded. Two years later the Sheriff accused William senior, whom he termed an "old devil", of obstructing tax gathering and leading an attack by thirty men on the collectors, who fled to St John's Church.

From the 1240s the FitzJohns were among several families locked in a feud with the Scotts. In 1270 William's son Peter had to prove he was alive after Richard Scott was charged at William's behest with killing him in a Christmas brawl (the man actually slain was Robert Robelin). The next year Peter led a gang to wreck St Leonard's Fair. William and Peter were arraigned for a string of offences, but again the King intervened; they enjoyed the patronage of John de Warenne, Earl of Surrey. On Henry's death Augustine, Richard, Peter, Robert and Michael FitzJohn were arrested and banished. Augustine was back by 1285, when he, too, tried to break up St Leonard's Fair. Richard, now a merchant operating from Dutch ports, was with Michael FitzJohn among thirteen former bailiffs accused in 1289 of pocketing taxes, and in 1296 two of his ships, the *Seynt John Cogge* and the *Welfare*, survived the Gascon expedition. Michael lost his *Rodeship* but, like Augustine Valeyns, did not drown as later records imply; as bailiff in 1293 he made peace with the King to regain the town's privileges, taken away after two royal officials were clapped into gaol. Shortly after Richard FitzJohn died in 1299, one of his ships was seized by Dunwich pirates, whose ranks Peter's son William would soon join. After Henry FitzJohn served as a bailiff in 1319 we hear little more. No FitzJohn ever sat in Parliament; maybe it was just as well.

Reginald FitzRobert was one of two burgesses who in 1198 rendered the Crown five years' back taxes. In 1214 Nicholas FitzRobert supervised the fitting-out of royal galleys; he was granted the manor of Westhall for meeting the crews' unpaid wages. He may well have helped tackle unwelcome baronial visitors the next year. In 1217 Henry III appointed him keeper of the coasts of Suffolk, Norfolk and Essex, a combined military and judicial office, but he could not stop the barons of the Cinque Ports pillaging the 1219 Yarmouth herring fair. That year Laurence FitzRobert, maybe a brother, led resistance to a suit against the town's trading community from the merchants of London; the bailiffs, also including Jocelyn FitzRichard, refused under Dunwich's new charter to answer outside the town. The suit was settled nine years later with the Dunwich traders paying less than one fifth of the sum claimed. Reiner FitzRobert received safe-conduct in

1224 to trade in wine and salt with Poitou; his name suggests that his father had married a girl from a German port. And in 1245 Gerald FitzRobert had a ship wrecked on the King's service near Deganwy.

The FitzWilliams joined the FitzRichards and others in 1216 in a plunderous attack on Walberswick that outraged Margery Cressy, lady of the manor. In 1245 John FitzWilliam, too, had a ship wrecked at Deganwy. Three years later the family was among those taken to law by the Scotts. They then took a low profile until 1330, when Thomas FitzWilliam sat in Parliament. The next year the shipowner Augustine FitzWilliam joined with the mayor and bailiffs in the violent seizure at Southwold of a ship belonging to Anastasia Butt of Walberswick. And in 1339 his ship the *James*, and the *Redcog* in which he had a share, were among six Dunwich ships that plundered the Flemish vessel the *Taret* when ordered to Antwerp by Edward III. Augustine's real claim to fame, though, is as Dunwich's final mayor in 1346. By 1385 the family had followed the Falaises in adopting an English name: Augustine Williamson served in Parliament.

The FitzJoces changed their name to Joce. In 1243 Robert FitzJoce sued for and got his share in a cargo of wool and hides on a ship from Pevensey held in Dunwich harbour. John FitzJoce, with Wiliam FitzJohn, led the attack in 1268 on visiting taxmen, and four years later was accused by Richard Scott of complicity in his son Robert's murder; Alexander and Roger FitzJoce were already in custody. In the early 1280s Ipswich merchants refused to pay £57 to Augustine FitzJoce for wine he had brought them from Gascony in his ship the *All Saints*; recovering the debt entailed heavy legal costs. In 1287 John Joce was among twenty-one mariners and merchants charged with impeding the mayoral court, and another John Jo(y)ce sat in Parliament in 1313.

The FitzAugustines became the Austins. Andrew FitzAugustine was the third owner to lose a ship near Deganwy in 1245. Soon after, they were among merchants sued by the Scotts for restraint of trade. Roger Austin captained the *Margarete* safely through the Gascon tragedy of 1296 and Willliam sat in nine Parliaments from 1300 to 1327, also serving as mayor; in 1304 he presented Dunwich's petition for £500 to make up for harbour dues lost through blockage of its haven. Thomas Austin, who sat in Parliament intermittently from 1331 to 1348, had a shop in the market-place; another William Austin was a Dunwich MP in 1340 and 1343. After the Black Death the name disappears.

The Scotts were the only family with a street named after them—Scotts Lane. They came originally from Scotland, hence the name; there were also Skets who may have been related. Eager to make their mark, Gerard, Luke and Richard Scott fell out with

Dunwich's Anglo-Norman "establishment". In 1248 the King tried at Colchester to settle the dispute; eight years later an assize at Dunwich made no headway and in 1258 Roger Bigod was called in. The Scotts gave up litigation as a bad job; in 1260 Luke and Richard were convicted of seizing a German ship laden with corn, ashes and pitch—it was returned after English ships were held at Hamburg. Perhaps through piracy, they became men of substance; the aged but practical Luke Scott was elected a bailiff after the disaster of 1287. Richard was also a keen huntsman, receiving from Henry III the right of "free-warren" in Dunwich, Minsmere, Westleton and Middleton. By 1264 he held the manor of Minsmere, living at Scotts Hall.

In 1263 Gerard Scott charged Nicholas Percival and others with murdering his son Robert. Parker blamed the FitzJohns, concluding that a feud between them and the Scotts reached its height around 1270 with the murder of Robert Robelin; the FitzJohns backed the prosecution of Richard Scott and twelve others. Richard stood trial in 1272 and was acquitted, having meanwhile been cleared of murdering Peter FitzJohn on the testimony of the alleged victim! Richard also tried and failed to get a third Joce—two were already in prison—convicted of killing Robert. Richard Scott last appears in 1274, losing a lawsuit at Dunwich Assizes over possession of a ship—further proof to him that piracy was the best policy.

Thomas Scott is listed in 1289 as one of the allegedly dishonest former bailiffs, but after this the family mellowed. Warinus Sket sat in three Parliaments between 1310 and 1314, and Matthew Scot in five from 1332 to 1347, appearing in the royal subsidy list for 1327. William Scott, bailiff, died in 1328 when men sent by Sir Edmund Clavering burned down the booth where he was collecting harbour dues. In 1334 Richard Skot owned a conde—a vantage-point for directing the inshore fishing fleet—in St Nicholas' parish. But in 1363 John Scott sold Scotts Hall to the Bedingfields, either to join the exodus or because the Black Death had left him without heirs.

As the Valeyns' influence waned, the originally humble Helmeths became Dunwich's most respected family. Six became mayor, even more than the Valeyns: Peter in 1260, John in 1271, Peter in 1299 and 1318, William in 1328 (the year of the second catastrophe) and Robert in 1342. Merchants though apparently not ship owners, they had the luck to own a prime waterfront site. In 1253 a new cut to replace the haven blocked by the encroaching Kingsholme was made through William Helmet's land; he charged each ship 4d to pass through and 4d for mooring. In 1334 Peter Helmeth (one or several) had property in St John's, St Peter's and St Leonard's parishes worth 4s in all; Nicholas Helmet had a plot assessed at 6d in St Peter's. One Peter Helmeth appears in the records of Dutch merchants who traded with Dunwich from the fourteenth century; another sat in the Parliaments of 1379, 1385 and 1400 and was a bailiff in 1405. They then disappear.

The Codouns were latecomers to Dunwich politics and probably to the guild, though a Constantine Codoun was living there by 1239. Geoffrey and Edmund Codun were among the throng who in 1287 impeded the mayoral court. They gave land to

The gates of Greyfriars still stand, almost the last remains of medieval Dunwich. Through the most can be seen the ruin of the friary itself.
Author

49

help relocate Greyfriars, and in 1302 Edward Codoun served as a bailiff. In 1307 Robert, bailiff four years earlier, sat as an MP; between then and 1451 Codouns represented Dunwich in eighteen Parliaments. Edmund, while never an MP, was a man of substance in the 1320s; Peter held the manor of Westleton Cliffs in 1337 and Richard Codun's *Plentye* was among the ships that attacked the *Taret*. By 1408 Robert Codoun, an MP in 1395, was Dunwich's largest tax payer, with Peter, maybe his brother, close behind; they were seemingly partners trading with the Dutch. Peter, an MP in 1407 and 1410, was probably the Peter Codoun buried in Greyfriars Church. The next generation produced a Robert and a Richard, brothers or cousins. Marriage to Elizabeth Francis in 1430 brought Robert Shaddingfield Hall, the family home for several centuries; he kept his Dunwich connections, serving eight times as bailiff and in 1442 and 1451 as an MP, but his progeny let them lapse. Richard remained, his family's fortunes waning with the town; he owned land at Theberton and sat in the Parliaments of 1431 and 1449. Nicholas Cuddon left his pightle to Greyfriars in 1521, and the subsidy list for 1524 mentions a William Codon. The last Codouns probably left in the mid-sixteenth century.

The mayors who followed John de Valeyns must have been next in importance. Luke Richer, mayor in 1227, was the first of four in his family to hold the office, the last being Augustine in 1330. Stephen Richer held land worth 10d in All Saints' parish in 1334. There had been Odes in Dunwich since at least 1198, when one, probably a merchant or seafarer, was fined £1 in Kent. John Ode was the first of five mayors between 1228 and 1314. Roger Ode had a one-third share in the *Redcog*, which he captained to Gascony in 1337; two years later the ship took part in the attack on the *Taret*. The Russells figure early—William was mayor in 1233 and Thomas in 1247—then vanish until 1426, when Richard Russell built the tower of Walberswick church; he was an MP in 1427 (with his brother Thomas) and 1432. The Barnards provided four mayors, the last in 1332. Some were seagoing merchants; William went down with one of his two ships in passage from Bordeaux to Sandwich. His brother Robert was a royal tax collector. Walter Barnard, twice mayor in the 1320s, had a shop; in 1331 Constantine Barnard was granted a nine feet by six feet pitch in the market and three years later was assessed 21d on sizable premises in St John's parish.

We hear a good deal too of the Paynes, Illes, Boytons, Battings and Cooks. The Paynes were shopkeepers; three served as mayor between 1252 and 1333, the last, John, having an emporium near the market-place. While mayor, he oversaw the attack on Anastasia Butt's ship. William and Edmund Payne were among nine Dunwich men remanded to Ipswich gaol, accused of robbery at

Yarmouth and attacking Flemish merchants. In 1545 John Payne sailed as mate of the *Jamys* on a hazardous winter voyage to Iceland . . . and John Payne of Dunwich was a sponsor of Gardner's history in 1754.

Robert and Richard Ille (brothers or father and son) were traders; Richard was among those accused in 1287 of impeding the mayoral court. In 1324 Augustine Ille was one of fourteen notables held in the town gaol to answer for the death of parson William de Brom; in 1331 he was involved in the seizure of Mrs Butt's ship and in 1337 he sat in Parliament.

Roger Boyton was mayor in 1270, and Constantine one of two bailiffs who supervised construction of a galley for the Gascon expedition; Reginald Boyton captained the *Nicholas*, returning safely. Augustine Boyton was an MP in 1308 and Constantine mayor in 1315. In 1334 Clement and Gerard Boyton had moderate holdings in St Martin's parish.

Eustace Battings was one of the bailiffs of the late 1260s later alleged to have had their hands in the till, and Humfrey Battenge was thrice mayor between 1308 and 1320. In the next generation Augustine Battinge and the heirs of another so-named held property in St Martin's and St John's parishes worth a hefty 69 pence; it included thirteen houses, one with six families.

The Cooks are first heard of in 1235: Reginald Cock commanded one of Dunwich's two royal galleys. John Cock was a Flanders trader and one of the ex-bailiffs accused of cooking the books. Cooks—John, John again, Robert and William—served in six Parliaments between 1311 and 1395; maybe they were ancestors of Clement, Henry and Richard Coke, who sat for Dunwich in the seventeenth century.

Notables buried at Blackfriars included Dame Joan Weyland, sister of an Earl of Suffolk, and her husband John; Sir Ralph Wingfield and Thomas Brewes, son of a Dunwich MP. And among those interred at Greyfriars were Sir Hubert Dernford, Sir Peter Mellis . . . and the heart of Dame Hawise Poynings.

CASTRI ORFORDENSIS IN
ORIENTEM PROSPECTVS.

Low Life 7

A NY PORT is prone to rowdiness and vice, smuggling and piracy. Any commercial centre has its "bad eggs" impatient with honest dealing. And any town contains men who cannot coexist with their neighbours. Dunwich in its heyday was no exception. We can only imagine the farrago of theft, burglary, assault, soliciting and drunkenness that came before the bailiffs; the records of their court went missing in Stuart times. For example, quayside taverns must have figured heavily in its proceedings, but the name of not one survives. Yet we do know how justice was dispensed, and of some major cases heard at Dunwich assizes by the king's justices.

Anglo-Saxon justice was conducted with community business at the court leet on the hill by which St James' Hospital was built. By 1066 the hundred court at Blythburgh had secured the right to summon suspects, those refusing to go being fined. Anyone tried at Dunwich for a capital offence was sent to Blythburgh for sentence, their goods being forfeit to the lord of Dunwich—first Edric, then the Malets. The Saxon system of punishment by compensation was replaced (mainly for Normans) by trial by ordeal, but its county and hundred courts survived almost into Tudor times. Henry II set up a system of visiting justices; the Dunwich assizes, held every couple of years in the Guildhall, heard cases referred by the justiciar on a writ from the King. Thus the Scotts aired their complaints against the Dunwich "establishment" before Henry III; he urged the two sides to settle, but in vain, and eight years later the justices heard the case at Dunwich. They, too, failed and Roger Bigod was brought in to find a solution, again unsuccessfully. The King sent his justices on their rounds as much to raise money (£200 at one Dunwich assize alone) as to enforce the law. Nor was the process always swift—the great lawsuit between London and Dunwich merchants in the early thirteenth century took eleven hearings in various venues to decide.

Much of the courts' time was taken up with commercial disputes and trading offences; in 1197 Reginald of Dunwich was fined £1 for "wine contrary to assize". As commerce grew more sophisticated, they had to deal with tax evasion and various forms of fraud. Yet the most noted embezzlers, the masters of the hospitals, went free; Robert FitzReginald was charged in 1243 with selling items from the Maison Dieu, but he had no right to be there. A line had also to be drawn between theft, genuine disputes over

Opposite page: *Orford Castle, said to have cost fourteen hundred pounds to build in 1165.*

53

ownership and claims arising from merchants laying-off their stake in a vessel or cargo against shipwreck or attack. In 1233, for example, Dionys FitzRalph and his wife were made to pay Richard FitzAlexander 20 marks in respect of a horse he had sold them, a loan he had made to Robert de Cressy, a share he had taken for them in a ship and compensation for damage to it.

John's charters set up the bailiffs' court and modified the Norman system for graver matters. Anyone charged with felony or homicide could demand trial by a jury of twenty-four of his neighbours; trial by battle was limited to the death of a foreigner. At first judicial and civic business was transacted at the same bailiffs' meeting; the court that lower-town dissidents impeded in 1287 would have been one such. But specific courts evolved until Dunwich could boast a court of record, magistrates' court, bailiffs' civil court, Court of Admiralty and coroner's court. Between these and the assizes were first the county and hundred courts and later quarter sessions sitting at Dunwich. After the justices stopped coming at the end of Edward I's reign, serious cases were sent to the next assize within reach. Minor offenders might be put in the stocks, which in 1784 still stood at the seaward end of St James' Street. They bore the legend:

> Fear God and honour the King,
> or else to the stocks I will you bring.

There, with a placard round his neck stating his offence, the miscreant had to sit while neighbours jeered or pelted him with rotten vegetables.

Bailiffs and justices alike could send offenders to the town gaol, in the custody of the borough sheriff (not to be confused with the county sheriff, whose jurisdiction in Dunwich John's charters virtually ended). It probably resembled the sheriff's office in a Western and was not escape-proof, two inmates breaking out in 1290 alone. Dangerous or important prisoners were sent somewhere secure like Orford Castle. The original gaol, probably to seaward of the market-place, was washed away in one of the first great storms; the lock-up used in the late Middle Ages, on the western side of town, succumbed in 1715, after which the shell of Greyfriars was used.

The Dunwich assize and the courts that came after had their fill of sordid crime. All manner of folk appeared, including in 1407 Walter, rector of St John's, who somehow escaped with a fine for rape. They also had to deal with repeated acts of brigandage between Dunwich and its neighbours, mayor John Payne and his bailiffs appearing in the dock after seizing Anastasia Butt's ship and, allegedly, murdering sixteen men.

If a serious crime was not cleared up, the whole town was

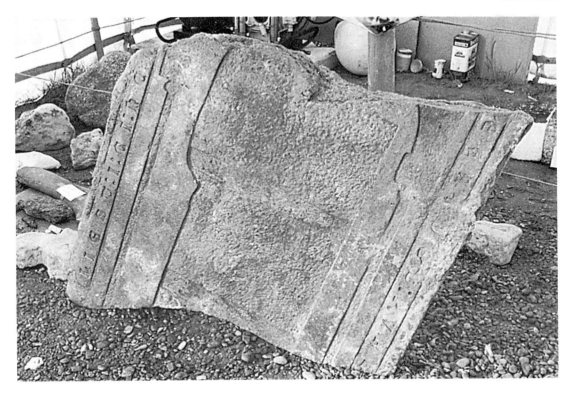

punished: in 1193 the burgesses were fined 40 marks for an unsolved murder. The arrest of several notables after a spate of murders in the thirteenth century probably stemmed not from guilt but from failure to find the culprit. And after the unsolved murder of William de Brom, former vicar of St Peter's, fourteen leading citizens including Augustine Ille and Roger Battisford were clapped in gaol; they were freed around Easter, 1324. Parker suspected Alexander Beccles, who had been sacked as parson of St Nicholas' in 1317 and whose son was among those held. Dunwich was also "amerced" several times, notably for sending corn to Flanders without a licence in 1197. It was also amerced £5 for the escape of William Miller of Hoxne in 1290, when Richard Holbrook, one of the bailiffs, was also fined £5 for letting John of Kelsale go. In 1371 the town was fined for the "escape of felons", then let off.

There is no record of executions in Dunwich; the beheading of Roger FitzJohn after his escape from North Elmham gaol in 1266 probably took place where he was caught. Gilbert de Birlingham was held in Dunwich gaol, then executed in 1272[17], but we do not

Part of the top of a 13th century tomb from one of Dunwich's medieval churches, recovered from the sea by Stuart Bacon's divers in 1979. Segment Publications.

know where. Throughout the Middle Ages the death penalty, save for treason, piracy (on occasion) and, later, heresy was seldom invoked. Moreover, John put a virtual end to trial by battle, which often led to the death of the accused—or the complainant. William of Dunwich resorted to it in 1182 to settle a suit with a forger named Jordan; he lost, but escaped with his life. In 1237 Edmund of Dunwich offered to fight five men or more to settle a grievance, but was denied his wish.

A grisly crime from 1263 is recounted in files, now at Holyrood House, that followed Henry III round his kingdom and fell into Scottish hands[18]. Gerald Scott swore that outside Nicholas Percival's gate in St Leonard's parish, Percival attacked his son Robert:

> with a Cologne sword and gave him a blow on the head five thumbs' length and depth as far as the bone, so that he lived lingering till the night of the Friday and died. Also William de Suthwold . . . assaulted Robert with an Irish hatchet and struck him a blow on the head four thumbs' length and depth to the brain. Also Alexander FitzJoce . . . with a Cologne sword struck him a blow on the head in length four thumbs, also Roger FitzJoce, by striking with a falchion, also Joce Percival for wickedly with Thomas Brodeye and Richard Marre holding Robert while the felony was committed.

Robert Scott did well to live on for five days with such wounds. The case had a sequel in 1272 when Richard Scott tried and failed to implicate John FitzJoce.

At Christmas, 1269, Dunwich was rocked by the murder of Robert Robelin, after which both Richard Scott and Peter FitzJohn (whose family thought he too had been killed and accused Scott) left town in a hurry. Robelin's nephew, backed by the FitzJohns, accused Richard Scott and twelve others. Two years later Scott was tried and acquitted, paying costs of £28 16s 6d; fifteen long years later, Leonard FitzThomas was convicted and imprisoned at Dunwich assizes.

Often in Dunwich's turbulent history, a man in fear of his life sought sanctuary in one of its churches—not that this always prevented bloodshed. In 1258 William and Augustine FitzJohn and Augustine FitzAndrew, going home from William FitzJohn senior's house, were set upon with swords and cudgels by Richard, Edmund, John and Philip Brun. They fled for All Saints' but the Bruns caught them, William and the two Augustines killing Edmund and John Brun; they successfully pleaded self-defence at the assizes. Ten years later taxmen sent in by the county Sheriff after defiance from the same William FitzJohn fled to St John's to escape thirty armed men led by him and John FitzJoce. They were manhandled, injured, pelted with mud and dung, and robbed of documents, three gold rings and money they had collected. The

Sheriff warned that unless the hold of "malicious people" over Dunwich was broken, traders would stay away.

Fugitives most often made for the Temple, where half-a-dozen knights were on hand to deter anyone tempted to force the issue; four outsiders are known to have taken refuge there. The Blackfriars took in Albert of Jena when he landed at Dunwich, pursued by those he had wronged on the Continent. And when John de Oyntur was caught stealing lead from the shell of St Nicholas' Church, he fled to St John's; as a local man, that was probably not enough to save him.

Between the justices' visits, the county sheriff or knights of the shire could be called to enforce their decisions. For example, the twenty-one townsmen claimed in 1287 to have impeded the mayoral court were also said to have sworn to frustrate judgments of the assize and to have misappropriated fines imposed by it. The knights Richard de Boyland and William de Pakenham were empowered to hear the case and remand the guilty to appear before the King.

The neglected ruins of Greyfriars with the also-derelict All Saints' church beyond, around 1848. From Hamlet Watling's sketch book. Dunwich Museum

Neighbours

8

DUNWICH and its neighbours were not always on bad terms. Most of the time they co-existed, helping each other over common problems and trading to mutual advantage. But the proximity of a waning, monopolistic port to covetous neighbours made some conflict inevitable.

The three small villages that ringed the town were usually on good terms with it, often being under the lordship of a wealthy Dunwich figure eager for prestige. Minsmere, a good mile to the south, suffered like Dunwich from the action of the sea. Originally the coastal forest sloped gently to the shore, but the waves ate into ever higher ground until Minsmere, too, sat atop a cliff; by tradition a church there was lost before the Conquest. In Dunwich's heyday, Minsmere was a fishing hamlet controlled by the rumbustious Scott family; the ancient Scotts Hall, a mile inland and later owned by the Vannecks, is more farmhouse than stately home. Minsmere came into its own in the eighteenth century when the coast teemed with smugglers.

Westleton, two and a half miles inland, was always mainly a farming village. The parish and manor took in a length of estuary shore, but its lords never sought control over the port. However, the opening of a market at Westleton brought a complaint from Dunwich in 1304 that dealings there were losing it £10 a year. Edward II was unmoved and legitimized the market; it probably dealt in goods landed at nearby ports which the Dunwich guild felt its members should handle. Not long after, he granted the manor of Westleton to Augustine de la Falaise.

Dingle lies a mile or so north of Dunwich on the former estuary shore; formerly in Westleton, it became part of Dunwich parish in 1982. Great Dingle lies on the tip of firm land across the marshes from Walberswick, and Little Dingle halfway along the track from Dunwich; in Gardner's time each settlement had one house "suitable for a husbandman". Dingle Great Hill and Dingle Little Hill, both at Great Dingle, may have been places of importance; it has been suggested that one was the meeting-place of the Suffolk *thing* (assembly) in late Anglo-Saxon times, and the other of that for Blything hundred. Gardner wrote that on Great Hill there had been a signal station for shipping; it could have been used to direct fishing boats, or to warn of Angles, Vikings or pirates. The Knights Templar had a chapel at Dingle; as there was no church there, it could have served as a "mission" for local

Opposite page:
Blythburgh, from the marshes over which the Blyth still floods at the highest tides.
Russell Edwards

59

people, some of them tenants of the Templars. An ancient stone coffin served as a farm trough at Dingle; did it originate there or was it saved from old Dunwich?

The Dingle headland divided Dunwich's section of estuary, including the original haven, from the northern arm leading to Blythburgh and Walberswick . . . and Southwold beyond. Dunwich's bitterest relations were with them, disputes over the estuary and its commerce leading to armed raids, piracy and murder. The catalyst was the particular force of nature that extended the Kingsholme spit to block Dunwich harbour: the waters forced a new channel that favoured these rivals just as Dunwich itself was first threatened by erosion.

Blythburgh, centre of Blything hundred, had been a place of note since King Anna moved there from Rendlesham. Endowed with a priory, it viewed booming Dunwich in the eleventh and twelfth centuries with a mixture of condescension and jealousy. As Dunwich fell into eclipse, Blythburgh and Walberswick, which came within its manor, were quick to capitalize; each eventually built churches grander than any Dunwich had boasted, Blythburgh's becoming known as "the cathedral of the marshes".

By John's reign there were arguments over Dunwich's claim to tax their traders and over the estuary north of Dingle; boundary disputes as the haven shifted; anger at fortunes being made and lost through the whim of nature; an exodus of flooded-out Dunwich folk to Blythburgh and Walberswick; and sheer cussedness on all sides. In 1216 merchants and common men from Dunwich launched a raid on Walberswick; they set fire to houses, burned the chapel of the manor house (Lady Margery Cressy held the manor, providing one knight to serve the King) and removed an image of St John. Lady Margery sued them for a massive £400 in a church court; they counter-claimed in the civil courts and won. She accused Dunwich of flouting her ancient liberties, including the rights to "wreck" on the landward side of the estuary and to operate a ferry across the Blyth. The bailiffs claimed the right under charter to defend the case in Dunwich, where in 1228 the justices heard it. They ruled that Dunwich could not limit the number of fishing and merchant craft from Blythburgh and Walberswick, provided those of twelve oars or more paid 5s a year toll, and that Lady Margery must not lure Dunwich folk away without royal permission; maybe not only flooding had caused the exodus.

Lady Margery's son Sir Hugh called a meeting at Westleton in 1231 with the justices, Dunwich Corporation and lawyers for the Earl of Gloucester, lord of Southwold, to settle the rights and liberties of each[19]. It agreed that the estuary south of Dingle—with the haven—belonged to Dunwich, which could charge each ship anchoring 4d; the rest came under Blythburgh, whose lord could do likewise. Ships for Blythburgh and Southwold using the haven enjoyed a pre-Conquest right of free passage and Dunwich could not tax them. The next dispute was over the right of wreck at Walberswick. Blythburgh and Southwold each claimed it, but Dunwich, arguing that the proceeds would go to the King, surprisingly won the decision. Emboldened, the burgesses began to hunt at Walberswick; Robert Clavering, who became lord of Blythburgh by marrying the last de Cressy's widow, complained and they were ordered to stop.

Around 1249 the haven was blocked and a new outlet forced to the north; Blythburgh and Walberswick took full advantage. Dunwich gained Henry III's help in reopening the haven and "stopping up a certain port north of Dunwich". Robert Clavering retaliated, adding a market at Walberswick to his legal one at Blythburgh and urging Walberswick fishermen to sell there, paying tolls to him and depriving Dunwich of harbour dues. He was within his rights under the 1231 agreement but did not know it, and no one in Dunwich was going to remind him. In April, 1281, Dunwich men raided Walberswick, carrying off oars, sails, anchors and other booty. Clavering prosecuted them, but the justices held that Dunwich had been distraining for lawful tolls and customs. When the waters burst through decisively near Walberswick in 1287 Dunwich again lost heavily; it petitioned Edward I and he ordered the new haven to be blocked again. Dunwich asked Southwold and Walberswick to help foot the bill, but not surprisingly they refused. Their redoubled efforts to woo shipping from Dunwich led Edward II to decree that all goods or fish brought in by ships based at the quays by the new haven must be sold at Dunwich, on pain of forfeiture. John Howard, sheriff of the county, found the ruling hard to enforce.

In 1328 the elements reopened what was now the natural mouth of the Blyth, blocking the original haven for good. Mariners bound for Dunwich had to sail within hailing distance of Walberswick and Sir Edmund Clavering stationed men in a waterside stockade to intimidate them. Ships reaching Dunwich had to pay harbour dues, collected from the tollhouse on Kingsholme; Sir Edmund, not content with his growing income, sent men to burn it down. They killed William Scott, the bailiff collecting the dues, broke the arms of his helper William de Radenhale and took away three boats, horses and oxen. Clavering went on to overplay his hand, proposing the revocation of Dunwich's liberties in Parliament and being rebuffed.

Dunwich, though weakened, was in no mood to accept humiliation. In 1330 Mayor John Payne led a party to seize a ship on Southwold beach owned by Anastasia Butt of Walberswick, remove the cargo, beat up the crew and scuttle it. By the time the case got to court, sixteen men were alleged to have been killed. (No more is heard of the claim, strangely if it were true.) Dunwich and Blythburgh were now on such bad terms that Edward III complained of almost daily "assemblies of men at arms, burnings, homicides, robberies etc between the men of Dunwich on the one part and John and Edmund Clavering on the other"[20]. The King ordered Dunwich to desist, and summoned Sir Edmund to his council for a rebuke. Yet the feud continued until 1345.

A new lord of Blythburgh, Sir Robert Swillington, annexed Kingsholme in 1381, then challenged Dunwich's claims to tax his tenants. He won exemption for goods brought into the estuary in their own craft, then in 1398 induced them to withhold all tolls from Dunwich. His son Sir Roger was ordered to return "Oldhaven and Kingsholme" to Dunwich, and went to law. He had Blythburgh's charter rights confirmed in 1404, then found a copy of the 1231 agreement and persuaded the King to order a further inquiry. This upheld Blythburgh's right to tax ships in its half of the estuary, but guaranteed Dunwich mariners passage to the sea. Sir Roger had to give up Kingsholme to Dunwich in return for an annual rent of a root of ginger; it was also ruled that there was no such place, parts of the spit being properly named Lenaldsmarsh, Middlemarsh and Churchmarsh[21].

A sixteen-year dispute followed over Dunwich's efforts to tax market traders from Blythburgh, who claimed exemption under ancient charters and would not acknowledge the Dunwich bushel, the taxable measure of salt, corn, malt and other dry goods (the tax was 4d a bushel, paid by the importer). Nor would John Hopton, next lord of Blythburgh, tolerate the presence at Walberswick quay of the Dunwich "meter" to collect 2d on each consignment of salt landed; he made a bushel of his own (larger, no doubt), and employed his own meter.

As Blythburgh, too, went into decline as its channel silted up, competition for diminishing trade became desperate. On 24th March, 1412, Johannes Thomaissone, a Zealand merchant bringing his ship into the haven for Blythburgh, was "impeded and disturbed" by a mob led by Thomas Clerk of Dunwich. Summoned to explain himself, Clerk won a royal pardon; the town was evidently proud of him as it later sent him to Parliament. Blythburgh men were as ready to seize Dunwich-bound ships and unload them at Walberswick. After one such incident Dunwich sent its serjeant to arrest the miscreants, but Hopton ordered his retainers to seize the serjeant's mace for a day to show he was not to be trifled with. He argued that the north side of the latest haven was part of his manor; the matter was resolved in 1451, Henry VI pardoning Hopton and Dunwich dropping its claim to 210 roods of river bank between the haven and the marshes in return for the right to anchor and dry nets there. Boundary disputes continued until the late seventeenth century, when Sir Charles Blois erected a mark on Kingsholme, later known as Sir Charles' Post.

Relations with Southwold deteriorated in the late fourteenth century. Dunwich merchants, seeing a threat to what was left of their trade in Southwold's new market, tried to put it out of business and in 1371 were ordered to leave it alone. Shifts in the coastline led in 1384 to a dispute over rights to one stretch that lasted well into the next century. And in 1408 Henry IV exempted small Southwold craft using the Dunwich river from tolls. In 1490 Southwold, now growing fast, was incorporated by Henry VII; Dunwich put this down to pique at its having backed his enemies in the Wars of the Roses. The next year the Dunwich MP Sir Edmund Jenney managed to secure an uneasy truce between the two towns. A century later, Southwold finally killed Dunwich's hopes of recovery by cutting a new river mouth at the spot best suited to it. Yet their greatest dispute was yet to come: the case of the puncheon of whisky that all but bankrupted Dunwich between 1827 and 1831.

Turning to larger towns further afield, Dunwich had less contact, and trouble, with those to the south. There were few causes for discord with Ipswich, and Aldeburgh had no interest in disputes over control of the haven. There was little friction with Leiston, just five miles away as the crow flies, whose abbey was founded with benefactions from Dunwich. But in Edward I's time its abbot tried to levy tolls on shipping and collect taxes in Middleton, just inland from Westleton, where Dunwich considered it had rights.

Of the increasingly powerful ports to the north, Yarmouth, though more distant, caused more trouble than Lowestoft. In 1233 its bailiffs were ordered to stop harrassing the men of Dunwich and let them enter and leave their port in peace, and in 1254 the two towns' seamen were so absorbed by a dispute that they ignored Henry III's summons to his fleet. Queen Eleanor enforced the order, forbidding them "on pain of their lands, life and limbs from causing any damage or impediment to them by reason of contentions between them". In 1661 Dunwich, Orford, Aldeburgh and Ipswich petitioned that Lowestoft be allowed to fish free of interference from Yarmouth; tension continued until a boundary was set in 1741. Yet they could work together when it suited them, as in 1282 when they fitted out a squadron with Ipswich to combat a serious outbreak of piracy.

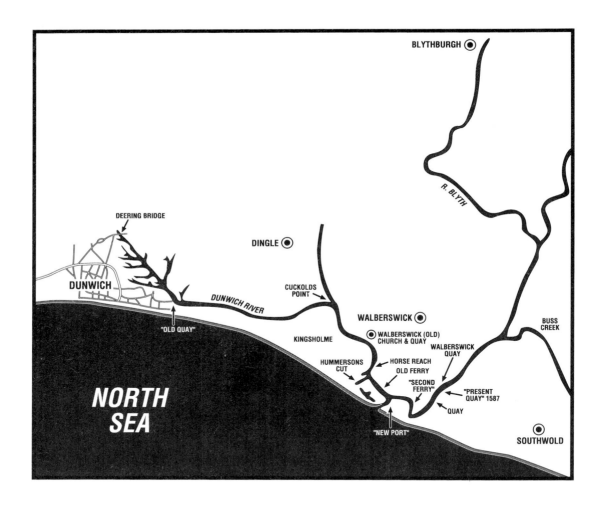

THE PORT OF DUNWICH

Sea Changes   9

DUNWICH'S rise and fall were each products of a process of coastal change that first created a sheltered anchorage, then destroyed it. While the tearing away of the town by the sea was dramatic, the blockage of its harbour, as an indirect result of erosion, was the fatal blow; hence its decline even when land loss was minimal.

The anchorage was formed as the sea rose after the last Ice Age to sever Britain from the Continent. The lower valleys of what are now the Dunwich river and a tributary to its north were flooded, merging off Great Dingle to form an estuary into which flowed the Blyth, round a headland on which Walberswick now stands. At times the Blyth also reached the sea north of Southwold (which was thus an island) along a channel known as Buss Creek.

The sandy cliffs of this coast have always been prone to erosion. The main current off Dunwich runs north and south, held close in by offshore banks; as the southward pull is stronger, sand and shingle dislodged are swept toward Orford Ness, which is still growing. Likewise erosion north of Dunwich caused a spit— Kingsholme—to creep southward across the estuary. At first the spit merely narrowed the haven, but it came to block it altogether after severe storms, the waters within finding a new way to the sea unless man intervened—and eventually even if he did. The rivers slowed, narrowing to little more than streams (the Blyth today is impressive only when its mudflats are flooded). Mud that would once have been washed out to sea stayed in the shrinking estuary, open water gave way to marshes and the haven became too shallow for shipping.

By the late twelfth century, Kingsholme stretched far enough across the haven to obstruct it and flood low-lying areas of the town. The slump in Dunwich's seagoing trade around 1203 and Henry III's readiness to finance a dyke in 1222 suggest that there had been a continuing problem. Around 1249 the haven was blocked outright and a new outlet forced further north. Dunwich, realizing this would benefit Blythburgh and Walberswick, had its channel reopened and the new one stopped up. The efforts of the Dunwich navvies were largely undone on New Year's night, 1287; though not completely blocked, the haven was obstructed enough

Opposite page: The haven in Dunwich's years of decline. Adapted by Adam Green from Ralph Agas' map of 1587, showing the town and haven as they were then, and identifying channels to the sea, ferries and quays that had fallen into disuse before then.

for water driven into the estuary by the storm to burst through near Walberswick. Dunwich again had its channel cleared and its rivals filled in, but from then on, strenuous efforts to keep it navigable were negated by storms and high tides once or twice a year that blocked it with sand, mud and shingle.

The issue was settled on 14th January, 1328. A furious north-east wind not only hurled the sea against the cliffs to tear away more of the town, but choked the haven. The waters inside built up again, causing severe floods when the people could least cope, then broke through Kingsholme two-thirds of the way to the present mouth of the Blyth. Dunwich's stone quay was swamped and a wooden replacement erected; it served for over three centuries until shipping abandoned the dwindling Dunwich river. Its mouth sealed, that river now meandered north through encroaching marshes to the point, close to Walberswick and Southwold, where the now-dominant Blyth cut across Kingsholme.

Repeated efforts were made to open a lasting cut close to the original haven, but in vain (though in 1739 nature briefly turned back the clock). Shipping for Dunwich shared the new channel, and royal influence was enlisted to direct fish and trade back to the town from its brasher rivals. By 1399, however, this haven too was blocked by shingle. A third, closer to Dunwich, was dug—even for the modest-sized ships of the day it must have been quite an undertaking—and lasted until 1464, by when nature had altered its course several times. When it, too was blocked Hummerston's Cut was dug, close to where the waters had broken through in 1328. Its sandbars or "passely-sands" became highly dangerous, and as ships still faced a lengthy, narrow and shallow creek to the quay Dunwich's now modest traffic declined further. Saxton's map of Suffolk, dated 1575, shows the Dunwich river as a mere tributary of the Blyth; Moll's of 1724 omits it altogether.

In 1589 Ralph Agas proposed one more cut to tip the balance back to Dunwich, but on 12th April, 1590, Southwold and Walberswick pre-emptively opened their own near the present mouth of the Blyth. Dunwich spent £300 taking Southwold to court, but to little effect. In 1614, however, the new cut too was blocked, harming all the ports using it. Tobias Gentleman wrote that year that Dunwich harbour was "now almost ruined"[22]; in 1618 Robert Reyce described its river where it joined the Blyth as "a little brooke"[23]. A public subscription for £6,600 was launched in 1619 to revive the haven and its ports; some work was done with modest results, but regular efforts were needed (as today) to keep even the lower reaches of the Blyth navigable. By the 1720s, Defoe could quote the rhyme:

> Swoul [Southwold] and Dunwich and Walberswick,
> All go in at one lousie creek

Such craft as still sailed from Dunwich landed their wares on the shore and, if small enough, were beached there. But as submerged rubble made it dangerous for ships of any size to put in to the beach, most seagoing craft had to berth in the mouth of the Blyth.

Erosion usually takes its toll in a couple of hours each year when waves surge over the beach to attack the cliff—most effectively when the shingle has been scoured away, leaving less-resistant sand. In 1911 the Royal Commission on Coastal Erosion observed:

> It is curious that the erosion ... does not appear to have been continuous, but to have occurred to a serious extent for periods of years followed by times when little change has beenaf13 recorded.

The rate of loss before 1066 is unknown, but according to Domesday anything from one hundred to 240 acres was lost in the next twenty years. We can only guess how consistently the Eastwood shrank in the next two centuries, yet Dunwich's unpreparedness for the cataclysm of 1287 suggests erosion had slowed, with the cliff edge still clear of the town. That storm did not just eat a few yards further into the cliffs; it swept the town's eastern fringe headlong into the sea. The storm of 1328 took a similar toll, and erosion continued until 1385, the sea nearing the perimeter of Blackfriars. There it virtually halted, only resuming in earnest early in the sixteenth century when it closed on St John's Church.

At least 440 yards (1,320 feet) has been lost since the 1580s. At first erosion was slow; the market cross was close to the edge in 1590, yet survived until 1677. It accelerated to sweep away most of Dunwich's remaining landmarks, then slowed again for the late eighteenth century and most of the nineteenth. In 1772 there was 210 feet between All Saints' and the cliff; a century later enough still remained for children to play safely. The pace quickened again: between the 1870s and 1919, when all but the last sliver of All Saints' fell to the shore, the sea advanced a little over 147 feet (the length of the church and a little more). Its churchyard lost thirty-one feet in two years at the turn of the century and Temple Hill (which has gone since the First World War) fifty-five feet; this compares with a total 660 feet (on average five feet a year) lost between 1837 and 1961[24]. The royal commission, which included Rider Haggard, reported that in the sixty-eight years to 1906, Dunwich's 5¼ miles of coast had shed 170 acres. At 2½ acres per year, this accords with the twenty-acre loss in six years cited by Dunwich Corporation in 1831.

The greatest storms have not always been great eroders, as witness the east coast floods of 1953, when tides rose eight feet above normal and hundreds were drowned. J. A. Steers, the

authority on British coastal change, noted that at Dunwich "the cliff was scarcely affected; at its southern end, overlooking Minsmere Level, perhaps a foot or two was eroded away". Noting that more was lost at Covehithe and Easton Bavents, he concluded that "along this coast the sea attacks in a series of bites". It always has; during the rapid erosion of 1902 to 1904, the cliffs either side of the points measured lost even more, while movement at Minsmere was minimal.

Since the storm of 1328 trapped the Dunwich river inside Kingsholme, the coast has retreated almost half a mile, forcing it inland; at times its submerged former course and the piling of old inlets are visible from the cliff top. The successive mouths of the estuary were last exposed in Gardner's time: in 1739, 1746 and 1749

> the shingle and sand were so abluted by the vehemence of the fierce waves of the sea which at these times overflowed the beach, that the foundations of houses, and the banks, on each side of the New Port and Hummerston's Cut were exposed to open view.

The final stretch of the Dunwich river was known as Horse Reach, probably after a ferry that once crossed it; seagoing traffic must effectively have ended by the late seventeenth century.

Gardner wrote that the marshes flooded in his time, more often after a sluice failed in 1743; a windmill was erected to pump the water out. Recently flood tides have again broken through to the marshes, and in 1989 the shingle vanished from Dunwich beach; the sea took six feet from the cliffs near the site of Bridgegate, forcing emergency action to save the Maison Dieu car park and the meadows beyond from flooding. Are Dunwich and Dingle once again to become headlands in an unfriendly sea?

Opposite page: *The decline and fall of All Saints' church; still in use, 1750; after twenty years of neglect, 1776.*
Dunwich Museum

Fisheries 10

FISHERMEN must have put out from Dunwich haven long before Roman times. As they grew more intrepid and demand for fish increased, they graduated from coracles to rowing boats to sailing craft and eventually "busses" with high bow and stern. Dunwich's fishery probably preceded its seagoing commerce, but the two became linked, especially through the Iceland trade.

The shoals of herring that swept down the east coast brought the greatest reward, making Dunwich at the Conquest Suffolk's, and possibly England's, premier fishing port. Its tribute of sixty-six thousand herrings was the largest in a fishery stretching north to Gorleston, compared with sixty thousand from Beccles and Southwold's twenty-five thousand. Ely Abbey probably held its property in Dunwich to secure supplies of herrings; two centuries later it was still guaranteed twenty-four thousand a year. Nor did the local clergy go short; their yearly due totalled 15,377 herrings, the most affluent taking 4,020 and the poorest just 30[25].

The fishery and herring fair ran from Michaelmas (29th September) to Martinmas (11th November). Churches were dedicated to St Michael and St Martin, and the first borough seal depicted a ship and four fishes; the bailiff's seal simply showed a herring. The shoals swam close inshore, clearly visible from the cliff top; from vantage points called conders or condes on Cock Hill, in St Nicholas' parish and possibly at Dingle, men with boughs would direct the boats to them. The catch from a season barely six weeks long had to keep Dunwich through the year: borough accounts for 1287–88, a very difficult time, show £4 16s 3½d spent on beacons and conders. Many Dunwich men no doubt left regular jobs on shore when the shoals appeared.

Fishermen from Walberswick, Blythburgh, Southwold and Easton Bavents had to pay dues to Dunwich: Walberswick's twelve-oared boats paid 6s 8d four times a year, craft from Southwold 4s and from Easton 1s; each fishing boat entering the port paid a further 2s. In time Walberswick was exempted and some other communities stopped paying, but as late as 1606 fishing boats sailing from Dunwich and craft trading to "Westmona, the North Seas, Island and Farra" were ordered to pay 8s every September. When these payments lapsed, Dunwich lost an important part of its income.

Many craft landing herrings had followed the shoals from ports as far away as north-east Scotland. Likewise some Dunwich

Opposite page: *Further decline of All Saints' church; collapse as the cliff edge draws near, 1886; the end draws nigh, 1904.* Dunwich Museum

boats sailed north to intercept the herrings, landing catches in Yorkshire and even Scottish ports. The largest Dunwich ships to take part were the Iceland barks, which returned from their four-month stint in Arctic waters to discharge their haul of cod, then went after herrings.

The herring fair was regulated by the barons of the Cinque Ports so that Dunwich gained full benefit and no one cornered the market. Advance ordering was barred, because if catches were poor this would leave none for open sale or would push up prices; a skipper who sold his catch before tying up at the Daine could be sent to prison. Fish were unloaded by the "pykers" who sold them in the market; theirs was a long day, the fair lasting from sunrise to sunset to give every bidder a chance. Fish were packed in thirty-two gallon barrels, which had to contain one thousand "white" or raw herrings, or halves or quarters. There was a fine of 3s 4d for not packing and salting them to the very bottom; a gauger, packer and searcher received 2d each for checking.

Red herrings (kippers) and sprats, the next most traded fish, were handled by the cade, a reed frame which held them in straw bound with rope yarn. A cade contained six hundred kippers or one thousand red sprats. Defoe was to write:

> Here also, and at Swole, or Southole . . . they cure sprats in the same manner as they do herrings at Yarmouth; that is to say, speaking their own language, they make red sprats, or to speak good English, they make sprats red.

By his time Dunwich kippers were things of the past, and sprats were fished for, as now, from the shore. In 1944 Michael Barne wrote to Ernest Read Cooper: "How I wish I was sprattling and lining from Dunwich beach as of yore, though I can't say I enjoyed the frosty mornings very much, before sunrise." Flatfish and cod too are still taken; a few boats line the shingle near the site of Bridgegate, launched and hauled back over wooden runners or "skeets". But the smokehouses for "making red sprats" are no more.

Dunwich also had a fine eel fishery, hence those sent to King John in return for its liberties. They were caught at sea, but also in the estuary and the marshes that superseded it by the traditional method of "pritching". Blow-holes in the mud give the eel away; the pritch, a spear with five hooks turned inwards and now illegal, is jabbed down hard until the eel is trapped and can be pulled out writhing.

The herring fishery was strongest in the eleventh and twelfth centuries; the first signs of decline were King John's waiving of his tribute in 1206 and the exemption of all Suffolk fishermen from the "fortieth" tax in 1233. Whenever the haven was blocked,

The 20th century sign of the Ship Inn, depicting a typical craft of medieval Dunwich. Russell Edwards

Dunwich fishermen must have launched their boats from the shore and landed their catches there. Herrings long remained a staple of the town's economy; as late as 1463 a Dunwich MP took his salary in fish. And when Yarmouth and later Lowestoft acquired more efficient drifting fleets, the older ports suffered together. The end of the monasteries and the break with Rome depressed demand for fish, but there were local factors too. Blythburgh's fishery was hit not only by the suppression of its priory but by silting of the upper Blyth, while Walberswick, having prospered through the confirmation of its right to land fish at its quay duty-free (a further blow to Dunwich), went into sharp decline in the early seventeenth century. A much reduced herring fishery continued, but the benefit no longer went to Dunwich; by 1621 fish was landed on the

73

beach and transshipped to King's Lynn. A company was formed in 1670 under Charles II's patronage to revive the deep-sea fishery; by then Lowestoft had twenty-five seagoing fishing craft, Pakefield and Kirkley fourteen, Southwold eight, Aldeburgh and Corton two each and Dunwich just one.

Suffolk men fished in Icelandic waters for centuries before the Danes, in 1490, conceded their right to do so. Walberswick was sending thirteen barks by 1151, and Dunwich twenty or so by the late thirteenth century. Survival in such treacherous seas was a tribute to the men and their ships, which as late as the 1530s averaged only fifty tons. St Peter's parish register notes that on 30th July, 1541, four Dunwich men were "buried in ye sea", and in 1536 Robert Kingston had to account to an Admiralty court for leaving six sick crewmen in Iceland. The barks were heavily armed to ward off pirates, but Dunwich men were not blameless; after one crew raided a port in the Orkneys and shanghaied several of its mariners, King James V of Scotland complained to Henry VIII that "the English who go to Iceland for fishing take slaves and plunder".

The barks sailed in March with grain or other cargo to be traded in Icelandic ports for furs and local goods. They went on to fish not just for cod, ling and mackerel but sturgeon and whale. Whaling from a ship smaller than the hunted animal must have been hazardous, but whale oil, like walrus ivory, sold well in Dunwich. In July or early August the ships, their holds full of salted fish, sailed for home to be in time for the herring fishery.

The Iceland fleet expanded during Dunwich's early Tudor revival, though by now much of its catch was taken direct to London. In 1529, thirty-two ships sailed from Dunwich, Southwold, Easton Bavents and Covehithe; in 1533, twenty-two from Dunwich and seven each from Lowestoft and Orwell. The accounts survive of a voyage in 1545–46 by the *Jamys* of Dunwich, with a crew of thirty-one headed by "Sander of Dunwhyche, maister under God, John Payne maister maet, John Foxe the gonner, and Edward Albright, souldier". Its promoter, Sir Thomas Darcy of St Osyth, her master and her "marchant", Jeffrey Smyth, were bold to the point of recklessness: she sailed alone on 1st December into the season when spray freezes on the rigging; even today ships are swamped by huge waves. The *Jamys* took for use or sale forty coombs of wheat, twelve bushels of peas for soup, four thousand biscuits, sixty stone of beef and forty-three "butz of bier"[26]. All bar one were Dunwich men, several having Dutch names; they were a large part of a seagoing population which throughout the sixteenth century never reached two hundred.

Thomas a Berry, who left Dunwich for Walberswick at this time, took the *Mary Walsingham* to Iceland in 1536 with a ton of salt,

4½ hundredweight of wheat, two pipes of beer and two flitches of bacon. For self-defence he trusted less in the grace of God, under which he hired her, than in a cannon, two "sarpentines", four "hackebuses", ten bows, two sheaves of arrows and a firkin of gunpowder. The trade was lucrative (a ship hired for £120 could make £700 profit) and her owner Henry Tooley sent her north at least seven times; in 1532 he sold two thousand dry cod in London for £33 6s 8d, and in 1538 four hundred ling for £18.

The Iceland fleet must have seemed a fixture in 1577 when Frobisher, on his second voyage in search of the North-west Passage, met it and put letters home on board. But the Dunwich contingent was shrinking. As late as 1614 Dunwich, Walberswick and Southwold had over fifty barks between them, but the end came in 1640 when a single Dunwich bark, the *Robert*, sailed for Iceland. A small-scale trade continued through the late seventeenth century from Southwold, Aldeburgh and Lowestoft; it was over by 1785, when a witness to a parliamentary committee blamed its demise on government salt regulations, "millstones around the neck of the fishing trade".

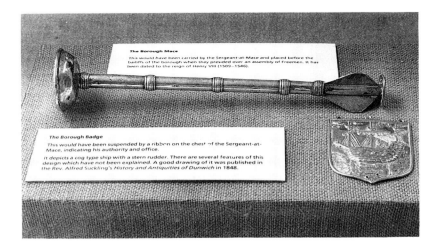

The early Tudor mace with its unusual bolt shape and the borough badge, also of silver.
Dunwich Museum

Seagoing Trade 11

WITH its sheltered anchorage and ready market, Dunwich was a major port for overseas and coasting trade. There was foreign-going trade in Roman times, and by the seventh century Dunwich ships reached Frisia, Sweden, the Rhineland and France. Imports such as pottery and metalware and exports of wool and corn grew steadily, checked only temporarily by the Danes. All newcomers—Romans, Angles, Vikings, Normans—fostered trade with their homelands, and the arrival of the "Franci" after the Conquest was a further boost. The closest ties were with the Low Countries; its ships were regular visitors, men with Dutch names crewed Iceland barks in Tudor times and Dutchmen settled in Dunwich as late as the seventeenth century. Ships came also from Denmark, Germany, France, Scandinavia, Spain and the Mediterranean. (In 1258 a Crusader from Acre sent a cargo, but as it was seized on arrival he may not have done so again.) The many foreign seamen with time on their hands as their ships discharged one cargo and took on another made Dunwich a Babel of accents—and a fairly lively place.

The size of the fine imposed in 1197 for trading with Flanders may have reflected Dunwich's prestige as much as the scale of the offence; Ipswich, Yarmouth and Orford got off comparatively lightly. The non-collection of the fine, and returns for 1203 showing Dunwich's foreign trade at an alarmingly low level, suggest disruption by blockages of the haven. Trade between then and 1287 could have increased despite such problems, levelled off or gone into decline; most likely it expanded, but slowly. Dunwich (the strength thereof was terror and fear) was certainly still the leading Suffolk port, just ahead of Ipswich; an embargo on foreign trade in 1229 applied to them alone.

Dunwich had in 1279 "80 great ships" of which "few towns in England had the like"; one, on the Gascon wine trade, was a giant of at least 125 tons. Its exports now included grain and salt for many destinations, cloth and wool for France, Germany and the Low Countries, and cloth for the Baltic lands and Iceland. The export of wool, which lasted into the eighteenth century, was not always above board: smuggling began when Edward I, anxious to establish a viable weaving industry, curbed wool exports and put a duty on what was allowed out. Flemish weavers would not forgo their staple, and "owlers" were soon shipping wool by night from Dunwich, Orford, Bawdsey (Goseford) and Orwell. Nor was wool the only contraband. In 1307 Dunwich and other east coast ports were ordered not to export corn, livestock, horses, armour, money

Opposite page: *Panels in Dunwich Museum depicting flat bottomed boats, typical of the tenth century, built with long wedge-shaped overlapping planks. The upper panel shows the building, and lower panel the sailing of such vessels.*

or gold and silverware without a licence; the edibles could go to Gascony and the rest Edward I needed for his Scottish war. In 1364 the export of gold, silver and jewels was banned, no doubt in an effort to prop up the currency. With stakes high and valuables easier to hide than bales of wool, the merchants and seafarers of Dunwich can have obeyed such orders only when it suited them.

The range of Dunwich's imports was impressive. Its ships brought wine from Poitou and Gascony (the port's most celebrated trade) and stone from Caen to build churches. Alum was imported from Bordeaux, and potash for making soap from Hamburg, which also sent corn and pitch. Pottery came from Rouen and Andenne in Belgium; steel from Spain, France and Scandinavia; fine skins from Spain; flax, bowstaves and wax from Prussia; cloth from Flanders (much of it woven from Suffolk wool); and pitch, tar and furs from Norway, Sweden and Iceland. Armour and weapons figured among the imports, and spices from the Indies were offloaded to Dunwich ships at Dutch ports.

Not all imports were beneficial. As a crusader port, Dunwich gained not only the Knights Templar but the lepers of St James's; incipient lepers travelled on the first ships to return. Ships berthing at Dunwich may also have carried the plague: whether the Black Death was brought direct from the Continent or by travellers from elsewhere in England (who might well have come by sea), it was certainly introduced to England by ship-borne rats.

If only because of the appalling state of the roads, Dunwich had a strong coastal trade with other English ports. Corn figured prominently; in 1211 King John paid £5 6s 8d for four ships to carry grain to King's Lynn, and Richard Wodehewer of St Osyth was licensed in 1375 to ship it to London. Peas, beans, malt, flour and dairy produce were also sent to London markets. There was a heavy salt traffic, though where it was panned is a mystery; as late as 1560 the *Peter* took a cargo of salt to the Forth. Coal came from Newcastle and pottery from Scarborough, possibly in ships that took cargo to Hull and went on with other goods; much of the work for Dunwich ships was between third ports. There was also a heavy seasonal trade in herring, Dunwich-landed fish being shipped to London, Southampton and probably further afield.

Nor did the ships just carry cargo; travellers with a choice would rather go by coaster than by road. Merchantmen from Dunwich to continental ports such as Hamburg, Antwerp, Rouen and Bordeaux also took passengers. Dunwich was a port of passage for some Crusaders and saw off a few pilgrims to such great continental shrines as Compostella in Spain. Compostella's sea-shell badges have been found at Dunwich and there was a link with St James's Hospital, but the only Suffolk ports known to have been licensed for pilgrim voyages were Ipswich and Southwold.

Merchants suffered even more than fishermen from the deterioration of the harbour. Their ships were larger, and while fish could be landed on the beach, cargo needed a quay. Commerce slipped away, first to the other ports of the haven and then further afield, and Dunwich's plight became acute; in 1364 Edward III urged Newcastle, Norwich and Yarmouth to give priority to trade with it. A century later efforts were made to revive trade with Hull, but by 1576 that too was dead. Foreign ships continued to use the haven—and be fought over by Dunwich and Walberswick—until the late fifteenth century, but probably not much longer. Coins of this period from Venice and Brabant have been found at Dunwich; whether seventeenth-century Nuremberg tokens and eighteenth-century Danish coins were the fruits of commerce it is harder to say. As late as 1566, Dunwich had more mariners, 166, than any other Suffolk port but Southwold, and one ship over one hundred tons. In 1572 a register compiled by Thomas Colshill, surveyor of customs in London, gave Dunwich one ship of fifty to one hundred tons, three of twenty to fifty and two under twenty. By then, however, Aldeburgh had more seamen, pushing Dunwich into third place, and only Gorleston and Orford had fewer ships. The haven's coastal trade outlasted that to the Continent and the Iceland fleet, but with ships docking at Walberswick. Defoe wrote:

> Dunwich, however ruined, retains some share of trade, as particularly for the shipping of butter, cheese and corn, which is so great a business in this county, that it employs a great many people and ships also; and this port lies right against the particular part of the country for butter, as Framlingham, Halstead etc. Also a very great quantity of corn is bought up hereabout for the London market—for . . . all the counties in England contribute something towards the subsistence of the great city of London, of which the butter here is a very considerable article; as also coarse cheese . . . used chiefly for the King's ships.
>
> It is remarkable that this town is now so much washed away by the sea, that what little trade they have is carried on by Walberswick, a little town near Swole, the vessels coming in there, because the ruines of Dunwich make the shore there unsafe and uneasy to the boats.

The coal trade lasted longest. By 1733 cargoes from Newcastle were split with Walberswick and Southwold. Soon after, violent storms shifted the offshore debris enough for some colliers to come alongside the beach; the coal was unloaded in round wicker baskets. The very last Dunwich merchant ship was the *Heart of Oak*, a forty-five to fifty tonner built at Southwold in 1836 for Joseph Dix, sergeant-at-mace and host to the poet Edward Fitzgerald. She plied each summer to Hartlepool for coal, wintering in the haven. A gantry was run into the sea to swing her cargo ashore; at other times it served as a diving-board for local children. The *Heart of Oak* was last sailed between 1884 and 1887 by Charles English, and was broken up at Southwold in the 1890s, bringing Dunwich's career as a merchant port to a surprisingly recent end.

Naval Service and   12
Shipbuilding

DUNWICH has a place in England's naval history from pre-Norman times to the Spanish Armada. When a king needed to reinforce his navy, move troops or supplies or combat piracy, its ships were impressed. The town was ordered to build and man ships for naval service, and, at times, warships were based in its haven. Dunwich and its shipping were also targets: the Roman fleet had to repel Anglo-Saxon raiders, and Dunwich ships were doubtless plundered by the Vikings. King Alfred's navy guarded the Suffolk coast and when Danish attacks resumed Ethelred the Unready strengthened it, ordering groups of communities to build ships of sixty oars apiece or find the money for them. At least one such vessel must have been built and fitted out at Dunwich when the first call came in 1008; more were supplied over the centuries as successive kings ran down the fleet, then had to expand it when caught short.

Naval records begin in 1173, when Dunwich was ordered to send twenty ships to Sandwich "for the safe keeping of the sea": to deal with pirates. In 1205 King John sent three galleys (out of a fleet of fifty-four) to join two already in the haven, as many as were based on London; the next year he paid £26 5s toward their upkeep. In 1209 three royal galleys, repaired there for £57, were sailed to Portsmouth. When John could not pay their crews, Nicholas FitzRobert footed the bill and was rewarded with the manor of Westhall; he was also paid £41 4s 1d for the purchase and stowage of masts, sails, ropes and pikes. In the mid-1230s two royal galleys were based at Dunwich, and in 1257 the town built and fitted out a galley of fifty-six oars and a barge of twenty-eight for £132 11s 8d. According to Parker the barge was used only once, in 1260, when it was loaned for a year to Richard, Duke of Gloucester. The galley never saw action and in 1305 Edward I gave it to the Greyfriars, probably as timbers for their resited building.

Up to Tudor times, Dunwich built merchantmen on the understanding that the Crown could commandeer them. Most were cogs, with a high prow and single square-rigged sail. Each had two officers: larger vessels two rectors, smaller ones a rector and a constable. Even merchants who did not usually go to sea probably took charge of their (or others') ships when required to.

The commonest tasks were to patrol coastal waters against enemy fleets or pirates, sail north to support campaigns against the

Opposite page:
Medieval pilgrims beginning their voyage. From John Lyegate's Life of St Edmund, *c. 1433. Many pilgrims travelled from Dunwich in its heyday, but most travelling abroad actually sailed from Southwold or Ipswich.* British Library.

Scots, and take troops and supplies to France during the endless wars to hold the king's lands across the Channel. Ships were commandeered, for instance, to carry corn to Rouen in 1203 for Richard I's forces defending Normandy. In 1211 King John hired thirty Dunwich ships to ferry his army to Ireland, and four to take corn to King's Lynn. Then in 1216 Dunwich was among twenty-one towns to send ships to the Thames estuary in a vain attempt to stop the Dauphin joining rebel barons; they returned a year later after Henry III's fleet triumphed in the Channel. In 1225 Dunwich was alerted in case Ipswich failed to provide three ships to transport horses to France, and in 1229 Henry asked it for forty armed ships to help ferry his army to Poitou, settling for thirty, one eighth of the whole. In 1235 the town ignored a call to send a ship to Winchelsea at its own expense, but with its neighbours it did provide ten ships to escort Henry's sister Isabella from the Orwell to marry the Emperor Frederick. 1240 saw a Dunwich ship in Danish ports on royal service, and in 1242 five ships with crossbowmen were called for an abortive Gascon campaign. Ships ordered to Deganwy in 1245 to take Henry's army to Ireland were away so long that Geoffrey of Dunwich, owner of *La Damaysel*, was paid 30 marks compensation. He was luckier than John Fitzwilliam, Andrew FitzAugustine and Gerald FitzRobert, whose ships were wrecked; the King told the borough to reimburse them from what it owed him.

Dunwich was often bracketed with the Cinque Ports of Kent and east Sussex, whose barons supervised the herring fair. In 1242 Henry III urged the ports and the "approved men of Dunwich" to ravage the French coast and its commerce. And in January, 1254, he commanded:

> all their ships able to carry 16 horses . . . to be at Portsmouth on the octave of Easter next ready for the crossing of the Queen, Edward the King's son, Richard Earl of Gloucester, the King's brother, and other magnates coming to him in Gascony.

Locked in a dispute, Dunwich and Yarmouth ignored the call. Queen Eleanor ordered that:

> the good men of Yarmouth and Dunwich shall go with the fleet to Gascony with the Queen, and forbids them on pain of their land, life and limbs from causing any damage or impediment to them by reason of any contentions between them.

Such demands could leave Dunwich exposed. In 1264 the town complained that with twenty-three ships impressed to fetch wine from Gascony detained at Bordeaux, it was undefended; Henry III allowed *La Blome*, which had slipped away to Winchelsea and been arrested there, home to fill the breach. Each port's share of the burden varied from one campaign to the next. For Edward I's first Scottish war, Dunwich was asked for just four ships; Bawdsey and Harwich had to send eleven between them, Ipswich seven, Orford four and Goseford two. In 1298 all ships in Suffolk and Norfolk were called to royal service, but three years later only one Dunwich ship was sought toward a fleet of seventy.

Just eight years after the storm of 1287, Dunwich showed its resilience by building and equipping eleven ships for Edward's Gascon campaign. Accounts audited by bailiffs Constantine Boyton and John Bullock priced one galley at £277 5s 11½d; it had 120 oars, its sails took five hundred ells of various-coloured cloth, and thirty-three ells of linen were needed for banners and streamers that must have made it a splendid sight. A hundred plates and a hundred dishes were also provided. The eleven ships sailed from Plymouth the next January under the King's brother Edmund, Earl of Lancaster, and the Earl of Lincoln. They were the *Nandicu* (owned by Robert and John Ince), captained by Nicholas Honeman, with a crew of seventy-two; the *Seynte Marie Cogge* (Andrew Terry and the two Inces), captained by Roger de la More with seventy men aboard; the *Margarete* (Robert Cullyng), with Roger Austin and a crew of seventy; the *Seynt John Cogge* and the *Welfare* (Richard FitzJohn), captained by Robert Denys with sixty hands, and "B. of Plymouth" with forty; the *Leonard* (Valentine Richman), under Captain Arnold, with a crew of sixty; the *Rodeship* (Robert Sparke), with Walter Gynys and sixty men aboard; the *Godyer* (Richard Morehead), with Captain Gerard and forty crew; a second *Rodeship* (Michael FitzJohn), with forty crew and captained by Augustine de Valeyns; the *Nicholas* (Roger Thurston), again with forty men, under Reginald Boyton; and the *Brekehons* (Robert Bullock), with forty-five crew, captained by William Bullock[27].

The expedition was disastrous, with four of the ships—the *Nandicu*, the *Leonard*, the *Godyer* and a *Rodeship*—lost in a futile attack on Bordeaux. A document from 1341 states that they went down with all hands: 212 men plus those in command. But nothing was said of casualties until then, and Augustine de Valeyns sat in Parliament two years after his "death". The seven surviving ships limped home in late spring. Agreed compensation went unpaid, and in 1327 Dunwich petitioned Edward III for £200 for the lost ships and £1,220 10s for the crews' wages; he set the sum against the town's debt to him.

Wars with Scotland and France coincided with a rash of lawlessness that led in 1316 to Sir John de Botetourt being given charge of the coast from the Thames to the Tweed. Yet few calls were made on Dunwich; maybe it was felt to have suffered enough. When Edward I needed ships in 1301 for his Scottish campaign, he sought just one towards a fleet of eighty. A second was ordered to Berwick with provisions, staying seventeen weeks. Three years later Dunwich's MPs tried in vain to have its quota of ships for requisition limited to ten because of the losses in the Gironde. Yet it was 1307 before another ship was sought for the Scottish wars; the King died before it could be sent. In 1310 one ship was sent for Edward II's Scottish campaign, and in the year of Bannockburn two; the choice led to claims that owners of the best ships were paying bribes to stop them being requisitioned.

In 1319 Dunwich and several other towns sent ships on an experimental risk-sharing basis. For three to four months they met all expenses, after which the cost fell to the Crown; if ships were captured, the victorious owner kept the prize while the King took the crew for ransom. The scheme was not repeated until 1380; when Parliament secured a formal system of payment, shipowners had to hope for the best. When in 1322 Edward II, fearing invasion from Flanders, approached several ports including Dunwich, he was offered just one ship; in 1324 two Dunwich ships stayed put when ordered to Plymouth to carry forty tuns of wine amid fears of war with France. For nine months from December, 1326, Queen Isabella—to whose dowry Dunwich had been forced to "donate" £47 10s—was expected with a force of English exiles and French mercenaries intent on dethroning her husband: this time the ships of Dunwich and its neighbours did gather in the Orwell, only for her to land unopposed at Walton.

Dunwich shipowners were given a respite after the disaster of 1328. But once their cogs returned to the Pool of London on the corn run they were fair game, and in February, 1336, Peter Cliff's *Margaret* was commandeered there. Peter's father intervened at Court to have her freed in return for a promise to sail her to Gascony that spring to fetch wine for the royal cellars.

The early stages of the Hundred Years' War with France imposed heavy demands, coinciding with renewed efforts to unblock the harbour. Dunwich's decline was hastened by the loss of both ships and men—five hundred according to one no doubt exaggerated account. In the first campaign, which ended in defeat off Middleburg in September, 1338, nine Dunwich ships joined a Suffolk fleet of forty, with 1,295 men. It assembled in June off Bawdsey and Goseford, crossed to Antwerp and cruised off Flanders until the fatal engagement. The Dunwich ships were: the *Redcog*, commanded by Roger Ode, with a crew of forty-three whose wages for one twenty-seven-day period totalled £15 3s 9d; the *Godbefore*, Andrew Litester with forty men (£14 3s 6d); the *Sainte Marie*, William Tutepeny, thirty-one men (£11 16s 1d); the *Godyer*, John Tutepeny, and the *Welfare*, John Frese senior, each thirty-one men (£11 2s 9d); the *Margaret*, Stephen Batman, twenty-three hands (£8 12s 11½d); the *Katerine*, William Crele, with twenty-three men (£7 11s 10½d); another *Margaret*, Edward Sorel, fifteen men (£5 11s 4½d); and the *Plente*, Stephen Frese, with a crew of twenty-eight (£10 5s 10½d).

Dunwich provided six of the sixty-four ships that escorted Edward III from Flanders the next year: the *Redcog*, the *Plente*, one of the *Margarets*, the *Katerine*, the *James* and the *Goste*. Halfway to Antwerp they met the *Taret*, a Flemish ship bound from the Mediterranean for the same port under royal protection, and plundered cargo worth £16,527 17s 1d. Edward compensated her owners and gave sixty-four men involved the choice of paying restitution or facing trial. When they chose the latter, he lost his nerve and pardoned them in return for three years' naval service. The *Redcog* and the *Margaret* saw action again in 1340 at Sluys, a costly victory over 140 French ships in the Scheldt.

In 1342 Dunwich volunteered four ships to join fourteen from Ipswich, fifteen from Goseford and one from Orford to quell unrest in Brittany. Having landed troops at Brest, the *Welfare*, *Margaret* and *Sainte* Marie sailed home; the bailiffs were ordered to arrest their masters for desertion. Two years later one ship was sent, and in 1347 six with 102 mariners joined a 105-strong fleet supporting the year-long siege of Calais, which fell that August. They took with them beef, mutton, pork (mostly salted), oats, beans, peas, cheese, fish (wet and dried), flour and ale. To ensure the men did not run short and that fair prices were charged, quartermasters were empowered to overrule other buyers in Dunwich market. The war at sea now subsided, which was just as well, as Dunwich was in a spiral of decline. Ships were sent in 1360 under a general requisition, but when in 1379 a squadron was raised against the French, Dunwich was not called on. One solitary vessel was supplied in 1417 for the passage of Henry V and his forces to France.

Early Tudor times brought a revival. For Henry VII's Scottish campaign in 1497, the *Antony* took on heavy guns from the Tower of London, a "demy curtows" of brass and "one bumbardell of brasses called portcolies"; the *John* had two guns "calld Pontfrett and Wyndsore". Lighter armaments borne by other ships were "taken by the host and ravenously despoiled upon Halidon Hill". Dunwich sent sixteen ships for Henry VIII's Scottish war from 1542 to 1544; the largest was sixty tons, against a maximum of 160. French prisoners were brought to Dunwich, including an admiral who was treated royally; Scots captives were sent home on foot. The borough gave them beer brewed at Leiston, a hundred herrings, kippers, oatmeal, eleven dozen loaves, butter and eleven stone of beef, and laid on "for the admirall dynr, xviij s". Another item in the accounts reads: "Payed for the Scotts suppr and brekefast, and conducting them forth to Estbridge: iii s. vj d. etc." During a Scottish campaign in 1560, the *Peter*, in the Forth on the salt trade, was commandeered for the siege of Leith. This time French prisoners were ferried straight to Calais.

Dunwich last supplied a vessel for the campaign against the Armada. Aldeburgh raised £590 and sent a ship named the *Marygold*; Dunwich £25 and a pinnace, the smallest acceptable craft. Walberswick, Southwold and Orford managed only £15 between them. What part the *Marygold* and its pinnace played in the famous victory we do not know. After this there was little left to commandeer, a point driven home in 1596 when a warship commanded by Walter Ger had to be sent to defend the herring fishery. In that year the bailiffs met at Snape bridge "to confer with the townsmen of Orford, Aldeburgh and other towns about·setting forth a ship in warlike condition for her Majesty's service." Dunwich thus made its contribution in kind, being assessed 20 marks toward maintaining the navy and raising at short notice armour, post-horses and powder for "the town's great ordnance". Yet when ship money was levied in 1637 the town was assessed £4, the least of any Suffolk port, toward provisioning a seven-hundred ton, 250-man ship for six months. Even this was later halved.

Shipbuilding, and especially fitting-out, had remained Dunwich's main industry well into its decline. The main shipbuilding families were Pett and Gentleman; they had their own employees but called in individual craftsmen for particular tasks. In 1436 Thomas Pears fitted out the *George of London* to sail against the enemies of Henry VI. And in 1463 Sir John Howard had the *Kervelle* built with workmen brought from Stoke-by-Nayland on the Essex border; either he wanted something out of the ordinary or Dunwich was short of craftsmen. Two years later the ship, a privateer maybe, was back for a refit, two new cables being provided at 12s a hundredweight. As the haven became less navigable, orders slackened and craftsmen moved away. In 1513, Dunwich caulkers were impressed to build galleys such as the *Royal Harry* at Woolwich; many did not return. The Petts left for Harwich by 1540, and Thomas Gentleman took his business to Southwold, where he died aged 98 in 1609.

Before long the industry all along the east coast fell on hard times. In 1685 Parliament passed a bill directing aid to Newcastle, Hull, Yarmouth, Ipswich, Aldeburgh, Dunwich, Walberswick, Woodbridge and Harwich, where "many stout shippes" had been built for "the coale and other trade", and imposing tolls on foreign-built coasters. But for Dunwich, and Walberswick which had built warships until the Civil War, it was a dead letter.

Ships might no longer be pressed into naval service, but seamen were . . . and in 1692 a press-gang seized Alderman Jeremiah Burlingham. Great pains were taken to impress only the poor, and when the Admiralty learned that an alderman had been hauled aboard the *Russell* as a common seaman, it ordered his release. An inquiry found that he was the victim of his political foes, Alderman John Benefice and Samuel Pacy. In the 1695 election, after Benefice's fall, his former patron Admiral Sir Robert Rich allegedly stationed a frigate offshore to press-gang his opponents. Many humble Dunwich men must have been impressed over the years; maybe Henry Green, who died in the wreck of HMS *Resolution* off Pevensey in 1703, was one.

The connection was kept more agreeably by the commissioning of HMS *Dunwich* in 1695. Built by Collins and Chatfield at Shoreham, she was a sixth rate of 250 tons, armed with twenty-four six-pound guns, 94 feet long and 24 feet 6 inches in the beam. She was in Admiral Hooke's fleet that attacked Cadiz in 1702 and ran the boom at Vigo, capturing twenty-three French and Spanish galleons and men-of-war. Five ships were lost, but HMS *Dunwich*, in the thick of the action, was unscathed though her captain was wounded. Her end was prosaic: she was scuttled at Plymouth in 1714 to form a breakwater. There was no other HMS *Dunwich*, but a sixty-ton coaster built at Ipswich in 1778 was named the *Dunwich*. This ship, whose first master was Thomas Archer of Walberswick, was sold on to a King's Lynn owner in 1803.

A postscript concerns the *Dunwich Rose*, a small pleasure boat built for Michael Barne in 1878, which ended its life in the East Indies during the Second World War under requisition by the Royal Navy. Maybe the Spanish Armada was not the last campaign in which a Dunwich vessel saw action.

The Dunwich Town Chest, washed ashore well before the Corporation bought it in 1596, it held the borough records for centuries, was stood on by schoolboys as a punishment and is now in the Dunwich Museum. Jack C Docwra.

Piracy and Wreck 13

WHEN in the early seventeenth century Dunwich and its neighbours listed the causes of their undoing, much was made of losses through piracy. It had been a problem at least since Roman times. Once the Angles settled, their trade was safe until the advent of the Vikings. After the Conquest they too were finally tamed, but the ensuing prosperity created fresh temptation. Regularly throughout the Middle Ages, Dunwich, Ipswich and Yarmouth sent ships kept in readiness for the king's fleet to patrol the coast against marauders from Dutch and German offshore islands and Flanders. Yet Dunwich men too were ready to abandon honest pursuits when a tempting prize hove into view.

War offered great scope for plunder. In 1216 the skippers of royal galleys based at Dunwich used the excuse of war with France to take Stephen de Croy's cargo of wool and hides; the loot was landed at Scarborough and only returned after royal threats. The next year they were in trouble again for seizing the goods of Roger FitzMichael of Rouen. In 1242 several Rouen ships at Dunwich lost their cargoes (wool and hides again) on this pretext, much of the goods vanishing before an account was made to the King. And in 1264 or so Dunwich men used the excuse of war to take twenty-eight tuns of wine from a ship from Picardy, holding the crew until the release of men and cargo was ordered. The opening of the Hundred Years' War offered rich pickings for shipowners who evaded, by luck or bribery, the commandeering of their craft for the King's fleet. And the episode of the *Taret* shows that those in royal service remained prone to piracy.

Ships were even at risk in Dunwich harbour: in 1243 Robert FitzReginald and Robert FitzJoce "arrested" a Pevensey ship there to recover 50 marks, two sacks of wool and forty hides it had brought for them. And in 1291 a Flemish merchantman was plundered. Local men also carried out the first recorded attack on a merchant ship off Dunwich, in 1260. Bound from Hamburg with corn and potash, it was boarded by a party led by Luke and Richard Scott; they ransacked its hold, but were forced to pay compensation. Luke claimed he had been "framed", and Henry III sent two judges to determine the truth. Much of the piracy off Dunwich, though, was the work of men from other English ports: in 1299 an inward-bound ship owned by Richard and Peter FitzJohn was seized and taken to Gillingham, where its cargo of wine, salt and armour was sold.

Opposite page:
An English 6th rate, the twin of HMS Dunwich, lying at anchor. Ironically this pencil and wash drawing is by Van de Velde the elder, the offical Dutch war artist at the battle of Sole Bay. National Maritime Museum

Beacons on Cock Hill, probably at Dingle and atop one or more church towers, warned Dunwich of approaching raiders. They must have been lit in 1282 when "Pirates of Zeland and Holland about Yarmouth and Donwich, did spoyle and robbe whosoever they met, slew many men and carryed away not a few shippes with all ye goodes in them"[28]. Florence of Holland sent them to avenge her father's death at the hands of the English; Suffolk ports were ordered to send ships to repel them. In 1295 the Zeelanders returned, attacking ships in the harbour and landing parties to loot the town. A French invasion was also feared, and Peter of Dunwich was put in charge of defences against both threats; two constables responsible for neighbouring sections of coast, William de Bovill and Reginald de Argentyn, deployed armed men on horseback under his orders. Yet lawlessness continued to grow along the entire east coast until the imposition in 1316 of what was effectively martial law.

Piracy on the Gascon wine run became so rife that the Warden of the Cinque Ports ordered ships to sail in convoy, even in sight of port, and make as smart a turn-round as possible. Skippers soon realized that they had *carte blanche* to hunt in packs, as in 1303 when eight ships returning from Gascony, including the *Pleyntie* of Dunwich, surprised a Spanish merchantman off St Mathieu in Brittany and made off with its tack and cargo. The Iceland fleet, too, was not above a spot of piracy, though it was also subject to attack. Humble herring craft were also vulnerable; in 1472 Dunwich petitioned the Lord Admiral of France to end the plunder of its fishing fleet by his countrymen.

Three ships owned by Richard FitzJohn's estate and James Reeve of London were robbed of cargo worth £4,000 in the Dutch port of Merland by men sent by Katherine, Lady of Vorne. When the Count of Flanders ignored calls for recompense, Edward I ordered the seizure of Flemish cargoes in English ports. In 1308 William FitzJohn went one further, taking goods worth £44 belonging to Walter le Fleming of York from a ship near Dunwich. Not long after, nine Dunwich men were in Ipswich gaol awaiting trial for a string of robberies at Yarmouth and attacks on Stephen Drayton, John de Belton and nine Flemish merchants; Parker reckoned all were hanged, as none appears in later tax records. Richard Sparrow, who helped plunder a Flemish ship at Orford, was luckier; he was pardoned and lived to a ripe old age as a baker in St Leonard's parish.

In 1311 Dunkirkers seized the *Grace* of Yarmouth off Dunwich, forced the crew to leave, took money and goods worth £60 and set about the ship with axes, and in 1317 pirates from Sluys attacked a Boston wool ship between Dunwich and Orford. In 1330 Dunwich men led by Mayor John Payne, two of whose

family had been held at Ipswich, seized Anastasia Butt's ship at Southwold. As Dunwich lost trade to Blythburgh and Walberswick, attempts to coerce ships into docking there had the ring of piracy, as in 1412 when Johannes Thomaissone's was "diverted" by Thomas Clerk and party. Moreover, Zeeland ships were attacked in the port in 1383 and 1457, the miscreants being fined.

Under Henry VIII, at a time of relative quiet, the law on evidence in piracy cases was changed to make convictions easier. One Dunwich man to suffer was William Woodd, fined in 1578. The next year a burgess found with plunder in his house refused to pay his fine and was sent to London to be dealt with. Piracy revived in the early seventeenth century; in 1622 Dunwich, Southwold and Walberswick asked to be excused their share of a levy for tackling it because of their financial state and in 1626 the Corporation apparently tried to buy them off with 2s 6d. The last recorded harrassment of Dunwich ships—the last because the fleet was disappearing, not through the end of piracy—came in 1627, when after a plea from the town and its neighbours four Newcastle ships were sent to protect the herring fishery from Dunkirkers.

The other great danger facing mariners was of shipwreck, often in distant waters. In 1260 Robert Neville, keeper of Bamburgh Castle, was ordered to hand over to John Sparcunte three pieces of wax from a wrecked Dunwich ship when survivors appeared. Five years later the notorious men of Romney were ordered to return to merchants from Pamplona cargo washed from a Dunwich ship off what is now Dungeness. And in 1274 William Barnard and a Spanish merchant sailed from Bordeaux, a cargo of alum in a second ship; his ship was lost with all hands but the alum reached Sandwich safely[29].

The waters close to Dunwich were safe in calm weather—save at times for submerged debris—but the storms that tore into the cliffs could also swamp a ship and grind it to matchwood. Wrecks were common; a typical entry in the parish accounts for 1604 reads: "To a Scotchman which lost his shippe laden with wyne, 6d." The first major wreck recorded is that of Hugh of Boves's fleet in 1215. The loss of life was awesome, but this would not have stopped locals looting the debris. Dunwich folk attached great importance to the right of wreck: to claim items washed on to the shore. They must have been tempted, as the Cornish were, to "engineer" wrecks by giving false signals, or simply to let them happen. King John exempted the burgesses of Dunwich from wreck elsewhere in the kingdom without granting them the right on their own shore. A special assize had to be held at Dunwich to resolve the claims of Dunwich, Westleton and Blythburgh; it gave Dunwich the right to wreck over most of the estuary shore and the coast below its cliffs.

The poverty that overcame first Dunwich and then its neighbours increased the importance of what was found, hence the ruinous lawsuit with Southwold over a puncheon of whisky beached in 1827. The corporation ruled in 1413 that proceeds of wreck should be split between itself and the finder, but if anyone "not a freeman dwelling within the borough shall find any wreck, he shall have nothing, save for his labour". The year before, Bartholomew Lomb had found a sail on the shore and sold it for 5s; maybe the bailiffs were piqued at not receiving half-a-crown. In 1419 John Moreff claimed £3 0s 8d and Robert Thorpe 19s 11½d; two years later John Sadilbow valued at 40d a pipe of wine he had found.

Dunwich's greatest catch was the town chest, a grand Dutch affair finely painted in the seventeenth century and fitted with massive clasps, which housed the borough records in the Town Hall. Bought by the corporation in 1596, it is thought to have been washed ashore well before and could be up to two centuries older. Read Cooper recalled that generations of Dunwich schoolboys were stood on it as a punishment, wearing off much of the paint.

The danger to shipping grew as the haven bore less resemblance to seafarers' charts. In 1367 a Prussian ship carrying flax, bowstaves and wax "was cast by a storm upon the soil of the King at Dunwich, between the present port of Dunwich and the former one called Old Haven"[30]. Which was it making for? Wrecks were common in the late fifteenth and early sixteenth centuries on the hazardous passage through Hummerson's Cut where the "passely-sands" had built up. Yet probably the worst, which inspired Agnes Strickland to write the tragic Victorian poem "Dunwich Fair", occurred at Southwold on 25th June, 1616. A boat bringing revellers from St James's Fair fouled a cable and capsized with the loss of twenty-two lives, among them Edward and Elizabeth Younges, children of the Reverend Christopher Younges, vicar of Southwold. The grieving father wrote in his parish register:

> They were drowned in the haven coming from Donwich Fayer, on St James' Day in a bote, by reason of one cable lying overwharf the haven; for by reason that the men that brought them down was so negligent, that when they were redie to come ashore the bote broke loose, and so the force of the tide carried the bote against the cable and so overwhelmed. The number of them were XXII, but they were not all found.

RELIGIOUS LIFE AND FOUNDATIONS

A Religious Centre 14

THE CHURCH so influenced medieval life that it is hard to separate the spiritual from the secular. Churches were more than spiritual centres; the clergy were often the only people who could read, and life was governed by the church calendar. Dunwich's most important day was Michaelmas: 29th September, when the herring fishery began, freemen of the borough were sworn and half the annual fee-farm was handed to the Crown. Early November was almost as busy; on the 2nd (All Souls' Day) the Knights Templar held court to collect rents and give pardons; from the 5th to the 7th came the revelry of St Leonard's Fair; and on the 11th, Martinmas, the herring fleet returned to port. Other important dates were 25th and 26th July, St James's Day and the day after, when the other fair was held, and Easter, when the rest of the fee-farm fell due.

When the Church revived after the Viking anarchy, Dunwich did not regain its bishop. It became the centre of a deanery whose emblem was a single-masted ship with the brother apostles Andrew and Peter aboard, and which by 1256 had forty-eight churches. Dunwich itself had just one church in 1066, but by 1086 there were three, by 1175 seven and in 1256 six—well short of the seventy of tradition; the evidence for two more is dubious. Between them, the churches and religious houses of medieval Dunwich offered townspeople a choice of a good twenty burial-places.

Up to the Conquest, Dunwich's only church was under the purview of Edric of Laxfield. After it, the town's new lord oversaw an ambitious building programme; when Robert Malet founded Eye Priory, he granted it all churches in Dunwich built and under construction. He assured the monks an income, plus "extras" including the profit from St Leonard's Fair. In 1291 the priory was collecting £40 2s 2d a year from Dunwich, by its dissolution under Henry VIII much less. The abbot of Ely, also, collected 1 mark plus 24,000 herrings—the King sometimes had to order Dunwich to hand them over, especially when catches declined—and for a time

Opposite page: *Three of the unforgettable 'chain of churches'; from the top, Southwold, Walberswick and Blythburgh, taken from the surround of Gardner's map.*

the archdeacon of Suffolk imposed a "holy-days-toll" of ½d on every cart of goods or food sold in Dunwich on Sundays, and 2d from every butcher. Leiston and Sibton abbeys also had an interest; Dunwich burgesses had helped endow Leiston Abbey, but its abbot in 1295 tried to levy tolls on shipping, to the anger of the town, which took him to court.

The only house of monks known to have been set up at Dunwich was the Benedictine cell of Eye Priory. Though the teachers brought from Canterbury for Felix's school must have been monks, there is no evidence of a monastery in Anglo-Saxon Dunwich. Indeed, Sigebert's promotion of monasteries elsewhere suggests there was not: surely we would have heard of one at Dunwich. And when monasteries thrived again after the Vikings, Dunwich was again left out.

Dunwich folk would have seen more of the town's Franciscan and Dominican friars than of the monks: they were more numerous and did not stay in to study and pray, preferring to seek alms and do good works. The cell and the friaries represented the three most numerous orders; the Augustinian, Cistercian and Carmelite friars, whose houses were mostly founded later, never reached Dunwich although the Augustinians were strong in Suffolk. Maybe they could tell by the mid-thirteenth century that Dunwich would shortly be seeking alms rather than giving them. Unlike the monks, who withdrew to Eye, both orders of friars showed commitment as the sea advanced. The Franciscans found a new site just inland; the Dominicans did plan to move to Blythburgh but stayed put in the event.

The town could boast three more religious houses: St James' Hospital for lepers and the poor, the Maison Dieu for the poor and mentally ill and handicapped, and the small but wealthy preceptory of the Knights Templar which provided a touch of class until the order was suppressed at the start of the fourteenth century; it continued in more modest hands for over two hundred years.

When Pevsner wrote that "the chain of churches which runs Lowestoft–Kessingland–Covehithe–Southwold–Walberswick–Blythburgh–Aldeburgh is unforgettable", the omission of Dunwich reflected more than the obvious fact that its medieval churches were no more. Some of them were large, but they boasted neither outstanding architecture nor rich decoration. The benefactions that embellished Suffolk's great churches reached their full flood only after 1450, long after Dunwich went into decline. Modest donations to Dunwich churches are recorded and we know of statues and stained glass, but had they been much more than shells of flint and masonry the iconoclast Dowsing would have stayed longer in 1643.

The number of churches tells us little about Dunwich's size.

Ipswich, smaller at the time of Domesday, had nine then against Dunwich's three; by the fifteenth century, when it had left Dunwich far behind, it still had only fourteen. The advance of the sea drove one of Dunwich's monastic houses inland and led a second to prepare to, and All Saints' probably owed its rebuilding in the 1330s to the destruction of other churches and its extension in 1537 to the imminent loss of St John's. But when Dunwich masons set to work in the 1420s, it was to build fine towers at Kessingland and Walberswick, not to replace their own lost churches.

It was probably the workaday nature of their churches that commended them to Dunwich people. Though there was occasional friction with the church authorities, like the dispute in 1281 over the actions of Bishop Middleton's tax collectors, relations between the clergy and their flocks seem to have been good. The priests rarely indulged in excesses and did their best to meet the needs of a seafaring and trading population; through the catastrophes that shook the town from 1287, they must have done much to hold together a populace close to panic. It is notable that when Tudor Dunwich was threatened, it was St John's Church rather than any secular building that the people tried to save.

Pilgrim badges found at Dunwich, now in its Museum.
Russell Edwards

Nor did the Church cash in on the town's past. Writers who dispute that Felix conducted his mission from Dunwich would say there was nothing to exploit, emphasizing that the monks apparently did not claim their cell as the old episcopal seat until it had been washed away. Yet little is made of Felix's memory anywhere in East Anglia. If the clergy and people of Dunwich were aware of Felix's role, it meant little to them. No effort was made to recover his remains when in Canute's time they were moved from Soham to Ramsey, or later. Felix's feast day in early March was absent from the Dunwich calendar, and such miracles as are recorded owe nothing to him; when in the twelfth century Ralph the schoolmaster was cured of a swelling in his throat, it was St Etheldreda, founder of Ely Abbey and daughter of Anna, Felix's later patron, whom he invoked. When Nicholas Gonomanaway's belly was grotesquely swelled in 1278 by a dropsy, he was carried to Bury, where on drinking holy water and invoking St Edmund, he "vomited forth a great quantity of poison", filling two bowls, and was cured. Felix was not in the same league.

Pilgrims thus flowed out of the town rather than in, most taking King John's Road for Bury, stopping overnight at Fressingfield. Others struck north for Norwich and the shrine of Our Lady at Walsingham. The more ambitious took ship for Compostella in Spain, or Mont St Michel off the Norman coast; badges from both have been found at Dunwich. The most devout made pilgrimages to Rome and Jerusalem; the Templars had their own VIP chapel for the latter.

Its Churches and   15
Chapels

All Saints'

THE LAST of Dunwich's medieval parish churches is the best known, as its abandoned shell stood starkly atop the cliff before toppling into the sea from 1904 onwards, the camera recording its gradual loss. Though large, All Saints' was conspicuously lacking in finery and artistic flourishes. Gardner, writing as the last services were being held, described it as "esteemed but mean", and a century later Suckling termed it "probably the least imposing fabric in the town". Its most striking feature was the embattled buttressed tower at its west end, with a base sixteen feet by ten feet, some sixty feet high and topped by a weathercock and statues of the angels Gabriel, Michael, Raphael and Uriel, one of which fell before the cliff had reached it. The tower was a landmark to seamen, and for a century after closure, Trinity House kept it from collapse.

Built of stone and flint, All Saints' stood at the west end of the town, its tower overlooking the Palesdyke; the north aisle abutted Scotts Lane. Its length, 147 feet, rivalled the churches of Blythburgh (128 feet), Walberswick (130 feet), Southwold (144 feet) and Lowestoft (184 feet). But it lacked their height and volume, owing its length to one extension or possibly two, or even the grafting of the main structure on to a smaller original. A nave ninety-one feet long and twenty-two feet wide, with five bays and a southern porch, linked the tower to a chancel of two bays with a further door to the south; this measured forty feet by twenty-one feet. There was also a north aisle, rebuilt in 1537—maybe to take the parishioners of St John's, who were still fighting to save their own church—and demolished in 1725.

All Saints' in its final form dated from the mid-fourteenth century; its tower and the octagonal shafts between nave and aisle were in the Perpendicular style fashionable from the 1330s. But it may once have looked very different. The parish was there by 1175, when John of Oxford was confirmed as Bishop of Norwich. A Purbeck marble coffin lid found under the floor in 1904 seems to date from the thirteenth century, and tax returns for 1291 list All Saints' as a rectory. Thus the church lost so recently must have replaced an older structure or been a rebuild obliterating what went before. Its final style dated from a time when at least two

Opposite page: *All Saints' church; the loss of more stonework to the sea, 1906 and 1913.*

Dunwich churches had been lost to the sea and a third was about to close; rebuilding and extension of the church furthest inland would have made sense in the years between the great storm of 1328 and the Black Death.

Less is known about All Saints' in Dunwich's heyday than about churches lost long since. It was not fashionable; the parish was far less wealthy than St Nicholas' or St John's. In 1258 William and Augustine FitzJohn and Augustine FitzAndrew took refuge there from the Brun brothers, whom they slew in what they claimed was self-defence; John Grimsby also hid there from his enemies. Later John Lewk, a Dunwich MP from 1421 to 1430, left 6s 8d to finish the east window. All Saints' status rose with the re-building of its aisle in 1537, bequests for which had been made over the previous decade, and with the closure of St John's seven years later; it also benefited from the end of Eye Priory, to which it had been paying £10 13s 4d a year since at least 1291. When St Peter's closed in the 1650s, All Saints' became Dunwich's only parish church.

All Saints' did have some modest embellishments. Dowsing in 1644 destroyed "30 superstitious pictures, and 28 cherubims, and a Cross on the Chancel". There was some stained glass, notably in the aisle, and an image of Mary Magdalene. The floor of the nave was dotted with memorial plates and two more substantial brasses: to Thomas Cooper, shipowner, merchant and four times bailiff, who died in 1576, and Robert Spatchett (died 1624), ten times a bailiff. The tower had a clock, and three bells cast in 1626, 1678 and (optimist-ically) 1725; the first may well have been salvaged from St Peter's.

By 1597 the state of the parish was disturbing Bishop Redman of Norwich. The curate, Robert Watkinson, did not "instruct the yowthe in the Catachisme—he practizeth physicke"; Nicholas Cooper and Richard Friende "were churchwardens five or six years together and never made their accompte". The decay spread to the fabric of the church, which Gardner described as "tottering", with interior walls afflicted by "an incurable spreading leprosy". Sale of materials from the aisle paid for repairs (and probably for the last of the bells), but the decline continued. By 1754 services were held once a fortnight from Lady Day to Michaelmas, and monthly for the rest of the year. There was no resident parson; services were taken by a neighbouring vicar for £2 a year plus refreshments.

In the late 1750s, with Dunwich's fortunes at their nadir, All Saints' was abandoned. The sea was still seventy yards away; closure was due to the state of the building and the inability of a community of barely a hundred souls to keep financing repairs. Its deterioration was now abetted by souvenir-hunters, among them Daniel Bonhote, law clerk to Henry Negus of Harleston and town clerk of Dunwich. On 29th August, 1770, he visited All Saints', writing:

Having never been in the Church, a decayed and almost ruinous building, curiosity and a desire for gratifying that of my friend, induced me to take a survey of the inside. When on my entrance the first thing which presented itself to my view was a majestic owl flying from the desk . . . On the floor and pews is nothing but the worlds of that bird and dirt driven off the top, some part of which is exposed to the boisterous element. Dangerous as my situation was I ventured to scrape off with my foot the dirt from the Stones that appeared to be laid over some bodies but could find no inscriptions. At last I spyed the brasses which I send herewith.

The most notable brass he took was Thomas Cooper's. Bearing effigies of himself, his wife Jane, son Michael and six daughters, it read:

Here Thomas Cooper sutym Bayly of this Towne, inclosed is Claie,
Which is the restynge place of fleash, untill the latter Day
Of one sonne and daughters syx, the lord him parent made,
Ere cruell death did worke his spite, of fickle life did fade.
Who deceased ye XVII of Maye in ye yeare of our Lord 1576.

Bonhote sent it to John Ives, a Yarmouth antiquary who died soon after aged only 26. His collection was sold and the brass vanished for a century and a half, turning up in Strangers' Hall, Norwich,

Only the tower of All Saints' church remained by 1918.

101

with a piece missing. Norwich Corporation agreed to return it and on 29th April, 1928, it was unveiled on the wall of St James' Church by the Bishop of St Edmundsbury.

Articles of worth, starting with the church bells, were salvaged and stored. The roof lost its lead in 1778, collapsing in the winter of 1784–85. As the graveyard was well clear of the cliff edge, burials continued into the 1820s. In 1826, with a new parish church planned, the lead was sold for £124 15s 6d and the bells for £70 8s. A man named Parker was transported to the colonies for stealing a bell he found in the ruins and some of the lead.

By the 1870s the east gable and parts of the chancel had fallen, though Trinity House kept the tower erect. Then the sea arrived: in February, 1904, the east end went over the cliff. The marble coffin lid was exposed, and also a fifteenth-century stone coffin, now at St James' with the Cooper brass and a magisterial chair dated 1705, apparently one of a set. The church succumbed arch by arch, until on 12th November, 1919, most of the tower crashed to the shore. The rest followed in January, 1922, save for the final buttress, which was re-erected in St James' churchyard.

The ruins of All Saints' now lie in twenty feet of water. A large part of the tower fell across earlier rubble. The western tip of the churchyard just survives, with two gravestones almost unseen among the bushes; one is to Jacob Forester, who died in 1796. For several decades a third, to John Brinkley Easy, who died aged 23 in 1826, stood proudly a few yards from the cliff edge. But late in 1990, as parishioners prepared to move it to safety in St James' churchyard, a sudden and massive cliff fall swept it to the shore, leaving it buried in a pile of debris.

St Bartholomew's

Dunwich had several churches of which we know very little; St Bartholomew's was one. It could have been one of the three founded by 1086; the document showing that All Saints' was there in 1175 confirms its presence by then. The Register of Eye shows that both it and St Michael's were lost to the sea by 1331, and the priory wanted the income from Laxfield church as compensation. But how long before did it vanish? St Bartholomew's is not listed in the Valuation of Norwich of 1254 which also omits St Michael's, yet would the monks have waited until 1331 to seek recompense? The church could have been flooded early on, or been a casualty of either the tempest of 1287 or that of 1328—which last would account for the compensation claim.

Either way, St Bartholomew's was presumably in the extreme north or east of the town; the fact that no record survives of land in its parish suggests that all was lost at much the same time.

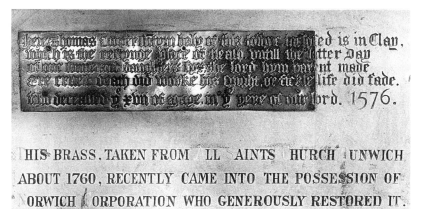

The brass to Thomas Cooper, former bailiff of Dunwich, who died in 1576, was the finest in All Saints'. It was removed from the church after closure and since 1928 has adorned the wall of the new St James' church.
Russell Edwards

"St Felix's"

There is no evidence that there ever was a church dedicated to St Felix, as some antiquarians have claimed. "St Felix's church" is sometimes used as shorthand for Dunwich's first church, and East Anglia's first bishop could hardly have dedicated a church to himself. Nor is there proof that Dunwich's sole church in 1066 was that founded by Felix four centuries before; given the turbulent events in between, it may very well not have been.

St James'

The chapel of St James' leper hospital (though not for the lepers themselves) apparently began as a church in its own right before the hospital was founded at the end of the twelfth century. The ruin that stands beside today's parish church is almost certainly Norman and may be based on an older church; the ground plan of St James' has a decidedly Saxon feel. Moreover, it is close to the Leet Hill where community business was transacted before the Conquest. It could have been one of Dunwich's Domesday churches, left stranded when the Palesdyke was thrown up: there is a tantalizingly uncorroborated reference to a one-time parish of St James' in a thirteenth-century document in the British Library. Townsfolk took an interest in the church and often worshipped there, and the later importance of St James' Fair underlines the connection.

Stow, writing when the church was still in use, described it as "a grete one, and a large, after the oulde fashion"; Gardner, since whose time most of the decay has occurred, rated it "not much unlike the antient form of the eastern churches". Its graceful lines and continental feel contrasted sharply with the rough-hewn All Saints'. St James' was 107 feet long, with a fine rounded arch separating the nave, sixty feet by twenty-four, from the choir, twenty-two feet by twenty. A further arch led to the apse, eighteen feet in diameter, where a round-headed window overlooks twelve arched recesses for seats. The church was used until around 1685, by when it was in a sorry state. Dowsing ignored it, yet there was one painting said by former worshippers to have been visible to the end; Gardner speculated that it could have been of a leper, a king, the founder of the hospital or simply St James.

In the nineteenth century the new St James' Church was built alongside. Burials, suspended in 1536, resumed, pride of place going to a Barne family mausoleum in the heart of the old church. Since the Second World War, its ruin has come under official protection, though in summer tall weeds obscure it.

St James' hospital chapel ruins today; the Barne family vault is in the foreground.
Russell Edwards

St John the Baptist

St John's was Dunwich's leading church until St Nicholas' was founded, and again from the 1330s until its own demise two centuries later; it was also its best loved. An imposing cruciform building with aisle, chancel, north and south naves and a central tower, it was well appointed, with a chapel to St Nicholas in the north aisle and statues or images of John the Baptist, St Mary Magdalene and Anne, mother of the Virgin Mary. Two guilds were affiliated: St John's, which met in the church, and St Katharine's, with a separate chapel of its own.

The church withstood the tempests of 1287 and 1328, and by 1334, partly by default, had Dunwich's largest parish with ninety-one taxable properties, forty-seven of them shops, against forty-two in St Nicholas', thirty-four each in St Martin's and St Peter's and thirty-three in both All Saints' and St Leonard's. Alone with St Leonard's, it could still meet the quota for its patrons. Its first known vicar is James de Langton, installed in 1340; after St Nicholas' closed, it gained a rector. One of the first, Walter, was convicted of rape in 1407. St John's was also a place of sanctuary; John de Oyntur fled there when hue and cry was raised against him for stealing lead from the shell of St Nicholas'.

In 1507 John Weybread left 10 marks for a tabernacle in St John's, and as late as 1538 Margaret Haliday was buried in the south aisle. And on the dissolution of Eye Priory in 1536 the 13s 4d a year St John's still paid the monks was diverted to the Duke of Norfolk, with the advowson of the parish, last exercised the next year when William Syward was appointed vicar.

Yet by 1510 funds were being raised to build "the pere against Saint John's church"—a breakwater to stop the sea undermining it. And in 1542 the struggle to save St John's became desperate: the churchwardens sold most of its plate for £21, "bestowed in making a pere for the defence of the church and of the whole town". Two years later more plate was sold for £17, "bestowed likewise in making a pere". Not long after, with the church's east end on the cliff edge, parishioners gave up and began to salvage what they could before it was lost, starting with the bells. Parts of the parish outlived the church, their revenues passing in 1545 to Anthony Rous, but few if any relics have survived.

Much of St John's was dismantled as the waves ate into the cliff below. And beneath a large gravestone in the chancel a stone coffin was discovered with the corpse of a man which, according to Gardner, fell to dust when stirred. He wore "a pair of boots picked like Crakows" (shoes with pointed toes bent upwards) and "on his breast stood two chalices of a coarse metal". Who was he? One suggestion at the time was William Rufus, but he was more likely a cleric or possibly a knight, and not necessarily the first occupant of the grave. The find raises questions over the age of St John's; Parker, noting its central position, reckoned that it probably stood on the site of Dunwich's first church, after several rebuildings. But there is no more chance of finding out than of identifying the man with the pointed shoes.

St Leonard's

St Leonard's Church stood in the north of the town, east of the Daine. The record of the Scott murder case of 1263 mentions "the King's street in the parish of St Leonard's stretching westward from the houses of the Friars Minor to the port", and the part of Kingsholme nearest the town was known as Churchmarsh or Lenaldsmarsh. When the church was founded is a mystery. It was not listed in the diocesan document of 1175, but as there are other omissions it could have been there by then. The transfer of the fair from St Lawrence's to St Leonard's Day early in the twelfth century could have coincided with its foundation or been a sign that it was well established. It was certainly active by the late 1220s when a papal judge settled a dispute over a chapel built in the parish by the Brothers of the Hospital of Jerusalem, which the monks of Eye claimed was diverting revenue from St Leonard's, and thus from them. The Hospitallers promised not to entice parishioners to pay tithes, hear Mass or be baptized; the monks undertook to respect the brothers' privileges.

St Leonard's was a fixture in 1270, when Roger Cristepeny gave the monks land in the parish for the good of his soul, and survived the storms of 1287 and 1328. There were still thirty-three taxable properties in the parish in 1334, twelve of them houses, and the church was giving the monks their due in 1342. But soon after, St Leonard's either succumbed to the sea—there is no later mention of ruins—or was abandoned, maybe during the Black Death. Parts of the parish survived for over a century more, a will proved in 1450 involving a house in the parish "antiently called St Leonard's". The last surviving link with the church was an oblong seal of "Richard, Priest of St Linnart" which Gardner, who saw it dated to 1334; it has since vanished.

St Martin's

St Martin's was functioning by 1175, and could have been one of the Domesday churches. By 1226 it had a rector; a papal court at Ipswich ruled against him in a dispute with the monks of Eye. Its parish, in the east of the town, lost many of its hundred or so houses in 1287. From 1308 St Martin's was often without a priest; it survived the disaster of 1328, but by 1334 the parish was down to thirty-four tax-payers, and in 1342 only seven houses remained. Nicholas of Spexhall became rector in 1335, but when he left, no priest would serve as there were no gifts to be collected, and St Martin's closed. It soon succumbed to the sea; there is no later mention of ruins. Again, some land in the parish survived; in 1408 the owner of a plot gave it to the Temple, not something he would have done were it about to be washed away.

St Michael's

We know very little of St Michael's Church—not even its location, dimensions or dates of foundation and loss. It was there in 1175 and could have been since Domesday, and it would be logical to suppose that it went in the storm of 1328, as in 1331 Eye Priory sought the revenues of Laxfield Church to offset the loss of it and St Bartholomew's. The absence of both churches from the Valuation of Norwich almost eighty years before could mean that they had gone by then, but why would the monks have waited so long? Church and parish must have been in the eastern extremity of the town, unless they were close to the port and were flooded out. The fact that the herring fishery started at Michaelmas could imply a link between church and fishing fleet that might put it near the quayside.

St Nicholas'

Dunwich's rise and fall are epitomized in St Nicholas' Church, endowed in palmy days and abandoned as fortunes declined. It was almost certainly not there at Domesday: dedications to St Nicholas were rare until 1089, when a church was built at Bari to house his supposed relics. After that churches to him spread rapidly in Europe's great trading centres: Utrecht, Hamburg, Stockholm, Bergen, Newcastle, Yarmouth, Harwich, Ipswich, Bristol, Liverpool . . . and Dunwich. The church was probably built, and the parish imposed on the existing structure, at the start of the twelfth century, and certainly by 1175. Stow wrote:

> The portion of Seynt Nicholles was 16 marks, and . . . of all the other 5 pryshes was but 6 marks a pece, whereby it plainly apereth that St Nicholles pryshe was the greatest psh, and the best benefice of them all, viz. it was almost worth any three of all the rest.

Dunwich's merchants must have made this the town's most ornate church, with carvings and paintings abounding and some impressive graves. It had at least two clergy; in 1334 Roger, the rector, and John Methwold, the chaplain, fell out over tithes. But was the founding of chapels to St Nicholas at St John's and St

107

Peter's an attempt to head off the imposition of such a church or to fill a gap after its closure?

The church lay south-east of St John's, a hundred yards beyond Blackfriars. Camden wrote:

> St Nicholas', the form of which, as also of St John's Church was thus, they were inclosed both on the North and South, and the Steeples in the Middle, like Cathedral-churches now in use, and as the manner of old Cathedrals was.

By its west door was a four-acre field successfully claimed in 1201 by Christina Swetyng from the parson of St Peter's for 1 mark; otherwise the parish was very built-up, with some three hundred houses in its prime.

The parish survived the storm of 1287 just about intact; it cannot have reached to the eastern edge of town. It lost some houses to the sea in the years that followed, at times having to do without a fully qualified priest as its revenues and congregation shrank, then was hard hit by the tempest of 1328. By 1334 only forty-two tax returns were being made, though some covered several sites. Further erosion or departure of the wealthy reduced this by 1342 to just eighteen houses; the Prior of Eye went without his dues through the "debility of the parish". St Nicholas' survived the Black Death, Thomas de Sterston being installed as rector in 1352, but was abandoned soon after; valuables were removed to safe keeping, and John de Oyntur stole lead from the roof. The church fell into ruins and, probably in the mid-fifteenth century, was washed into the sea. A piece of its masonry was built into a new house as a keystone; it bore the legend "S C Nicholae ora pro nobis" ("St Nicholas, pray for us"). The churchyard was joined in 1413 to the Dominicans' friary grounds; its last graves survived until 1740.

St Patrick's

Some antiquaries have said that a church at Dunwich was dedicated to St Patrick, but there is no evidence for this. Such a church would have a strong claim to be the oldest. There are only eight English churches dedicated to St Patrick, but Felix was reared in the Irish tradition. It is conceivable that he dedicated a church to St Patrick out of respect for Fursa—but if he did, it did not last into the Middle Ages.

St Peter's

St Peter's, the last but one of the old parish churches to be lost, stood just inland of the market-place between Duck Street and the

High Road. A local gentleman, Thomas Lemarr, described it soon after its loss as "a spacious fine old church, nearly as long as Blythburgh". Its layout was simple: tower, nave and chancel. But Lemarr wrote that it was "curiously glased with painted glass" with "many gravestones with inscriptions upon brass". Dowsing noted "63 Cherubims, 60 at least of JESUS, written in Capital Letters, on the Roof; and 40 superstitious Pictures; and a Cross on top of the Steeple". Inside were a chapel to St Nicholas on the north side, and the "altar of the Trinity", either the main altar or one in a side chapel. There was also in the parish, maybe with its own chapel, a society described in a will of 1525 as "Jhesus Gilde".

The church could have been there in Norman times. It was listed in 1175 and the first known parson was Thomas, in 1202; at some stage it gained a rector. After 1303 when Sir Robert de Creke was priest-in-charge, a series of acolytes had to suffice. In 1315 William of Pont-Audemer in Normandy was ousted after a year as priest and replaced by the acolyte William de Brom, son of the master of the Maison Dieu. Eight years later de Brom was murdered.

St Peter's parish suffered gale damage in the two great storms. In 1334 it had thirty-four taxable properties, but in the next decade it was so impoverished that the Bishop of Norwich had to make a chaplain remain there for a pittance. In 1413 John of Eye, a carpenter repairing the chancel roof, was seriously injured in a fall from scaffolding. His work lasted just ninety-nine years, for in 1512 the chancel was rebuilt and maybe extended. In the 1540s the church sold its goods for £18 to "to keep the harbour in good repair" . . . probably to help St John's. John Day, the Protestant printer, was born in the parish and left money for a gift to the town to be erected in the church. And when Bishop Redman visited the parish in 1597, he was not satisfied with its spiritual life, finding Margaret Finly excommunicate and "vehemently suspected to be a witch", and Thomas Deane "having by his own confession two wives now living".

During the seventeenth century the cliff top crept toward St Peter's. But Dunwich was shrinking faster, and some thirty years before the sea reached the church, the last services were held. Lemarr wrote in the parish register: "Mr Brown, 20 years Vicar of Wenhaston, was ye last gt preached in or about 1654 or 1655, as Mr Driver a very ancient inhabitant there living to about 80 years of age has very often told me." St Peter's remained a mark (with All Saints') to ships edging along the Suffolk coast; one writer said of that journey in 1653: "Dunwich is the best beknown of all these foresaid places, it hath two steeples and on both sides some trees."

As the end neared, St Peter's was stripped of everything usable until only the walls remained. Nothing remarkable was found in the debris; the oldest tomb identified was that of John Melton, from 1481. The east gable crashed down the cliff on 11th December, 1688, and the rest of the building followed; the first part of the tower fell in the winter of 1697. Just before the rest went in 1702 the peal of four bells was removed to All Saints'. The graveyard outlived the church, succumbing in 1734; bones protruded from the cliff face.

Stuart Bacon puts the debris of St Peter's half a mile offshore. In 1972 his divers found part of a stone that had borne a brass matching one at Trotton, Sussex, that dates from 1310; it is now in the museum. The parish register is in the British Library; its title page bears an elaborate capital A, comprising several human faces. It is inscribed:

> A regester booke of all the marriages Crysteninges & burialles that hath ben in the parrishe of St Peters in Dunwich within the county of Suff sence the yeare of our Lord God 1539.

When St Peter's closed, the book was preserved by the Reverend Thomas Roose, vicar of Westleton.

The Seal of Greyfriars now in Dunwich Museum.
Russell Edwards

The Chapels

Dunwich also had at least four small chapels: meeting-places for guilds and clubs, chantries where masses were said for the departed, and exclusive burial-places. We know of St Anthony's, St Francis', St Katherine's and one set up by the Hospitallers; there may have been more. In prosperous times each probably had its own chaplain. All were dissolved after Henry VIII suppressed the monasteries, bar one: St Anthony's, whose location is unknown, may have been lost as early as 1328.

St Francis' Chapel, overlooking the port, was suppressed in 1545. The building survived as a house or an outhouse to a new dwelling; in 1595 the house and St Francis' Meadow to seaward were leased to George Waller. The building eventually fell into ruins, but in 1631 a five-hundred-year lease was optimistically taken on houses on the meadow. In 1740, wrote Gardner:

> The sea raged with such fury . . . that the foundations of St Francis' chapel, which had laid between the [Cock and Hen] hills, was discovered, where besides the ruins of walls were five round stones, near of a bigness, the dimensions of one were 4ft diameter, near two the thickness. There was likewise a circle of large stumps of piles, about 24ft circumference. The bounds of the cemetery were staked, within which the secret repositories of the dead were exposed to open view, several skeletons on the ouze, divested of their coverings, some keeping in pretty good order, others interrupted and scattered as the surges carried them. [Also] a stone coffin, when were human bones covered with tiles. Before a conveniency arrived for removing the coffin, it was broken in two pieces by the violence of the sea, which serve now as steps at each foot of Deering-bridge.

Parker thought the pillars could have been from a Roman temple.

St Katherine's Chapel, in St John's parish, was dissolved at much the same time as St Francis' and apparently washed away soon after. It had its own guild and was occasionally used for burials; in 1523 John Stone left it money for a pair of organs.

The fourth chapel, in St Leonard's parish, was there by the 1220s. Its founders were the Brothers of the Hospital of Jerusalem, who became the Knights Hospitallers. They could have abandoned it on acquiring the Temple a century later, or kept it on until its site was lost shortly after.

111

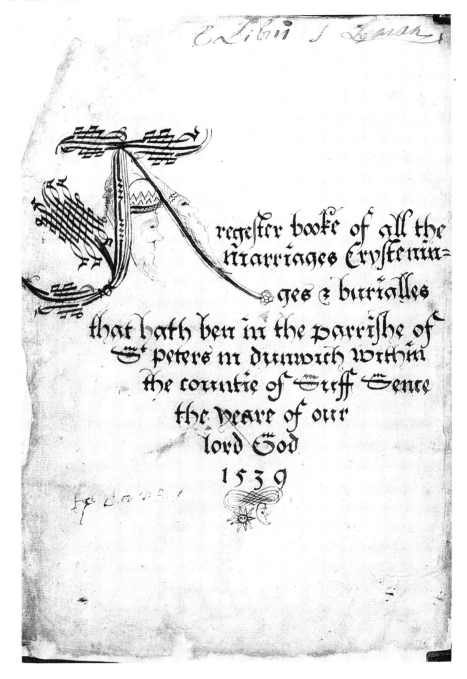

Monastic Houses 16

The Benedictine Cell

ONLY one order of monks is known to have settled at Dunwich: a cell of Benedictines, "black monks", attached to Eye Priory. The order was founded in the sixth century, but the monks may only have arrived after Robert Malet founded the priory, and even then maybe only a dozen of them. There were eight Benedictine monasteries in Suffolk, the main one being at Bury, and other cells at Felixstowe, Hoxne, Sudbury, Snape and Rumburgh. Only the Dunwich cell was linked to Eye, a satellite of Bernay Abbey in Normandy until Richard II severed the link in 1385. The monks withdrew to Eye when the cell was overcome by the sea; the fact that they did not consider rebuilding in Dunwich suggests it was lost in 1328 rather than in 1287, as the first disaster was seen as an isolated blow the town could survive.

The monks of Eye were later to claim that the cell had inherited Felix's seat. Blomefield wrote that it was used by bishops of Elmham into the tenth century; one can imagine the monks taking it on, with the "schools" mentioned in Malet's charter and maybe the Red Book, when all church property in Dunwich passed to them. The monks' legacy to Dunwich was the Covent Garden, bordering the south-western part of the Palesdyke near Gildengate. It was mainly known for its wild thyme and other herbs; Gardner suspected it had been their graveyard, as many human bones were found nearby during the storm of 1740.

Blackfriars

The Dominicans, known as friars preachers or black friars, were the only order in Dunwich to stay put until their suppression. Ringed by a stone wall with several gates, their house was in the south of St John's parish, about three hundred yards south-east of All Saints' between the market-place and Gildengate. Blackfriars was founded by Sir Roger Holish, with support from Henry III and Archbishop Grosseteste, himself a Suffolk man, at much the same time as houses at Ipswich and Sudbury. Building was under way by April, 1256, when Henry gave seven oaks from his forests in Essex; he may also have given the site. Confusion over when Blackfriars was established has arisen from a document implying that in 1227 Edward I sent twenty-four friars there 16s for two

Opposite page: *The parish register of St Peter's has survived, not least by virtue of its unusual title page with a capital 'A' bearing three human faces.*
British Library

113

days' food. Yet as the Dominicans only reached England in 1228, Edward must have directed his charity elsewhere, maybe to the Hospitallers whose arrival in Dunwich had caused a fuss the year before. The house and its forty to fifty friars remained in royal favour for some time; even if Edward I could not have fed them, Henry III did. In 1291 it was left £5 by Eleanor of Castile, and when the site was enlarged in 1349 Edward III gave his blessing.

Soon after the friars arrived, they fell out with the Dominicans of Norwich over where each could preach and seek alms. Geoffrey of Walsingham and William St Martin from Blackfriars met two of the Norwich friars at the Austin Friary at Herringfleet on 10th January, 1259, to settle the matter. Brother William of Nottingham, divinity reader to the Norwich friars, arbitrated, ruling that the Waveney should mark the boundary as it did between Norfolk and Suffolk; the parishes of Rushmere and Mendham, which straddled it, went to Dunwich. The rancour did not last; in 1271 William of Dunwich, a civic leader in Norwich and benefactor to the Franciscans there, left Blackfriars a garden.

The house was unscathed by the storm of 1287, though the friars must have joined in the rescue effort. And the sole sequel to that of 1328, the ensuing decay and the Black Death was the adding of five acres to its site by John de Wengefield, probably a forebear of the Sir Ralph Wingfield who was buried at Blackfriars. Many benefactors, starting with the founder, were interred there: Augustine Valeyns MP, a survivor of the Gascon expedition; Dame Joan Weyland, sister of an earl of Suffolk, and her husband John; Thomas Brewes, son of Robert Brewes, MP; Sir Rauf Offord; Sir Henry Laxfield; Sir Walter Hardishall; Sir Henry Harrold; and Richard Botyll of Leiston and his two wives.

In 1355 Blackfriars became embroiled in church intrigue, friar Thomas Hopman acting at the papal court for the Bishop of Ely in a dispute with the King, a patron of the house. The Prior was ordered to arrest him on his return for leaving the realm without a licence; whether he did is not recorded. There was also the occasional plea for sanctuary, as when Albert of Jena hammered on the door to escape continental justice.

By 1385 the sea was almost at the friars' perimeter wall and they prepared to move to Blythburgh. But for a century it hardly advanced, and the house was even compensated for its losses, gaining St Nicholas' churchyard in 1413. Dunwich folk had little to give; Thomas Reeve who donated 10s in 1482 hailed from Darsham.

Blackfriars was still a going concern when abolished in 1538, though the sea had been nibbling at its grounds for decades. The former prior, now Bishop of Dover, wrote to Thomas Cromwell that he had suppressed twenty friaries, among them the black and grey of Dunwich; he urged that lead from their roofs be moved to London or elsewhere as it was piled near the cliff edge. The friary's assets were its garden and orchard and two adjacent holdings worth £1 3s 4d a year; let briefly by the Crown, they passed in the 1540s to John Eyre, a major holder of monastic lands in East Anglia. The last of the building went over the cliff in 1717, part of the grounds surviving as farmland until later that century.

Greyfriars

The gates, perimeter wall and ruin of Greyfriars, the house of the Franciscans, the friars minor, are the most imposing survival of medieval Dunwich. Yet this was not their original home; that was threatened by the sea within sixty years of being built and was abandoned. The order was founded by Francis of Assisi in 1210, reaching England in 1224, two years before his death. Soon after his canonization in 1228, a friary was founded in Dunwich by Richard FitzJohn and his wife Alice; in 1230 Henry III gave it land in the north east of the town, at the seaward end of Dam Street. Dunwich became one of East Anglia's main Franciscan centres; in the order's third custody based on Cambridge, the house was equal to that at Ipswich and outranked those at Bury and Yarmouth. Its complement of forty friars or so was, however, much the same as Blackfriars'.

The storm of 1287 severely damaged the building and brought the cliff top uncomfortably close. The Valeyns, Falaises and Codouns found the friars a new seven-acre site well inland, just outside the Palesdyke between Middlegate and Bridgegate; with royal permission the rampart was levelled there in 1290 to keep them in touch with the town. The Franciscans sought permission to enclose the original friary site, arguing that it would be "indecent" for their graveyard to be put to secular uses. By the time it was given late in 1328, a second great storm had removed three-quarters of the site. Yet a remnant withstood the sea until at least 1455.

The builders of the new Greyfriars put round it a wall of stone and flint that lasted almost intact until a seaward section was levelled to give a clear line of fire to a Second World War anti-aircraft battery in the grounds. Only in the 1990s has it been threatened by the erosion of the cliffs. The well-preserved main gate on the Westleton road, which survived the passage of the guns unscathed, boasts an arch and a smaller doorway. The townspeople used two lesser gates, of which nothing survives. The friars' chapel was probably modest, given the simplicity of the order and the little time it devoted to religious observances, but there were stained-glass windows to St Cicely and St Andrew. The living quarters were

115

on the south side of a cloister, overhung by an upper floor probably housing the refectory. The roof was almost certainly made of timbers from the royal galley that had been mouldering in Dunwich harbour; in March, 1305, Edward I ordered the town to give the ship with "all its tackle and appurtenances" to the friars. It must thus have been twenty years after their first house became well-nigh uninhabitable before the replacement was complete.

The warden of Greyfriars up to 1482 was John Lacey, replaced that year by Nicholas Buckenham; in 1505 it was George Muse. Nicholas Wicet, ordained priest at Cambridge in 1484, was at Greyfriars in 1514 when he was left 3s 4d. Thomas of Dunwich, a Cambridge Franciscan ordained deacon in September, 1353, may also have had links with the house.

Greyfriars had more benefactors than its Dominican counterpart. In 1470 John Moreff left the friars 100 pence to sing for the souls of himself, his relatives and friends, and twelve years later Thomas Reeve left each house 10s. In 1521 Nicholas Cuddon left the Franciscans his pightle to sing a dirge for him. Benefactors buried in the chapel include Sir Robert Valence (Valeyns?) and Sir Hubert Dernford. Interred elsewhere in the friary were Dame Ida of Ilketshall; Sir Peter Mellis, his wife Dame Dunne and his mother

The ruins of Greyfriars, with the extension built by Sir George Downing in 1710. Dunwich Museum

Dame Anne; John and Margaret Francans; Dame Butler of Furnival; Austin of Cales and his wife Joan; John Falaise (who changed the family name to Cliff), his wife Beatrice and priest-son Augustine; the wife and daughter of Richard Phellip; and Peter Codun (probably the MP).

Also buried there was the heart of Dame Hawise Poynings, probably a fifteenth-century benefactor. In Gardner's time a labourer working in the ruin found a mole; when he went to put it outside he noticed a small earthen vessel topped by a brass plate inscribed "Ave Maria Gracca Plena" ("Hail Mary, full of grace"), and broke it open. Gardner wrote with regret: "This man being a servant durst not neglect his master's time to make diligent research, although he was inclined to think there were more things." He believed the heart had been placed in a niche, covered and secured with a buckle.

One of Greyfriars' seals, from the fifteenth century, was a pointed oval depicting John the Baptist under a canopied arch. Clothed in a camel skin whose head dangled at his feet, he held in his left hand a plaque of the Lamb of God, pointing to it with his right. Beside him knelt a friar, with a scroll reading: "S: JOH: ORA: P': ME" ("St John, pray for me"). The seal bore the legend "Sigillio Gardiani Fratrum Minor Donewycy" ("Seal of the Warden of the Friars Minor of Dunwich"). Another showed a ship with a large mainsail, a king seated at the bow and at the stern a bishop with crozier; it was inscribed "Sigillu' Fr'm Minor Donewic" ("Seal of the Friars Minor of Dunwich").

At its dissolution Greyfriars was Dunwich's premier religious house. Being inland from Blackfriars it was more of a prize, as its land and buildings had a future; they passed to John Eyre. Parts soon fell into ruin as much of its masonry was taken by builders, but the main building became a private house. Sir George Downing bought it as a summer home in 1710 and built a three-storey crenellated brick extension facing the sea, including a hall for civic business and prison cells. The Barnes bought the new building in 1807 as a farmhouse but demolished it around 1815.

Beside the heart of Dame Hawise, the site has yielded Roman tile fragments, numerous twelfth- and thirteenth-century half-pennies and farthings, the seal from a bull of the fifteenth-century pope Pius III, seventeenth-century Nuremberg counters, nails, pins, a pewter dish and fragments of window glass. A dig in 1936 uncovered a fine stone head.

The friary grounds were once noted for the Dunwich rose, a rare burnet with black hips found between Dunwich and Sizewell; the friars are said to have cultivated it, naming it the "holy flower". Today the Dunwich rose is hard to find. The friary enclosure survives in private hands, and the ruins, gateway and wall are now protected as an ancient monument.

Temple and Hospitals 17

The Temple

THE PRECEPTORY of the Knights Templar gave Dunwich a dash of colour. The Templars, founded in 1118 to guard the road to Jerusalem, became international bankers and were suppressed as heretics, their leader invoking a highly effective curse on the royal house of France. Probably because Dunwich had been a crusader port, the order set up a house there which, though having only seven members at its dissolution, amassed considerable wealth. It owned property in the town and at Westleton, Dingle and elsewhere, rents being paid at a "Temple court" on All Souls' Day, 2nd November; pardons were also available then, no doubt for a fee.

The Temple was in the south west of the town, just south and to seaward of Middlegate. The author of the *Index Monasticus* rated it the most important of the Templars' four houses in the Norwich diocese. Stow wrote in 1573 that its recently demolished church of St Mary and St John was "vaulted over, and the rofe of the same church and also the tyles ware leaded all over"; it was probably round, as were most of the order's churches. Attached to it, fine rather than large, were the knights' quarters and guest rooms for Templars passing through. There was also a chapel at Dingle, probably the building mentioned in a ledger of 1310 as having cost 2s 6d to rethatch. It had a chaplain, who no doubt ministered to the hamlet and said masses for its departed, and a clerk.

The knights in their ceremonial white mantle and red cross were a dashing sight, but the black or brown of the lower ranks would have been more often seen in the streets of Dunwich. Once the Crusades came to an effective end in 1204, the Templars had little to do but perform limited devotions and put their money to work. No doubt they helped Dunwich merchants raise capital for trading expeditions, the more so if there were no Jews in the town. It is, however, the Temple of which Stow noted that it was there "in the Jews time".

One would like to imagine the Templars on hand to resist the siege of 1173, pouring boiling oil onto attackers' heads and roving out to engage them. Individuals may have been, but the order probably set up shop some fifteen years later. Dunwich is not mentioned in the Inquest of Templars taken in 1185, but does appear in an addition after the original was bound. Richard I is said to have given the site—which would make 1189 the earliest

Opposite page: *The Maison Dieu, near the end of its life, 1690. Nathaniel Back's sketch redrawn by Hamlet Watling.* Dunwich Museum

119

date for foundation—and King John added to his grant. The Temple also owned one of England's very first windmills, let for half a mark a year.

Their fighting days behind them, the Dunwich Templars prospered, their lands augmented by benefactions and favoured further by Henry III. But their muscular reputation continued to attract sanctuary-seekers; more are recorded as fleeing to them than anywhere else in Dunwich. They sheltered Adam le Trompere of Chelmondiston, a self-confessed thief, in 1287; Reginald Sefare of Gislingham, where they had their other Suffolk preceptory; Henry Stelt of Colness and William Filisol of Little Ocle, Essex.

Eventually the Templars became scapegoats for disillusion with crusading, and the Church, dependent on them as bankers, began to feel the tail was wagging the dog. In 1308 Edward II had all 135 English Knights Templar arrested and their property seized; denying heresy, they were condemned to perpetual penance in 1310. They were the lucky ones: Philip the Fair had more than fifty French Templars burned at the stake. Pope Clement V disbanded the order in 1312.

John de Medefield was allowed to stay on as warden of the Temple for nine months at 9d a week; his assistant, Richard Osmunde, got 3d a day, the chaplain at Dingle 2d a day and his clerk 2d a week. The knights, confined to monasteries, were paid 4d a day; in 1313 the king ordered John de Eggemore, custodian of the manor (as the Temple's rights had become known), to pay arrears to Robert de Spaunton and John Coffyn. The house's assets were found to include gold and siver cups, seven gold rings, thirty-five gold florins, £111 14s 6¼d in a purse, a mattress worth 6d, nineteen lambs and a thousand herrings, two old carts, two chests containing papal bulls, a pair of organs (12d), four sets of vestments (29s 8d), a silver cross (18d), two gold chalices (16s and 3s), books of offices, two small chests with relics of the saints (no value!), stone from Normandy (13s 4d) and twenty cheeses (2s 6d).

The Pope granted the Templars' property to the more pliant Knights Hospitallers, but it was 1322 before Edward conformed. The Hospitallers were no strangers to Dunwich; having absorbed the Brothers of the Hospital of Jerusalem, they already had a chapel in St Leonard's parish. They now took on the Temple, holding services there and maybe at Dingle, and the manor with its court. But the house lost influence through the seepage of wealth from the town and the loss of its lands to the sea, partly offset by gaining a plot in St Martin's parish in 1408. The Hospitallers shared the fate of the monastic orders, being wound up in 1540; though their order was revived by Mary, its reprieve was brief. The Crown kept the goods of the Dunwich house, and on its dissolution in 1562 its lands and the lordship of the manor passed to Thomas Andrews. The Temple was demolished within ten years and its foundations washed away in Charles I's time; in 1979 divers recovered the marble matrix for the brass from a fourteenth-century knight's tomb near where it had stood.

St James' Hospital

The Crusaders brought back from the Holy Land not only wealth and tales of chivalry but the ghastly disease of leprosy. It was no stranger to England—in 1085 Hugh de Orwell, Bishop of London, died of it—but it now became a serious problem. A special synod in 1200 decided that groups of lepers might build their own churches and appoint priests to them.

St James' Hospital, "the Lazar", was intended both for lepers and for the poor, aged and sick who were reckoned in such straits that leprosy would hold no fear for them (the view that it is not communicable dates only from the twentieth century). Its purpose dictated its siting, outside the Palesdyke beside the church that became its chapel, with a "lepers' gate" by Deering Bridge. The hospital—the church, a separate lepers' chapel and a range of cottages—had the softest water in the village, from a "Holy Well" over the road; it vanished in the 1900s when a gravedigger broke the stratum that held water from an underground spring.

The hospital was founded late in Richard I's reign, conceivably by King John as Count of Mortain. The greatest-known benefactor was Walter de Riboff; around 1206 he granted "to the church and house and Hubert the chaplain and his successors, for the soul of Henry de Cressy and his own good estate" land in Dunwich, at Brandeston (forty acres), Heveningham and Carlton Colville, eight bushels of wheat at Michaelmas, two loaves daily from his oven, 1½ pints of ale from his brewhouse and the tithes of his mills. The chaplain received 5s a year and two "leprous brethren" shared a measure of corn each Michaelmas. Non-lepers in the house took communion and made offerings on feast days at Brandeston Church, and could be buried there. They seem not to have lived under a religious rule.

Before long the masters had their hands in the till. Stow wrote that both Dunwich hospitals were:

> now latelie greatly decayed and hendred by evyle masters . . . and other evil disposed parsons which doe sell away divers londs and rents . . . to the great hindrance of the poore people of the said hospitall, as plainly it is to be proved. I wolde to God these injuries and wrongs done to these 2 poor hospitalls myght be restored and reformed again to their former estate, for sewerely whoso ever shall doo it, shall do a good worke before God. I pray God brynge it soo to passe. Amen

121

One "sordid master" after another, in Gardner's words, plundered the hospital, to such effect that in 1252 Henry III ordered the mayor and bailiffs to investigate. In 1312 Edward II allowed the inmates to beg for a year as the hospital could not keep them; the permit was extended for three years and reissued for three-year periods in 1320 and 1330. William Cotterell's appointment as master of both hospitals and one at Orford in 1389 could have been a sign of their poverty, his greed or a recurrence of the Black Death—each hospital had a rapid succession of masters, Cotterell lasting only six months. In 1393 St James' and the Maison Dieu were again given a joint warden, Hugh Blythe[31].

St James' lost its final leper in 1536 at the latest; there were no more burials in its graveyard until the 1820s. Not belonging to a religious order, its other inmates survived the end of the monasteries. Those entering the hospital were supposed to leave their families behind, but in 1612 the Corporation ordered the "poor people" not to keep their children there, on pain of being told to leave themselves. The hospital's meagre treasures were hidden in its church, though neither Henry VIII's agents nor Dowsing troubled to visit. The sanctum burst open, to the surprise of the villagers, on 30th January, 1744. The house's revenues had shrunk to £26 by 1739 and £21 19s 8d fifteen years later. The master lived on 40s a year, and three or four paupers in one tumbledown house, all that remained of the buildings, shared the rest. At some point in the nineteenth century St James' closed, its funds passing to the Dunwich Town Trust.

The Maison Dieu

The Maison Dieu (Domus Dei or House of God) was really a large almshouse. A half-timbered range of buildings, it stood outside the Palesdyke between Bridgegate and the port; to seaward stood its chapel, dedicated to the Holy Trinity. A refuge for the poor and simple, it housed by 1251 a master appointed by the King, six brethren and several sisters, all living under a religious rule. Like St James', it was generously endowed, with houses and land in Dunwich bringing in 4s 6d a year, and land at Heveningham, Ellow and Blyford. The house's oval seal implied that it had been founded in the reign of Henry III or even by him: in the centre were three lions surmounted by a triple cross, the lowest hub of which bore two *fleurs-de-lis*. It was inscribed "SIGILLUM FRATRUM DOMUS DEI DE DONEWICO" ("Seal of the brethren of the house of God at Dunwich"); the sisters were evidently a later addition. Gifts to the house were mainly for upkeep: for example, a bequest in 1455 by Sybil Francis for the fabric of its chapel, 3s 4d from Richard Sharparew in 1512 for repairs and a gift in 1527 for paving in the chapel.

Stow said that the Maison Dieu had been:

> an house of grete privilege, and a place exempt, and was a very little proper house, and a proper lodgyn for the masters of the same for the tyme being to dwell in, as there hath been masters of the same Massendue in tymes past that hath been worshiple, viz. one there was of late days a Master of Arte, and another that was a Sqyer, and such like.

In 1251 it tried to recover articles taken and sold by Robert FitzReginald, but he died before they could be traced. John de Sancta Maria, King's chaplain, and in 1258 Robert Fulconis, a King's clerk, were brought in as master to restore the fortunes of the house, some of whose inmates had been sent packing as there was no money for food. Whatever good Fulconis did in thirty-two years there was undone by his successor, Robert de Sefeld, after whose removal in 1305 the inmates were allowed to beg for alms, six years before the lepers. Three years later Sefeld, now vicar of Brampton, offered to "take care of" almost £112 found by auditors at the Temple[32]. He was followed as master by Adam de Brom, whose son became priest of St Peter's and was murdered in 1323.

The Maison Dieu possessed the town's only known object of reverence: a cross reputed to have miraculous healing powers. In the mid-thirteenth century it vanished, turning up years later at St Osyth Abbey in Essex, where it had been taken by William Litequene, a brother of the Maison Dieu, when appointed a canon there. The house took the Abbot of St Osyth to court, a Dunwich jury swore that the cross was indeed the missing one, and it was returned to Adam de Brom in 1306. As the Abbot of St Osyth was patron of Blythburgh Priory and clearly had Dunwich connections, foul play cannot be ruled out.

On the dissolution of the monasteries, the Maison Dieu relaxed its rule and apparently abandoned its chapel. It was demolished in 1573 save for its south wall, which survived into the eighteenth century. From its estimated site, divers in 1981 recovered carved masonry imposts. With an annual income of £93 the house was better off than St James': in 1596 there was enough for a schoolmaster, Robert Aleyn, to teach the inmates. But by 1754 it was down to £11 17s 10d; the master received £2 and the balance was split between a few paupers who shared his quarters and others in a decrepit house. At one point in the eighteenth century there were only the master and four poor women.

The Maison Dieu faded from the scene before St James', its assets passing to the Town Trust and its site becoming the beach car park. But it lives on in a pair of nearby almshouses built by the trust in 1932 for £732. Ernest Read Cooper, a trustee, championed the scheme, writing:

> And so after nearly 400 years the prayer of that anonymous scribe [Stow] is to be brought to pass, and therein will be done "a good worke befor God" and let there be no more "evil masters and covetous persons." Amen.

DISASTER AND DECLINE

The Tempest, Act One

18

NOTHING could have prepared Dunwich for the disaster that struck on New Year's Eve, 1287—23rd March by our reckoning. Violent storms and high tides were nothing new, and the worst anyone could have foreseen was that the haven would be blocked yet again. Erosion had made little recent impact on the cliffs close to the town's eastern edge, so there was no reason for Dunwich folk to suppose as the storm blew up that they were at risk.

How wrong they were. Waves battered the cliffs until a slice of the town collapsed into the sea, the gale flattened buildings inland and the sea thundered over Kingsholme to swamp the lower town. One can imagine the panic as houses, churches, orchards, livestock and people were swept away and families confronted with death tried to flee. Alarm must have been almost as great away from the cliff edge as people rushed indoors to avoid falling trees and masonry, choked the streets leading up from the Daine as they fled the surging waters, and huddled in terror as their homes groaned in the gale.

The storm wrought havoc throughout East Anglia. John Eversden, the Benedictine chronicler of Bury St Edmunds, wrote that, "as well through ye vehemence of ye wind, as violence of ye sea, manby churches were overthrowne and destroyed . . . at Yarmouth, Donwich and Ipswich"; the province was "for the most part turned into a standing poole, so that an intolerable multitude of men were overflowed, and destroyed with the water".

As it subsided, a horrific sight confronted the survivors. A strip of the town a good hundred yards wide in places—maybe a tenth of the whole—had crashed to the shore, where a jumble of masonry, timber, trees, household objects and the corpses of adults, children, livestock and pets was being ground by the waves. The waves had swamped marshes and meadows inland and invaded the lower town, smashing to matchwood many ships that had been riding at anchor. Ships' timbers, rigging, nets, bodies and masonry almost blocked the haven, and to the delight of the mariners of

Opposite page:
Shipping from Dunwich's heyday, 1269 in the reign of Henry III. This stylised etching by Atkinson shows five contrasting types of vessel, that in the foreground obviously a warship. The quayside at Dunwich was mean and tumultuous, with none of the fortifications in this fictitious scene. National Maritime Museum

Blythburgh and Walberswick the water was starting to force a passage through Kingsholme that would suit them better. In the upper town fallen trees, houses, steeples and windmills blocked the streets or had crashed through the roofs of those who had sought shelter. It must have seemed that the Day of Judgement had come.

What actually had been lost? We know that churches were flattened or washed away, but which? How many houses had been swept into the sea, flooded out or crushed? How much of the Palesdyke had gone, assuming it flanked the seaward side of the town? How badly had Dunwich's merchant and fishing fleets been depleted? At this point fact gives way to guesswork.

Almost all the known churches of medieval Dunwich were still there well after 1287. There is only doubt over St Bartholomew's and St Michael's; the fact that Eye Priory did not seek recompense for them until 1331 suggests they were lost in 1328, but unless there were further churches of which we know nothing—or fanciful antiquaries were right about St Felix's and St Patrick's —they would have to be those lost in 1287. If any church fell and was replaced, some benefaction would surely have been noted. The storm could also have swept away the monks' cell, though that too may have gone in 1328. It certainly alarmed the Franciscans, who had built their friary in all innocence near the cliff edge; the sea tore away a corner of its grounds and the building suffered gale damage. They decided to make a new home on a sheltered site where it could be built to last, as it has. As for houses and shops, it is clear that some were lost with the town's eastern fringe, others by the harbour were engulfed, and more, notably in St Peter's parish, were flattened by the gale. St Michael's and St Bartholomew's parishes were also hard hit, though flooding may have done much of the damage. It would not be fanciful to suggest that in one night Dunwich lost over two hundred houses.

Dunwich now resembled an apple with a bite out of its top left-hand corner and a straight slice taken from its right side. However far the sea advanced that night, the length lost from its eastern perimeter was far greater, maybe four hundred yards. The last of the Eastwood had gone, and almost certainly any gate leading to it.

The effect on the town's economy was catastrophic. A number of its ships would have been away from port, though the outlook for any at sea that night was grim. But the Iceland barks would have been in, and with them many of Dunwich's merchant ships and those of other ports and lands. Some, like the royal galley, remarkably stayed afloat; others would have been driven on to the marshes and left high and dry, or dashed against the quay. The ship-yards, themselves hard hit, must have taken a while to get a fleet of any size seaworthy; it was eight years before Dunwich was asked to contribute to the King's fleet, and when it did fresh disaster struck.

Painfully, Dunwich set about the task of rebuilding. Rubble had to be dragged from the streets of the upper town, and crushed buildings, shingle and maritime debris from the lower—where little could be done until the waters subsided, which took some time. The first priority was to recover and bury the dead and find a church intact enough for masses to be said for them. The task must have been harrowing, with rotting bodies coming to light weeks and months later. Families who had escaped before their homes were washed away would have searched amid the scavengers on the rubble-strewn shore for their possessions; anything that could float would have been washed toward Aldeburgh, and what remained could be crushed by the waves or by masonry from falling churches.

If some civic notables were among the casualties and others did not rise to the occasion, that would explain why new leaders were now elected: Simon Baldock (bailiff eleven years before) became mayor and the bailiffs included "Luke Scott, bailiff twenty years before and pirate in the meantime"[33]. Discontent with the running of the town now come to a head, twenty-one mariners and merchants flouting the authority of the mayor and bailiffs. The royal reply to complaints from these notables is dated 12th October, so the challenge came either just before or just after the disaster. Parker saw the twenty-one as a force for good government, but that was not what the mayor told the King. He accused them of vowing to stop his court sitting, thwarting execution of the justices' judgements, abstracting fines and disrupting the peace. They also withheld their taxes, apparently suspecting the bailiffs of lining their pockets; that year, partly as a result of the disaster, just £12 8s 4d was collected toward the fee-farm. The protesters were remanded to prison to appear before the King; what they told him is not known, but in August, 1289, an inquiry was ordered into the finances of thirteen bailiffs who had served over the previous thirty years, and money was shaken out of their pockets.

The greybeards elected in 1287 were ousted the next year by novices, who in turn were sent packing in 1289. By 1293 the original clique was back in control—but not for long, as it took on the Crown and lost. The Sheriff of Norfolk and Suffolk sent Adam Church of Knodishall and Adam Skill of Westleton to enforce a writ distraining property in Dunwich. The bailiffs locked them up for a week, and the ensuing lawsuit ended in their being awarded 5 marks damages and the town forfeiting its privileges. Gardner noted that bailiff Michael FitzJohn "made peace with the King on payment of one mark, and one-half mark for John le Folur; the third defendant, Henry Ringulf, dead". Dunwich's liberties were restored, but the upheaval could explain why it sent no one to the Model Parliament of 1295. Two MPs did go the next year and two to York in 1298, the first whose names survive: Thomas Thorald and William "the Priest's son". The fact that such persons as William existed owed more to livings being held by men not in full holy orders than to sexual licence.

The only known new construction after the disaster was the rebuilding of Greyfriars safely inland; it apparently took twenty years to complete. Some of the dispossessed probably left town; others would have been put up by neighbours or in religious houses until there were homes for them. Fewer new houses were built than had been lost, hence the open spaces that began to appear. And quite a few must have been left precariously close to the new cliff edge, where further falls might take place at any time.

Reopening the port was a major task. A start was made by hauling debris from the haven to make it navigable and digging out the Daine from under tons of mud and shingle. Closing the new channel across Kingsholme took longer, not least because Blythburgh, Walberswick and Southwold were profiting from it. Dunwich complained to Edward I that merchants were putting in there rather than to the Daine, recalled that it had already had one such channel filled in and sought leave to do so again at its neighbours' expense. The King agreed, so the borough had the work done and claimed the cost as an extortionate £2,000. When its rivals understandably failed to pay, Dunwich urged Edward in 1304 to make them—but now put the cost at £500. Next it built a tollhouse on Kingsholme, with a bailiff and assistant rowing out to incoming ships to collect Dunwich's due. Walberswick saw this as provocation and in 1324 sent a gang to burn it down, killing the bailiff on duty. The odd ship still got through, so Walberswick embarked on a campaign of "persuasion" which in 1327 brought a complaint from Dunwich that merchants were being bullied into staying away.

A weakened Dunwich was more vulnerable than ever to privateers. In 1295 Zeeland pirates staged the boldest raid of all, not only sailing into the harbour to despoil ships at anchor but landing raiding parties who stripped the town of more of its wealth. By 1316 the combination of piracy and feuding between ports was causing such havoc that the defence of the entire east coast was entrusted to John de Botetourt. Despite this revival of the "Saxon Shore", the mayhem continued until the outbreak of the Hundred Years' War.

Dunwich may also now have had to face a final onslaught by the Bigods. Roger Bigod, the fifth Earl, refused to go to Gascony in 1297 while Edward went to Flanders, arguing that he was only bound to serve if the King were there too. "By God, sir Earl", Edward reputedly told him, "you shall go or hang!" Bigod replied: "By God, O King, I will neither go nor hang." Dunwich built and equipped eleven ships for the expedition, but four were sunk off Bordeaux—though not with all hands as was later claimed. With so many of its men away with that fleet the town was vulnerable; maybe the thought of loot influenced Bigod to stay behind. Redstone suggested that the final siege of Dunwich now took place, and that it was with the town in its weakened state that Bigod besieged it for six days, plundered it and carried off hostages to Kelsale. Documents studied by Parker put this siege in the late 1260s, but as they were written much later it is conceivable that the reference, like those to hundreds of sailors drowning off Gascony, was a slip of the pen and that the Bigods did strike for the last time in 1297.

Roger Bigod forced an imprisoned Edward to confirm his titles, but had to give up the earl marshal's rod in 1301. He died without issue in 1306 and the King's youngest son, Thomas, took his place, and the earldom of Norfolk. Edward II granted Dunwich, which had so long eluded the Bigods, to his paramour Hugh Despenser; on Despenser's execution in 1327, that too passed to Norfolk- —though it never brought the income he had been led to expect.

There was further drama at Epiphany, 1308, when the Templars were seized and charged with heresy; one can imagine the townspeople looking on as the proud and once gallant knights were frogmarched away to face likely death. In the event they suffered no such fate, being paid 4d a day to do penance in monasteries for the rest of their lives. The chaplains of the Temple and its chapel at Dingle stayed on for a time, also paid from the riches of the house on which Dunwich folk were no doubt allowed to feast their eyes as proof of cupidity.

The fact that other towns had been almost as hard-hit by the disaster of 1287 must have led Dunwich folk to overestimate their chances of recovery. It took a while to realize that they were being left behind, but by the end of Edward I's reign it was obvious. The port failed to regain all its trade, and rival fairs and markets, operated by manors and religious houses under royal licence, wooed commerce away; in 1322 Dunwich complained to Parliament that they were harming its finances. The rich began to slip away; we last hear of the Joces in 1313 and the FitzJohns in 1319. There was little more erosion, but alarmingly some homes away from danger were now being abandoned. Moreover, inmates of St James' Hospital and the Maison Dieu were having to beg for their keep, though this was partly due to embezzlement of their funds. In 1324 the royal Chancery, responding to a further petition, ordered an inquiry into how Dunwich had suffered from the sea; its findings were overtaken by events. The subsidy list for 1327 shows Dunwich contributing just £6 4s 4½d to the Exchequer, the least of any Suffolk borough; the biggest tax-payer, Richard Gerard, was assessed at just 10s. Yet the town's condition would soon become immeasurably worse.

The Tempest, Act Two

O N 14TH JANUARY, 1328, a second cataclysmic storm struck, violent north-east winds whipping up a high tide to tear away more of the town. The heart was ripped out of wealthy St Nicholas' parish, with all but thirty of its two hundred remaining houses sliding down the cliff or flattened by the gale. St Martin's Church was left on the cliff edge, and its parish lost three quarters of its hundred houses. Much of St Leonard's parish was overcome by the sea, with the church narrowly escaping. On higher ground, many houses round St Peter's and St Michael's churches and the monks' cell, once by their tradition the bishops' "palace", now succumbed. Most of the ruins of the first Greyfriars, not a century old, also thundered down the cliff. Several windmills were blown on their backs.

A second slice had been taken from the apple, though its core was still some way from the cliff edge. As much again was probably lost as in 1287, with more of the now-derelict Palesdyke. The death-toll can only be guessed at, but this time fewer families would have lingered.

This was also the moment when the haven was finally choked. Mountainous waves again tore ships from their moorings and swamped low-lying parts of the town, as well as Dingle and the meadows round the estuary. But this time, when the storm abated, Kingsholme was joined to the foreshore. The waters that had built up in the estuary had forced a channel across Kingsholme, two miles north of Dunwich and a mile short of today's river mouth; it was described as "very narrow and not deep", but there was no question of filling it in, as it was the only access Dunwich or its rivals now had to the sea. Dunwich erected a wooden quay to replace the Daine, which had been buried, and required all goods shipped through the new haven to be handled at its market, even if landed at Blythburgh, Walberswick or Southwold. Eager to cash in on its new accessibility, Walberswick manned a stockade to deter ships from sailing to Dunwich up what was now a creek. Dunwich swiftly retaliated; in 1330 Mayor John Payne led an attack on Anastasia Butt's ship on the Southwold foreshore which was later claimed to have cost sixteen lives. For a time the neighbouring ports were almost at war.

The disaster knocked the stuffing out of Dunwich by proving that lightning could strike twice; its people must have begun to

Opposite page: *Ships of the fourteenth and fifteenth centuries. Another etching by Atkinson.* National Maritime Museum

wonder if the entire town would eventually be swept to oblivion. And as they began the task of clearing up, sights were lower than in 1287—though All Saints' Church was rebuilt, maybe financed by the assets of lost churches. The town's economy was also left in a parlous state. In Henry II's time Dunwich had ranked fifth in aids paid to the Crown; now it was not among England's thirty wealthiest towns and was soon to default on its dues to the Prior of Eye. A summons to Parliament—rarely ignored by boroughs under Edward III—twice went unanswered. Tax returns for 1333/34 still show a substantial and balanced community, but also how much had been lost. St John's parish was now the largest with ninety-one taxable properties (some involving several houses or shops but also including land). St Nicholas', formerly with three hundred, could now muster just forty-two; there were thirty-four each in St Martin's and St Peter's, and thirty-three each in All Saints' and St Leonard's.

Dunwich's decline accelerated in the late 1330s. Erosion continued, with St Martin's Church lost by 1342 and just seven houses in its parish remaining. St Nicholas' parish was down to eighteen houses, but that was because patches of dereliction were now appearing in the formerly crowded central area. The wealthy and enterprising were moving to towns with a future; we last hear of the Barnards, Battings, Boytons and Richers in 1334, the Valeyns in 1338 (though there are later Valances), the Odes in 1339, the Cliffs in 1341 and the Austins in 1343. By then there were probably under three thousand inhabitants.

In 1346 Edward III deprived Dunwich of its mayor and halved the number of bailiffs; the line begun by John de Valeyns 130 years before ended with Augustine Fitzwilliam. This was probably when Dunwich gained its final seal, described thus by Gardner:

> A King standing in the hull of a ship riding in the waves without rudder and rigging expressed king Edward III protecting the community of this sea-port-town deprived of its late governors, the Mayor etc, and the loss of navigation by their port being choked.

By 1349, he quoted from a contemporary source, the "great part of the town, with upwards of 400 houses which paid rent to the fee-farm, with certain shops and windmills, had been devoured by the sea". This statement has created a misleading impression that all were lost in a single catastrophe, instead of over a period.

Further calamities had overtaken Dunwich by then. The opening of the Hundred Years' War reputedly caused heavy losses of men and ships—though partly because the Gascon tragedy has been wrongly attributed to this period. Dunwich could still boast a sizable fleet, sending nine ships with 262 men on the first expedition in 1338. One can only guess how many it lost between that abortive campaign and the siege of Calais nine years later, to which it sent six vessels. Men from the town also joined Edward III's army, maybe because there was little work for them; Henry Lodden, a Dunwich market trader, was among the victors of Crécy in 1346[34].

An even crueller scourge than war and the elements now struck . . . the Black Death. Ships bringing the good news of Crécy and Calais also brought rats carrying the bubonic plague that had reached the Middle East in 1346 and been borne to Europe by Genoese merchantmen. The first infected ship reached Melcombe, Dorset, from Calais on 7th July, 1348, and the plague spread like wildfire; it reached London that autumn, Sudbury by the end of March, 1349, and north Norfolk by late April. How it arrived in Dunwich—by land, by coaster or direct from the Continent—is not known, but early in 1349 it struck. A boil appeared on a groin or armpit, fever and vomiting of blood set in and the victim died of convulsions inside forty-eight hours. Amid panic, mass absolutions and numerous burials, often of the same people, half the people of Suffolk died, and there is no reason to suppose Dunwich got off lightly. A mass grave found when the foundations of St James's Church were dug in the 1820s may have held victims of the Black Death.

The clergy were at greatest risk, having to visit the sick and administer the last rites. In a year eight hundred parishes in the

Hamlet Watling's sketch of the new St James' church. Russell Edwards

gam ab eo: neque nocebo in ue
mea.

Contemporary drawing of a medieval warship from the 14th-century Luttrell Psalter. Almost a cartoon, it would have struck an instant chord with anyone who had grown up in sight of Dunwich haven—note the bowmen fore and aft.
British Library

Norwich diocese lost their priest, eighty-three of them twice; in two monasteries every single person died. The Bishop retired to Hoxne and appointed priests at a furious rate in June, July and August. St John's, Dunwich, had two new parsons in rapid succession, and the Maison Dieu three wardens. A petition of 1352 for a cut in the fee-farm lamented that Dunwich had been "wasted and diminished by the late mortal pestilence", as well as by piratical attacks on its fishermen.

By autumn the plague was dying down. Throughout Europe villages and even towns stood deserted and crops untilled amid gloom, cynicism and anarchy. Empty churches were not just caused by depopulation; an age of Godlessness was setting in. In Norwich ten parish churches out of sixty had gone by 1368; fourteen more became useless. The plague halted work on the towers of St Nicholas' Church, Yarmouth; its namesake at Dunwich was

134

abandoned soon after, the role of the town's premier church reverting to St John's.

Dunwich narrowly escaped the Peasants' Revolt of 1381, which despite its title brought to a head wider tensions; the disasters that had befallen the town had defused the animosity between upper and lower townsmen and the revolt passed it by. The dissident priest John Wraw of Beccles raised his banner at Leiston and marched inland, conflict ensuing at Sudbury and Bury St Edmunds before the revolt's brutal suppression by the Bishop of Norwich.

Though erosion seemingly slowed after the 1340s, the sea was almost at the perimeter of Blackfriars by 1385, having made a little bay; St John's Church to the north and seaward was not yet threatened. The Dominicans were alarmed enough to prepare to move to Blythburgh, but never left; the cliffs' resistance to a further storm in 1394 may have been decisive. The storm was probably responsible, though, for blocking the channel to the sea forced in 1328; at the turn of the century a new one was dug, closer to Dunwich.

There was now national concern over the state of Dunwich and its port. After an inquiry in 1354 into its plight, the fee-farm was cut from £65 a year to £14 10s 9d; even that was hard to raise. In 1364 Edward III urged merchants in Newcastle, Norwich and Yarmouth to trade with Dunwich. Gradually, the worst effects of the Black Death wore off, the economy of the region recovered and grand churches were erected along its coast—but not at Dunwich. This new prosperity passed by on the other side and more of the wealthy moved on: the Scotts sold Scotts Hall in 1363; the Williamsons are last heard of in 1385; the Cooks left soon after 1395; and in 1405 the Helmeths, almost the last link with the great days, vanish from the picture.

In the Shadows   20

DUNWICH entered the fifteenth century having lost more than half its people and many of its finest buildings, and with its harbour barely navigable. It could still boast up to two thousand inhabitants, three parish churches, two friaries, two hospitals, its Temple, a sizable fishing fleet, some merchant trade and at times busy shipyards. But it had lost most of its influence, though its condition was to improve a little as the century wore on.

The Duke of Norfolk had been responsible for the fee-farm, but when he was killed in a revolt in 1405 Dunwich became a town in the royal gift, from which a custodian (or favourite) raised what he could and passed what was due to the Crown. In 1447, for example, it was bestowed for life (which was not long) on William de la Pole, Earl of Suffolk. The Hopton family provided several custodians, beginning a long if peripheral connection with Dunwich. Henry VI imprisoned the first, William, for erratic handling of the fee-farm; he may not have been wholly to blame as Henry reduced the sum required to £12 2s 1d. John Hopton was both master of the Maison Dieu in 1466 and lord of Blythburgh until his death in the late 1480s. The family gained status through the Wars of the Roses and came into royal sinecures; Arthur Hopton was to serve as a Dunwich MP in 1571.

It was Henry VI who finally ended the conflict between Dunwich and Blythburgh. He settled a dispute over the shores of the latest haven in favour of Sir Roger Swillington, lord of Blythburgh, who in 1410 sugared the pill by leasing Dunwich the portion of Kingsholme—which Henry ruled was not the correct name but a colloquialism—as far as the haven. More important, he exempted Dunwich mariners from Blythburgh's tolls. Tension with Southwold, however, continued until 1490.

Dunwich now made a lasting contribution to the face of the Suffolk coast in the work of Richard Russell, who built the magnificent flint tower of Walberswick Church and almost certainly began that at Kessingland. He was typical of the class that came to the fore as the wealthy left: a respected artisan who served three times as bailiff and sat in Parliament. (Some parliamentary histories make him Speaker in 1423, but it was probably another Russell, John.) Russell rented property at 13 pence a year in Dunwich from 1427 to 1437 and probably died in 1441.

The ninety-foot tower at Walberswick, with battlements, corner buttresses and walls six feet thick, decorated with flushwork at the base and elegantly vaulted inside, was modelled on those at

Opposite page: *The fine tower of Walberswick church, the work of Dunwich stonemason Richard Russell, who also represented the town in Parliament.*
Russell Edwards

Tunstall and Halesworth; the church of which it was the first part is now three-quarters ruined. Russell and Adam Powle of Blythburgh contracted to build the tower on "the Tewesday next after the Feste of Seynt Mathie Apostle, the fourte Zeer of King Henry the Sexte" in September, 1426. They only had to work between Lady Day and Michaelmas, and were given a house and materials, "40 scheelynges of laughful money of Inglond" a year and a cade of herrings, plus a gown of livery each to last the entire project.

Russell died with only thirty feet of the buttressed tower of St Edmund's, Kessingland, completed; hence the less ornate style of the top. The doorway attracts most attention: an arch richly decorated with religious and secular emblems, under a frieze of quatrefoils and the seated figure of St Edmund.

From Russell's time, few out-and-out Dunwich men represented the town in Parliament. Thomas Pears, who fitted out the *George* of London for Henry VI and was nine times a bailiff, was one, serving three times between 1447 and 1456; his son or grandson William Pears sat in 1491. But of eighteen Dunwich MPs in the later fifteenth century only seven lived there; of the rest, eight were lawyers and two royal placemen. Fewer than ten per cent of borough MPs at this time were esquires, but in 1478 both Dunwich members were. It was on the way to becoming a rotten borough.

Lack of talent now that the wealthy had left was not the main reason. The custodian of the fee-farm might want to sit, or be represented, in Parliament, especially if revenues fell short. Dunwich was also hard pressed to pay its MPs: in 1463 John Strange took 1,100 herrings in lieu. And the electorate—the freemen of the borough convened by the county sheriff—had become very small, fluctuating in the late fifteenth century between seven and nineteen, and word spread that it could be easily controlled. It was a sign of the impotence of the still-numerous burgesses that while they favoured the house of York during the Wars of the Roses, Dunwich's MPs were usually Lancastrians; Strange was the one undisputed Yorkist. Henry VII paid off this score by incorporating Southwold, the navigation and industry of whose people, he said, "exceeded and excelled above the ancient privileged towns of these parts".

Dunwich came to be represented by a series of colourful figures, some of whom played a minor part in English history. Among the first were the Jenneys, six of whom were MPs, four for Dunwich. Sir William, a trimming Lancastrian, "a man of great power, made by the law", had been removed as a justice in 1448 because of conspiracies by his family in Suffolk. Sitting briefly for Horsham, Dunwich (1450–51) and Suffolk, he was reinstated by Edward IV and knighted the day before Richard III was crowned. His son Sir Edmund, of Theberton, sat for Dunwich in 1478 and

1489–90, being called in that last year to settle the borough's long-running disputes with Southwold. His younger brother Nicholas also sat briefly for Dunwich. Christopher Jenney represented the town from 1529 to 1536; a namesake was taken to Chancery for allegedly selling the same plot in St John's parish three times over.

John Sulyard, a Suffolk but not a Dunwich man, represented the town once before moving on to sit for Hindon, becoming one of Henry VII's justices. From 1485 until his charge's incarceration in the Tower, he was tutor to Edward, Prince of Wales, the elder of the little princes whose probable murder has cast Richard III as an arch-villain.

Three Dunwich MPs had links with the Pastons of Norfolk, whose letters are a literary classic. Robert Brewes, a lawyer who had been constable of Winchester Castle, sat for Dunwich in 1478; Richard III gave him a £10 annuity for "his good service to the King's father and the King". Brewes' sister Margery married John Paston in 1477. John Allen junior had represented Oxford and Yarmouth and was Clerk of the Signet to the Queen when elected for Dunwich in 1467. When his father died in 1453 the Pastons noted that he was "no well wisher to Sir John Falstaff". Finally Reynald Rous, a forebear of the earls of Stradbroke and placeman of the Duke of Norfolk, sat for Dunwich in three Parliaments. When he died in 1464, the Pastons considered him unworthy of mourning.

Having well-connected MPs did little for Dunwich. Edward IV attempted to steer trade back to it, but no thanks to them, as several were his sworn enemies. Dunwich mostly had to fend for itself, and did so with some success, activity picking up again as the century neared its close. Erosion had almost halted and a storm in 1471 which did widespread damage elsewhere in Suffolk apparently had little impact. The same year East Anglia was struck by one of the worst recurrences of the plague, an outbreak Sir John Paston described as "the most universal death that ever I wist in England"; Dunwich can hardly have escaped but there is no record of exceptional losses.

The town's main handicap was the continued deterioration of its port. The haven opened at the turn of the century was finally blocked in 1464 the notorious Hummerson's Cut was dug in its stead. The shrinkage of the creek to Dunwich quay drove ever more trade to its neighbours; Walberswick opened coasting links with Ipswich in 1495 and Lincoln in 1502. Moreover, the incorporation of Southwold cost Dunwich roughly half its income in harbour dues. Gardner, a Southwold man, thought Dunwich had brought this fate on itself by slighting "good King Henry [VI]" and failing to appreciate the favours it received from Edward IV. Richard III may have offered "my kingdom for a horse" at Bosworth Field, but Dunwich had backed the wrong one.

Tudor Dunwich

DUNWICH in the early sixteenth century was in better shape than at any other time since its heyday. The Iceland trade was thriving, its shipyards were busy, and the sea having stayed its hand for over a century prosperity was returning. In 1524 it had 223 tax-payers—five per cent of them foreigners, another encouraging sign—against 123 for Aldeburgh and Orford's ninety-two. Its tax bill had risen in a century from £12 5s 5d to £39 19s 1d—more than for Birmingham. Dunwich's largest tax-payer was Nicholas Baldwin, and other notable families were those of Gentleman, Cuddon (Codoun), Rabett, Moreff (Morris?), Howard and Coppyn. Sir George Coppyn, MP in 1542, became Clerk to the Crown in Chancery and was buried in St Martin's, Westminster, leaving £200 to build busses for the Dunwich fishery. Such benefactions from townspeople are another sign of prosperity. Dunwich's churches and religious foundations all benefited and almshouses were endowed by Peter Melton in 1515 and Peter Shelley (next to his own house, Bollyants) in 1537; John Barnett's widow left his house to the poor in 1556. Legislation was even passed to revive the bishopric of Dunwich, the town being one of several deemed worthy of a suffragan, but the measure lay dormant until 1934.

Man and the elements combined to halt the revival. The shipyards, which had been doing well despite growing difficulties over access, suffered first. Shipwrights of all trades were much in demand when Henry VIII embarked on yet another war with the French, and in 1513 they were impressed and taken to Woolwich. Few saw a reason to return, and Dunwich's shipbuilders moved to Southwold and other towns whose craftsmen did go back.

The sea was making inroads again by 1510, when two parishioners left money for building "the pere against St John's church", which shielded the foot of the cliff for thirty years before the threat became critical. The church's treasures were sold in 1542 and 1544 to finance a final attempt to fend off the sea; then St John's was demolished as it was undermined, leaving the market-place open to seaward. Erosion bit all along the cliff, materials from the dissolved religious houses being hastily moved from sites near the edge. By 1573 Stow could write: "there is three parts of the town drowned in the sea, and but the third part of the town now remaining".

The dissolution of the monasteries hit Dunwich hard. Black-friars and Greyfriars were closed by 1538, the Temple in 1540 and

Opposite page:
Southwold today. The final core of Dunwich's merchant class, notably the shipbuilder Thomas Gentleman, moved there in Elizabethan times, finally tilting the balance with Dunwich in favour of its northern neighbour.
Russell Edwards

a clutch of chapels and chantries six years later. Orders for fish from monasteries inland ceased, so the Dunwich fleet shrank rapidly. The revenues of Eye Priory were given in 1536 to the Duke of Suffolk, passing on his attainder to Anthony Rous; it had been drawing £10 13s 4d (the same as in 1291) from All Saints', 13s 4d from St John's and 26s 8d from remnants of other parishes. The friaries' buildings and lands passed to John Eyre and the Temple, crucially, first to the Crown and then, when Elizabeth I finally dissolved the Hospitallers, to Thomas Andrews, who became lord of the manor. Dissolution or the departure of a notable family also enabled Sir George Barne, Lord Mayor of London, to buy land in the borough in 1552; two centuries on, his descendants would take centre stage.

In 1553 Mary Tudor marched from Framlingham to claim the throne, put Lady Jane Grey to death and restore the Old Religion. That year Francis Yaxley sat as an MP for Dunwich; a gentleman from Eye, he was sent to France on Mary's business, was imprisoned by Elizabeth for "babbling" about her proposed marriage to Lord Robert Dudley and drowned in 1565 on a mission to Philip of Spain for Mary, Queen of Scots. Mary's support in Suffolk evaporated; when thirty-seven MPs, Catholic and Protestant, seceded from the Commons in 1555 "disgusted with the detestable penal laws which lit the torturing fires for the Protestants", Sir Edmund Rous, elected for Dunwich the year before, was among them.

Dunwich produced one major Reformation figure, John Day, the ardent Protestant who printed Foxe's Book of Martyrs. Born in St Peter's parish, he went to London and in 1546 began printing in Holborn Conduit with William Seres; their first book was *The Tragicall Death of David Beaton, Bishop of St Andrewes*. He soon struck out on his own, living and working in Aldersgate and selling through a shop in Cheapside. His 230 or so books—he was the most prolific printer of his day as well as probably the ablest since Caxton—bore the motto "Arise for it is Day". When Protestantism flowered under the young King Edward VI, Day published the most radical divines, and on Mary's accession he was arrested. Several of his patrons were burned at the stake, but Day was freed at the height of the persecution. Tradition has him fleeing to the Continent but he may have stayed in England: when Mary gave the Company of Stationers its charter, Day became its first liveryman.

With Elizabeth enthroned, Day set out to widen the breach with Rome, starting with Ridley's "Friendly Farewell", written before his burning at Oxford, and (with a Strasbourg imprint) "An Harborow for Faithfull and True Subjects", Bishop Aylmer's reply to John Knox's attack on the "monstrous regiment" of women rulers. Day had kept in touch with the Protestant exiles and took in several on their return, including John Foxe, who became his lodger and collaborator. Day, like Foxe, saw the printing press as God's instrument to secure the Reformation, writing in a preface to one of Latimer's sermons:

> Then must we as well live the word as talk the word, or else, if good life do not ensue and follow upon our reading to the example of other[s], we might as well spend that time in reading of profane histories, of Canterbury tales or a fit of Robin Hood.

Day, with Foxe his editor and reader, produced in three years the 1,600-page *Acts and Monuments of these Latter Times Touching Matters of the Church*, known ever since as Foxe's Book of Martyrs. While it was not confined to the Marian persecution, more than half dwelt on that "horrible and bloody time", with a message to Elizabeth that Providence had spared her from the fate of Latimer, Ridley and the rest.

Day was among the first music printers in England and also produced one of the first printed almanacs, a celebrated *Testimonie of Antiquities* and the first edition of Euclid in English. His patron, the same Archbishop Parker who owned a Gospel said to have belonged to St Felix, declared him "more ingenious and industrious than the rest". Parker himself edited Day's 1567 edition of Aelric's *Homily*, the first book printed in England to use Anglo-Saxon type, brought from the Continent by refugees he had sponsored, on their return.

What contact Day had with Dunwich is unclear, though he left money for a statue in St Peter's, probably destroyed by his fellow-zealot Dowsing. He may have gone home after his release from prison, and was almost certainly the "Master Deye" to whom Stow wrote on his visit in 1573; they knew each other and shared a patron in Archbishop Parker. Yet when Day died in 1584 he was buried in Little Bradley Church, near Haverhill. Married twice, he had twenty-six children; the brass depicts his second wife, their eleven living offspring and two who had died, over the epitaph:

> Here lies the DAYE that darkness could not blynd
> When popish fogges had overcast the sunne;
> This DAYE the cruel night did leave behynd,
> To view and show what bloudi ACTES weare donne
> He set a FOX to wright how MARTYRS runne,
> By death to lyfe FOX ventured paynes and health;
> To give them light DAYE spent in print his wealth,
> But God with gayn retorned his wealth agayne;
> And gave to him as he gave to the poore,
> Two wyves he had partakers of his payne;
> Each wyfe twelve babes and each of them one more,
> Als was the last increase of his stoore;
> Who mourning long for being left alone,
> Set upp this toombe, herself turnd to a stone.

MONUMENTAL BRASS AT LITTLE BRADLEY, SUFFOLK.

The final pun was the neatest, Day's widow having married William Stone; she later took Edward Grimston as a third husband. Day was also commemorated in a stained-glass window in the church given by the Stationers' Company; he was its master in 1580 and left it the copyright of thirty-six books to feed the poor. In 1926 a publishing house bearing his name was founded in New York.

Whatever her misgivings about Protestant zealots, Elizabeth was a friend of Dunwich. On her accession she confirmed its charters and added further privileges, said by a local bard to have fallen "like sunbeams on the blasted blossoms". Dunwich probably now acquired the surviving civic mace and badge. The unhallmarked silver mace is just 10½ inches long, weighing 11¾ ounces and shaped like a bolt or arrow, with the Tudor arms quartered on the broad end with those of the borough; its shape probably symbolizes the fate of St Edmund. The unusual square lozenge shape of the silver badge, bearing the arms of the borough, suggests it was modelled on an older original, dating maybe from King John's first charter.

On 5th February, 1570, the "Candlemas Storm" struck: a surge of sea and wind combined with floods caused by the thawing of snows that had lain since before Christmas. Norwich was worst hit, but according to Holinshed Dunwich, Yarmouth, Wisbech and King's Lynn also suffered "incredible damage"[35]. Southgate was swept into the sea and the last of Gildengate flattened. Soon afterwards Thomas Badby, the county receiver, wrote:

> The Queen's Majesty's towne of Dunwich is by rage and the surgies of the sea daylie wasted and devoured, and the haven of her highness' said towne, by divers rages of winds continually landed and barred, so as no Ships or Boats can enter in, or ought; to the utter decay of the said town which hathe theretofore well and faithfully served Her Majesty and her noble progenitors.

In 1577 she granted Dunwich the proceeds from the sale of lead, bells, glass and stone from Ingrave Church and the chancel of Kessingland Church. A second storm on 4th August hit Blythburgh hardest; the church spire collapsed during the second lesson, killing several worshippers and injuring others.

Not long after the Candlemas Storm, John Stow produced the earliest surviving description of Dunwich. He had often mentioned it in his potted versions of earlier chronicles, and when he eventually paid a visit he was spellbound. A letter from "Master Deye" asked him to discover how substantial Dunwich had once been, and whether there had been a mint, a castle, a mayor and so forth. Stow went through the borough records (many of them since lost) and compiled a reply that has survived in the British Library to be drawn on, often without Stow's critical judgement, by almost everyone who has written on Dunwich since.

Stow's reply was titled "A Declaration how by reason and conjecture to know what compass, and how much in quantitie the Town of Donwiche hath been of in old time past, and how much in quantitie it containeth now, Anno Dom. 1573, both in length and brede, and also how much the subbarbes of the said town containeth without the Palles Dyke, and the King's river, &c." There followed a serious attempt to separate fact from the myth that was building up. Stow estimated Dunwich's surviving two hundred acres, with 750 inhabitants, as a third or a quarter of the area once inside the Palesdyke, but added that without proof, "here is all my symple discretion can conjecture and gather thereof". He named six of the town's parishes—St Leonard's, St Peter's, St John's, St Martin's, St Nicholas' and All Saints'—noting which had gone; just six acres of St Nicholas' remained. He inferred that as three churches, two friaries, two hospitals and three chapels still stood, "the other . . . two parts of the town now drowned in the sea, should have placed in it parish churches and all other like buildings . . . But to sertifie you howe many and what they ware, I can not." He showed that "Master Deye" was a Dunwich man by adding: "I put the judgement thereof to your discretion, who can judge thereof a grete dele better than I."

Stow told of St Felix, of the church he was "credably reported" to have set up, of the division of the diocese and the bishops' removal from Elmham. Speculating that Felix's church, St John's and St Nicholas' had in turn been pre-eminent, he recalled the body in pointed-toed shoes found when St John's was demolished. He listed the town gates and described the Palesdyke, thrown up when:

> all that part of the town was of grete forse, and strong enowghe to keep out a greate number of people cuminge out of the lowe countrie, and out of the west pt, and in specially before any gones were had and known.

He believed the rampart had skirted the town to the east, but stressed that this was only a theory. Likewise he wrote:

> Touchen your note that you sent me concerning castelles, or any such lyke, I have none other profe for the same, but only as I have conjectured as is a foresaid, which is verie like to be true, for the este part of the towne next the sea could not be strong without a castle or such lyke.

He also reckoned Dunwich had probably had a mint. Stow noted that Dunwich had had a mayor and bailiffs but by the end of Edward I's reign was "soore decayed, and but small in quantitie". Once it no longer needed "soo many governors and rulers", "the Mayor sessed, and one of the Ballies also" (actually two). He ended by telling of a church at Minsmere reputedly lost to the sea long before, and of the civic insignia; he and "Deye" had evidently corresponded on the meaning of the borough coat of arms.

A further document in the British Library, dated 1590, has been attributed to Stow, but its approach suggests otherwise. It tells the Dunwich story less scientifically, quoting different sources, and dwells on the town's trade and fisheries, barely mentioned in Stow's account. The writer also states that "the Towne hath been greatly consumed with fire alsoe, soe that one quarter of the Towne remayneth not now of what it hath been at this daye being the last day of August, Anno dm. 1590". No record survives of such disasters, but fire did devastate Southwold in 1633, 1683 and 1749; there was a particular risk after great storms from lighted fires buried in ruins and embers blown by the wind. An appeal for funds to revive both towns in 1619 lists fires as a cause of their decline, and the map produced in 1589 by Ralph Agas and Joshua Kirby contains large blank areas, especially in the south-west of the town, that could well have been levelled by fire.

Agas, a Suffolk surveyor famed for his maps of London, Oxford and Cambridge, mapped Dunwich for the first time, depicting what then remained of the town—its streets, churches, ruins and built-up areas—though amazingly not identifying the market-place. The original has been lost; it was owned for a time by the Suffolk antiquary David Elisha Davy, and Horace Walpole wrote in his *Anecdotes of Painting in England* that George Vertue, a mid-eighteenth-century art historian, had seen "on a large skin of vellum a plan of the town and boundaries of Dunwich, in Suffolk, and several records made by Radalphus Agas in 1589". Fortunately Gardner had a copy made; this omitted a road, shown in the original, along the cliff top towards the site of Southgate.

With the map was a plan of the estuary, showing how the haven had shifted; this was relevant to the hopes Agas entertained of reviving the port. In a report to the Queen, he speculated on Dunwich's potential if money were spent on it, and recalled its great days:

> Touching the state of the Toune in times past, it appeareth as well by their Charter, as otherwise, that there hath benn a Bishoppes Sea, also a Minte, and a Market everie Daie in the week, And hath also for their sondrie faithfull and espetial Services, as making out at some one time eleven strong and well furnished Shyppes for the defence of the Realme at their owne Costes and Charges . . . from Time to time stood in high favour with the Kinges of this Land, of whome they have received most large and Liberal Graunts of Priviledges, Liberties, Customs, &c., besides sundrie Letters from such Kinges, written to the Burgesses here.

Agas showed his interest immediately after the defeat of the Armada, to which Dunwich made the token contribution of a pinnace. In 1579–80 Sir Robert Wingfield had found that guns installed at Aldeburgh, Dunwich, Southwold and Lowestoft to repel invaders were missing from their mounts and urged the towns to replace them. Nothing was done, and months later the Suffolk justices were ordered to put the ordnance of the four ports into battle-ready condition. In 1587 a "Queen's General" found defences still inadequate; he repeated the order, but reported that Dunwich was of little strategic significance. Robert Day, an engineer, supervised the installation of shore batteries at Aldeburgh, Southwold and Lowestoft; by 1596 Dunwich too had a "great ordnance" for which the town had to supply gunpowder.

As the Spanish war owed as much to religion as to politics, "Papists" were reckoned a threat to the State and a watch was kept on them: in 1583 Peter Poper was examined by the bailiffs after returning from Rome with "Popish trash". Bishop Redman's visitation in 1597 uncovered a measure of degeneracy—three parishioners having been fined for putting out in their fishing boat on the Sabbath—but no papists; by 1603 Dunwich deanery had just five "recusants", all probably Roman Catholics rather than extreme Protestants.

Dunwich could no longer afford 2s a day to pay MPs of its choice; the civic accounts for 1588–89, with £41 10s 3d spent and £41 12s 10d collected or left owing, explain the attraction of handing responsibility to a patron. Its MPs were now usually

Gardner's copy of Ralph Agas' map.

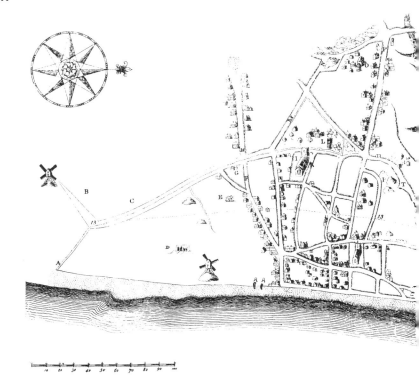

Suffolk gentry or nominees of powerful courtiers. Robert Hare, barrister, antiquary and benefactor of Cambridge University, was chosen in 1563 by Thomas Howard, Duke of Norfolk; he had taken part in Anne of Cleves' funeral, and held the sinecure of Clerk of the Pells until just before Norfolk's execution in 1572. Sir Anthony Wingfield, from a family with Dunwich connections for over three centuries, represented it in 1584 and 1586 after sitting for Orford; he had friends at Court and was Sheriff of Suffolk in 1597–98. He later held one of the two county seats. Sir John Suckling, father of the poet, was elected in 1601; briefly secretary to Sir Robert Cecil, Lord Treasurer, he went on to hold four other seats, serving as Receiver of Fines, Comptroller of the Royal Household and Secretary of State. John Aubrey said in his *Brief Lives* that the poet got his wit from his mother and his comely person from Sir John.

Robert Devereux, Earl of Essex, held the sinecure of High Steward of Dunwich, worth £5 a year, and in 1593 chose for one seat his friend Henry Savile, Warden of Merton College, Oxford, later Latin Secretary to the Queen and Provost of Eton. In 1597 he sought both seats and was given one, for his secretary Arthur Atye,

another scholar. Atye, one of twelve MPs to join the rebellion that cost Essex his head in 1601, had already represented Liverpool, Fowey and Shaftesbury, and under James I sat for Bere Alston; he preceded Suckling as Receiver of Fines. Attorney-General Coke gave the other seat to Clipsby Gawdy, whose family were involved with the Bedingfields and Riches in colonizing Virginia.

Dunwich at the end of the sixteenth century was a dismal place, its port and fishery declining fast, most artisans having followed its merchants away and many of the people holding off starvation by eating the sea peas that grew wild around the town. One of the few things to relieve the gloom were regular visits of companies presenting the plays that make the age unique in the theatre. In 1595 Dunwich paid 5s for a visit from "Lord Darbies players" and six years later 6s 8d for "Her Majesties Players", which could have included William Shakespeare. From 1598 to 1604 he was in a company licensed to play in any town in the country, and there is a tradition in Aldeburgh that he performed at Dunwich. Yet the town's surviving residents were not an easy house to please: in December 1597 6s was paid by Mr Allen, Scrivener, to "the Quene her Majestie's players, and yet much discontented."

A ROTTEN BOROUGH

Zeal, Battle and Riot   22

THE coronation of James I in 1603 was marked by "ringers, goners and drummers", and a peal of the town bells at St Peters. But no new dawn was at hand. During the seventeenth century Dunwich's trade dwindled, the last Iceland ship sailed and the herring fishery abated. Lawsuits over land and livestock replaced maritime disputes: in 1621 Thomas Mayor, a burgess, claimed before the Exchequer of Pleas in London the right to graze cattle and sheep on the south common, while Henry Gathercole, a former bailiff, swore that he had rented the land from Mayor and was entitled to drive the beasts away as a burgess and one of "Lez four and twenty". The court decided for Mayor.

The bailiffs' duties shrank with the town; their main function became to support the worthy poor and have the undeserving whipped. In moments of schizophrenia they did both: the accounts for 20th December, 1616, read: "Geven to a vagrant person that was whipped a/c to the statute, and to him that whipped him, vj d." Among those helped were "a maymed saylor that cam out of the Turkes galleis, vj d." (1610); "a German Minister that came out of the Palatinate cuntrye, 1s." (1638); "a poore ould man of 100 yeare old, 6d." (1640); and "a travailour that was taken in Turkye, and had his tong cut out of his head and maymed, now goeing to his friends, viij d." (1618).

Efforts were still made to revive the port; an appeal was launched in 1619 to restore Dunwich and its neighbours, Charles II backed a company to revive the coastal fishery and a tax was imposed in 1685 to stimulate shipbuilding. But the cause was lost, a visiting army officer writing in 1634[36]:

> I galloped to that ancient decayed corporation, Dunwich, sometime a most flourishing City and the seat of this first Diocese, which her bishop made happie with his fruitful Tillage about 1,000 years sithence amongst the people in the province in her infancy of the Christian Religion, which place hath had (if any report or history will carry credit) as many Religious Houses and Windmills in her as would afford each weeke one to grind both Spiritual and Temporal ffood for 230 of her Burgesses and as many gallant Topsayles as there were weekes in the yeere before swallowing Neptunes Waves devoured her up, that now so little is left of her as leave her I must without adding more.

Opposite page: *North prospect of Dunwich from Gardner's embellishment of Agas' map.*

151

Continuing erosion brought a migration to new, brick houses, outside the now-decayed Palesdyke on Middlegate Street and St James' Street and to streets well clear of the cliff edge. There were still some optimists: in 1631 Robert Bennett of Westhall signed a five-hundred year lease on houses on St Francis' Meadow which were to vanish in barely a century. In 1608 the southern end of the High Road was washed away; a diversion was put through land owned by Peter Willett. And in Charles I's time the Temple's foundations gave way after resisting the sea for some time. Yet the town still had some life. In 1633 the Corporation noted eight "tippling houses" even after a purge of unlicenced drinking dens.

Dunwich largely escaped the turmoil that culminated in the Civil War. As (just) a port, it could not object to the levying of ship money in 1637, especially as the assessment of £4, the lowest for any parliamentary borough, was halved because of its poverty. The town at this time did have "two great guns", but they were intended to point firmly out to sea. Suffolk was a Protestant stronghold though its gentry were not always strict, and when zealots ruled nationally, Dunwich acquiesced. Only one of its pre-Civil War MPs was a known Puritan, and Sir Valentine Knightley, elected in 1603 but opting to sit for his home county, was better known for dissipating his family estates in Northamptonshire. When Parliament took up arms against the King, Dunwich subscribed £5 5s a month, largely from the confiscated assets of papists, toward the army of the Eastern Association. The action never came close, though six hundred men mutinied over pay at Bungay in 1640 and there was a Royalist rising in parts of the county eight years later.

The greatest impact was made by William Dowsing, a Laxfield man of yeoman stock, who methodically destroyed church artefacts in the belief that they were idolatrous. Under legislation passed in August, 1643, the Earl of Manchester, general of the eastern counties, had him appointed parliamentary visitor to the churches of Suffolk, to remove altars and candlesticks and deface pictures and images. Between 6th January and 1st October, 1644, he fulfilled his mission with devastating thoroughness. He was busiest in January and February, visiting 150 places in fifty days; on 29th January alone he mutilated eleven churches at Ipswich. On 8th April he broke down 130 "superstitious pictures" at Southwold. His diary tells what happened next:

> Dunwich. April the 9th. At Peter's Parish. 63 Cherubims; 60 at least of JESUS, written in Capital letters, on the roof; and 40 superstitious Pictures, and a Cross on top of the Steeple. All was promised by the Churchwardens to be done.
>
> Allhallows. 30 superstitious Pictures; and 28 Cherubims; and a Cross on the Chancel.

He missed St James' Hospital chapel, which stayed in use until around 1685 and had at least one religious painting. But time was pressing; the same day he dealt with churches at Blyford, Blythburgh, Bramfield and (continuing the next day) Heveningham.

Dowsing could have ignored St Peter's, too, as its days were numbered. By 1650 a commission reviewing the presbytery set up to cover most of Blything hundred was noting "another church which is now fallen into decay, and out of use and fit to be taken down". The patron of the living was William Page, and the minister, on a stipend of £22, was William Browne—maybe the "orthodox preaching minister" for whom Anthony Bedingfield, a London mercer, left land at Bruisyard in 1652. The state of All Saints' parish as St Peter's closed was summed up in a report from two burgesses, William Farrar and Thomas Coppin:

> The living is impropriate to one Mr Dade who alloweth but £20 p.a. for the service of the [communicants]. The town is an ancient Corporation, but much impoverished by the beate of the sea, which hath already taken away the greatest part ... The inhabitants are generally weakened by losses at sea, and thereby disabled from expressing their wonted liberality for the worship of God, there being moreover no Parish about them, within any tolerable distance, for uniting as in some other places might have been desired.

One minister of All Saints' was Thomas Spatchett, probably not the subject of "a faithfull narrative of the wonderful and estraordinary fits which Mr Thomas Spatchett, late of Dunwich, was under by witchcraft", published in 1693. Other villagers were tainted by the black art: in 1597 Margaret Finly of St Peter's parish was "vehemently suspected to be a witche", and later Priscilla Collit claimed to have accepted 10s for her soul from the devil, who left without paying. Eliza Southerne stated that the devil had entered her bed in the form of a crab and nipped her, fetching blood with which he urged her to sign a fourteen-year mortgage on her soul.

Oliver Cromwell was less concerned with Dunwich's spiritual poverty than with the anomaly of its place in Parliament. While the borough supported him, he objected to the poorest town represented having two MPs when larger ones lacked a voice. In 1654 the Rump was asked to transfer Dunwich's seats to Aldeburgh, a town by now far more important. Cromwell's proposed redistribution closely resembled the reform of 1832; this part was defeated by seventy-two votes to fifty-nine.

Under the Commonwealth, trading with tokens was common and many tokens from Suffolk survive, just one of them issued in Dunwich. Worth a farthing, it is inscribed "Iohn Whittman" on the obverse and "of Dunwich" on the reverse. John Whitman was registrar of marriages in 1656, when he married an out-of-town couple with bailiff Alin Davison as witness. It was customary at this time for the banns to be published in the market-place and the marriage solemnized before the bailiffs.

Charles II, advised on his accession that Dunwich could not bear a tax burden unchanged since its early Tudor prosperity, cut the fee-farm to £7 2s 1d, payable toward Katharine of Braganza's marriage settlement. The bailiffs imagined the reduction would continue for the Queen's lifetime, but when she died in 1705 the Treasury claimed that the rent had reverted to £60 on Charles' death twenty years before and demanded £1,260.

Dunwich now engaged the interest of Samuel Pepys, who wrote in his naval minutes: "Look into the story of Dunwich on the coast of Suffolk, swallowed up by the sea and said to have been heretofore a great place." If he did enquire, he would have found it in decay. Stow had put the population at 750, but by 1674 there were just seventy tax-payers, three of them gentry, against 179 at Aldeburgh and sixty-two at Orford. Tax returns show 114 hearths, and houses with nineteen hearths between them were, significantly, lying empty.

It was thus not surprising that Dunwich relied increasingly on its patrons—at the Restoration the Rouses, whose forebears reputedly had William the Conqueror's leave to hunt in the Eastwood. Their Dunwich connection had been forged by 1437 when Reynald Rous was elected one of its MPs. Sir Anthony Rous bought the Hopton estate at Henham in 1544 and the next year the lands of Eye Priory, including those in Dunwich. The lordship of the manor, derived from the Temple's estate, devolved to Sir John Rous when he married Elizabeth Knyvett, whose father had bought it in 1628 from Ellis Rothwell. (Rothwell had acquired it in 1622 from the Andrews family, who had held it since the Temple was dissolved.)

John Rous was an ardent Royalist; when Cromwell's men came to Henham to arrest him, he hid in a hollow oak tree which the family used as a summer-house and had food brought to him by night. At the Restoration, Charles II made him a baronet and he was elected an MP for Dunwich—the fifth Rous to serve after Reynald, Sir Robert (1529), Sir Edmund (1554) and Sir John (1623–26). His son John, who succeeded to the baronetcy in the late 1660s, sold the lands and lordship of Dunwich to Colonel Charles Long; he became High Sheriff of Suffolk and after 1688 a secret Jacobite; the Henham oak witnessed toasts to "the King over the water". The sixth baronet, another Sir John, was in 1821 to take the title of Viscount Dunwich.

One Dunwich MP to suffer for his king was Sir John Pettus. Knighted by Charles I, he was captured by Cromwell at Lowestoft, raised a regiment of horse which scattered when ordered into action and was besieged at Bath and Bristol, where Colonel Charles

Fleetwood, a relative by marriage, spared him—also vouching for him when he faced expropriation. Pettus tried to prove his now-suspect loyalty by giving nearly £20,000 to help the King escape and fund the future Charles II; their correspondence put him in prison, but the Council of State freed him on £4,000 bail. By 1651 he was £5,900 in debt, which may explain why in 1655 he swore loyalty to Cromwell to become deputy governor of the royal mines, holding the post until his death in 1690. Charles II made him deputy lieutenant of Suffolk and colonel of a militia regiment; Dunwich complained of being left undefended when it was moved in 1667. Pettus sat for the borough from 1670 to 1677, losing King John's charters, lent him by Alderman Benefice; it was over 250 years before any reappeared. In 1672 his wife entered a nunnery and had him excommunicated, and in 1679 he was gaoled for debt, begging Archbishop Sancroft for a loan for his release. By 1683 he was "reduced to nothing".

Sir Philip Skippon, son of a Cromwellian major-general, served from 1677 to 1685, and in the assembly that offered William of Orange the crown; he was knighted in 1674. Dunwich's other member in 1688 was the Hon. Roger North, sixth son of the fourth Baron North. Sancroft's choice as steward of the see of Canterbury, he became solicitor-general to the Duke of York in 1684 and attorney-general to Queen Mary of Modena. North benefited from his brother Francis being Lord Chancellor, but while earning £4,000 a year he never took more than 20 guineas for a brief. With his brother's death, the ascendancy of Judge Jeffreys and the fall of James II, he lost influence and retired to Norfolk, writing a seven-hundred page apologia for his brother and Charles II. Married into a wealthy Jacobite family, North was executor for the court painter Sir Peter Lely, wrote on music and pioneered yachting along the Suffolk coast.

In 1652 the first Dutch war broke out, and the next May the Royal Navy suffered heavy losses in the Battle of the Gobbards. Wounded were put ashore at Ipswich, Aldeburgh, Dunwich and Southwold. Their people were expected to tend them, but their charity was limited; on 10th July, 1653, Admiral Monk wrote that their bailiffs were demanding payment for care of the sick "whereby the inhabitants began to be weary of them". Dunwich also saw the English fleet set sail from Sole (Southwold) Bay for the Battle of Lowestoft in 1666, and return to Southwold with two thousand Dutch prisoners.

On 7th June, 1672, a small crowd stood enthralled on Dunwich cliffs as the world's most powerful fleets, more than fifty thousand men in three hundred ships, met in the Battle of Sole Bay. The action stretched from Lowestoft to Orford, and the guns, 4,950 on the English and French side and 4,202 on the Dutch, were

heard at Yarmouth. Fog and smoke obscured much of the action, but the watchers were closest to an engagement between the Dutch and the French, who were later accused of avoiding the real fight. The official Dutch war artist Van de Velde the elder was sketching in the heart of the action, complaining that the combatants kept getting in the way; he later made drawings of the battle for Lord Dartmouth. It was also commemorated in verse, a local bard beginning:

> One day as I was sitting still
> Upon the side of Dunwich Hill
> And looking at the Ocean,
> By chance I saw de Ruyter's fleet
> With Royal James's squadron meet . . .

The allies were as surprised as the anonymous poet. Their fleet of 156 ships, fifty of them French, under the Duke of York was at anchor just north of Dunwich when a force of ninety-one men-of-war, fifty-four fireships and twenty-three tenders attacked, under the veteran Admiral de Ruyter. By going for the centre, de Ruyter split the allied fleet; it had so little warning that many ships cut their anchor cables in their haste to retaliate. The English sailed out of the bay on a northward tack; the French bore south.

The Duke's flagship the *Prince* was soon so damaged that he transferred to the *St Michael*, moving when she was disabled to the *London*. His second-in-command, the Earl of Sandwich, an opponent of the war who had a premonition that he would die in it, made a desperate stand in the *Royal James*. Two-thirds of the crew were killed as she held off attackers including the *Groot Hollandia*

The Battle of Sole Bay, 7th June 1672. One of two panels from sketches by Dutch war artist Van de Velde the elder.

for several hours. Sandwich then gave the Dutch the slip and sank or evaded three fireships before his luck ran out. The *Royal James* was caught by a fourth, and an explosion blew her to smithereens; it was three days before the Earl's body was found, identifiable only by the star on his chest. Divers began in the late 1980s to search for remains of the *Royal James*.

Though he had caught the allied fleet off guard, de Ruyter could only claim a favourable draw when the Dutch withdrew at dusk, the allies lacking strength to pursue them. He did settle one score: among the English dead was General Richard Nicolls, who had been sent in 1664 to conquer the New Netherlands and had renamed its main city New York. The allies lost two thousand men, mostly English, the *Royal James* and several fireships, and had eight ships badly damaged; the Dutch never disclosed their casualties but had two ships captured, two destroyed and eleven fireships expended. HMS *Greenwich* escorted the forty-eight-gun *Staveren* into Dunwich as prize; seventy-three prisoners were entrusted to the bailiffs until they could be sent to Harwich.

One of those bailiffs was Alderman John Benefice, who for twenty-two years in that capacity (and for a time as magistrate and borough coroner) exerted a corrupt and sinister influence. He cornered Dunwich's choice of MPs through the "outsetter" system, enrolling electors from as far away as Yorkshire to outvote the forty freemen. Benefice installed first Sir Thomas Allen, a Tory and a relative, and then Sir Robert Kemp, a local Whig landowner, as the borough's representatives in Parliament. In 1689 "King John" paraded his outsetters to elect Admiral Sir Robert Rich of

157

Roos Hall, Beccles, who had found him a post in the customs at Southwold. Rich, a Whig and a member of the Navy Board, had been implicated in the Rye House plot against Charles II; with the Stuarts in eclipse he could go into politics.

Greater tolerance of dissenters led in 1672 to Dunwich being briefly allowed a Congregational chapel. Yet freedom of speech remained limited, hence a report in 1682 that bailiff Matthew Daniel had termed the Duke of York "a Papistly rogue" and another citizen had called the King "a murtherer and his hands full of blood". The "Popish Plot", when the Whig opposition over-reached itself, had a direct effect on Dunwich. The court party demanded surrender of the charters of hostile boroughs, and on 5th May, 1687, James II remodelled the corporation. With each faction insisting its charter was valid, there were hotly contested elections in 1689, 1690, 1691 (a by-election), 1695 and 1698.

In 1692 "King John" went too far, having Alderman Jeremiah Burlingham snatched by a press-gang. Summoned before the Grand Assembly of Freemen to answer charges of corruption and abuse of power, he refused to attend and was stripped of his offices. Sir Robert remained patron, and his camp took William and Mary's endorsement of the original charters in 1694 as confirming the rights of outsetters; several hundred invaded Dunwich, stormed the Town Hall and "read and published" the document. The borough was now one of half a dozen (including Aldeburgh and Orford) with two sets of charters. The Jacobite "Old Corporation" ousted Rich's supporters, who formed a rival body and provocatively reinstated Benefice. Sir Robert now asked Thomas Neale, a respected county figure, to assess his position; he

The Battle of Sole Bay. The second panel of Van de Velde the elder's sketch on show at Southwold Museum. The difference between the date shown, 28th May, 1672, and the recorded date of the battle, 7th June, 1672 would have been caused by the alteration in the calendar.

advised that Benefice was a liability and Rich excluded him, to his chagrin, from the corporation[37].

Not that Sir Robert had changed his spots. The 1695 election was the stormiest of all with both sides claiming victory; the ensuing riot severely damaged the Town Hall. The Tories Woods and Bence received twenty-five votes against thirteen for Rich and Henry Heveningham, but the Sheriff declared the Whigs elected. The Old Corporation withheld its seal from the return, alleging abuses including the press-ganging of Tories by Sir Robert, who had had a frigate anchored offshore. The Whig majority at Westminster cynically upheld the election, and after a further defeat in 1698 the Old Corporation gave in. The factions compromised, accepting the most favourable parts of the 1687 and 1694 charters without undue concern for legality; conveniently neither charter was to hand (they were said by 1835 to be in the Tower of London). When Rich died in 1699, his seat passed quietly to a Tory.

There was by now even less of a borough to represent. One night in 1677 a furious storm brought the people from their beds as waves broke over the market-place. The market cross, under which stalls still opened weekly, was dismantled and lead from its roof auctioned to fit out new stalls to landward, with a butcher's shop the first priority. The same storm probably put paid to most remaining houses north of Maison Dieu Lane. Next to go was the shell of St Peter's Church, which had remained a mark for mariners. The east end collapsed in December, 1688, and most of the rest over the next nine years. After that, only part of the tower remained, falling in 1702 after the bells had been removed.

Patrons, Antiquaries 23
and Smugglers

DUNWICH touched rock-bottom in the eighteenth century. Its politics was marked by flagrant corruption before coming under largely benevolent patronage, its population fell to as low as a hundred, and the abandonment of All Saints' Church marked a final break with its past . . . just as that past was being fully chronicled for the first time.

The compromise over the charters created new scope for electoral manipulation. A master of the art was the Whig Sir Charles Blois (pronounced Bloyce), made a baronet in 1680, who had himself elected to the corporation and fifty-nine of his friends made freemen. The Bloises have been local landowners since Richard I's time, yet only Sir Charles ever represented Dunwich in Parliament, from 1698 to 1710. A loser in the 1708 election accused Blois and his fellow-member Sir Robert Kemp of bribery and "treating"; one freeman swore he had been given, and had drunk, a pail of beer and a bowl of punch. The drink flowed both for the insetters whose votes had to be bought and the outsetters Blois had brought to the poll. Sir Charles's election was voided on the technicality that he was a bailiff, but he took his seat anyway. It became clear that proof of corruption would lead at most to a couple of freemen losing their votes; in any case the complaints usually came from losers who had been outbid.

Sir George Downing, who sat for Dunwich almost continuously from 1710 to 1749, refined the process. The grandson of the minister after whom Downing Street was named first acquired property in Dunwich in 1708. In 1710 he fought Cambridgeshire as a Whig but was elected for Dunwich, bringing in almost ninety outsetters, during a flirtation with Toryism, and bought The Place, amid the ruins of Greyfriars. He and Kemp were ousted in 1714, arriving minus outsetters to find that they had been outspent by Sir Robert Rich, second son of the admiral, and Colonel Long, lord of the manor, who had countered Downing by housing his former tenants. In 1708 Rich had fought a duel not far away with Sir Edmund Bacon, running him through with effects which, wrote the diarist Narcissus Lutrell, were "supposed to be mortel". Sir Edmund lived until 1755.

Dunwich could not pay the fee-farm arrears that had built up since Charles II's death, and in 1718 the bailiffs and eight freemen

Opposite page: *Sir Joshua Vanneck, of Heveningham Hall, co-patron of the borough with Miles Barne from the late 1760's. From a print in Dunwich Museum.*

161

were imprisoned at Beccles; at trial the judge acquitted the borough, saying that where the debt could not be had, "the King must lose his right". The fee-farm was let at £5 a year to Downing, who claimed one Dunwich seat in return; this was never formally conceded but the freemen acquiesced, for a time letting him choose both MPs. Sir George now ensnared his freeman tenants by letting them run up rent arrears, then giving them notice to quit, suspended as long as they voted for him[38]. When the Town Hall and gaol were washed away, he built a replacement in the friary ruin, to which he added a three-storey extension; in 1720 he bought out the Kemps after their house opposite the inn burned down. Assuming the fee-farm greatly reduced his costs after the 1722 election, when he reckoned that "not less than £5,000 will carry it for the person who should be his partner". Colonel Long was ready to pay but was defeated, Sir Robert Rich offered each voter £50 yet also lost his seat. Once Downing had seen them off (Rich took seats in the south-west and became a field-marshal), there was no more need to inflate the electorate. From 234 in 1701 it now fell steadily until only thirteen freemen remained —who could be bribed economically.

Sir George, a supporter of Walpole—who had him knighted in his own right in 1732—and of Pelham, took little part in politics beyond his exertions to secure a seat. Married to a girl of 13 when just two years older, he was sent on a three-year Grand Tour and on his return would not acknowledge her. Though from a Beccles family, he was more at home at his Cambridgeshire seat, Gamlingay Park, than at Dunwich; the history of Downing College states that in his last years he led "a miserable, covetous and sordid existence there".

His first partner, Edward Vernon, who in 1740 became the hero of the War of Jenkins' Ear by capturing Porto Bello, never took his seat, preferring to represent Penrhyn, Cornwall. Thomas Wyndham was elected in 1727, and 1732 saw a bizarre triple return, the victors being registered as "Sir George Downing KB, William Morden, Sir Orleando Bridgeman (feign'd dead)". His fellow-MPs were placemen approved by Walpole, whose local credentials and mastery of patronage were impeccable; they paid Downing for the privilege.

Sir George's control reached its height in 1741, when his nephew Jacob Gerrard Downing was elected with him—only to be ousted six years later by Miles Barne, one of whose sons wrote: "Sir George Downing either residing at too great a distance or for want of an heir had not thought it worth his while to pay that attention to the freemen that they deserved." Dr Ormonde Pickard, in his study of Dunwich as a rotten borough, found that Sir George had fallen out with Jacob and quietly sold Barne the seat for £1,200. When Sir

George died in 1749, his nephew succeeded to the baronetcy and his seat. Sickly and short-tempered, he alienated the freemen who, led by Alderman Francis Robinson, a tenant farmer and trader, prepared to kick over the traces on his death. One beneficiary of Sir Jacob's patronage was Henry Fox, father of Charles James; defeated at New Windsor, he sat for Dunwich for two years from 1761 until created Lord Holland. It was written of Fox, who sat twenty-eight years in the Commons, the last as Leader of the House, that he could have been prime minister but "had not the spirit to undertake it". In 1761 Sir Jacob gave up his seat to Miles Barne.

The Barnes had held land in Dunwich since 1552, taking little part in its affairs. As Lord Mayor, Sir George Barne's interests were in London, where as an adventurer of the Muscovy Company he pioneered trade with Russia. His son Sir George, also Lord Mayor, owned the three-hundred-ton *Hercules*, the largest ship sent from the Thames against the Armada. Next came Sir William Barne of Woolwich, whose son became chaplain to Charles II. In 1744 Miles Barne bought the Sotterly estate, nine miles north of Dunwich, from Sir Thomas Playters, who had been able to ride from Beccles to Dunwich on his own land. And in 1754 he acquired the still sizable Dunwich estate from the Long family, becoming lord of the manor.

The freemen rallied to Miles Barne on Sir Jacob Downing's death in 1764. His widow, Lady Margaret, fought back; when Barne beat her nominee by thirteen votes to three she had the thirteen gaoled for fee-farm arrears from which Sir Jacob had exempted them. Barne and Sir Joshua Vanneck, banker to the Walpole ministry whose wealth created Heveningham Hall, stood bail, housed them when she evicted them and then took on the patronage of the borough. By agreement with Alderman Robinson each took one seat, and the number of freemen was fixed at thirty-two, half chosen by the patrons. A house was built where each entertained the freemen for a few weeks a year, and on civic occasions the corporation feasted at their expense. Lady Margaret went on to frustrate Sir George's bequest to found "Downing's College"; litigation prevented the first stone being laid until 1807. In the end the Downing holdings in Dunwich were split between Lady Margaret's heirs and the college; in 1802 the Barnes bought the college's part, then with the Vannecks' help acquired the rest. When they also bought the Rich family's holding, they owned almost the entire village.

By 1749 Dunwich was down to some hundred inhabitants in thirty-five houses, twenty fewer than in 1674 and mostly outside the old town. The sea in 1702 took the last of St Peter's tower, but the hurricane the next year that horrified Queen Anne and swept

Henry Winstanley away with his Eddystone lighthouse had little impact. A Dunwich seaman, Henry Green, drowned in HMS *Resolution*, one of thirteen warships lost; he was buried at Pevensey. Erosion took the gaol in 1715, the town hall ("by the force of the sea being dangerous to enter into"), in 1716 the last of Blackfriars in 1717 and by 1750 the last fourteen sizable houses on Duck Street and nearby fishery sheds. Gardner did not blame only the sea for the shrinkage, writing of the ploughed site of Middlegate: "Iam seges est ubi Troia fuit" ("Corn now grows where Troy once stood").

Dunwich struck the same note with Daniel Defoe, who paid a visit in 1722, aged 62. In his *Tour Through Great Britain* he wrote:

> Even this town seems to be in danger of being swallowed up; for Fame reports that once they had Fifty churches in the Town; I saw but one left, and that not half full of People. This town is a testimony to the decay of Public Things, things of the most durable nature; and as the old Poet expresses it,
>
> "By numerous Examples we may see,
> That towns and Cities Die, as wel as we."
>
> The ruins of Carthage, of the Great City of Jerusalem, or of antient Rome, are not at all wonderful to me; the Ruins of Nineveh, which are so entirely sunk, as 'tis doubtful where the City stood; the ruins of Babylon, or the great Persepolis; and their Capital Cities, which time and the Change of Monarchies have overthrown, the Capital Cities necessarily fell with them; But for a Private Town, a Sea-Port, and a Town of Commerce, to decay, as it were of itself (for we never read of Dunwich being Plunder'd, or Ruin'd, by any Disaster, at least not of late years); this I must confess, seems owing to nothing but the Fate of Things, by which we see that Towns, Kings, Countries, Families and Persons have all their Elevations, their Medium, their Declination, and even their Destruction in the Womb of Time, and the Course of Nature. It is true, this Town is manifestly decayed by the invasion of the Waters, and as other towns seem sufferers by the Sea or the Tide withdrawing from their Ports, such as Orford, Winchelsea in Kent, and the like; so this Town is, as it were, eaten up by the Sea, as above, and the still encroaching Ocean seems to threaten it with a fatal immersion in a few years more.
>
> It is remarkable that this Town is now so washed away by the Sea, that what little Trade they have is carry'd on by Walderswick, a little town near Swole, the Vessels coming in there because the Ruines of Dunwich make the Shore there unsafe and uneasie to the boats; from whence the Northern Coasting Seamen a rude verse of their own using, and I suppose of their own making, as follows:
>
> "Swoul, and Dunwich, and Walderswick,
> All go in at one lousie Creek."
>
> The Lousie Creek, in short, is a little river at Swoul, which our late famous Atlas-maker [Agas] calls a Good Harbour for Ships, and rendesvous for the Royal Navy, but that by the bye; the author it seems knew no better.

Miles Barne, Lord of the Manor from 1754 and an MP for Dunwich, 1764–1777. This print is in Dunwich Museum.

Defoe could not grasp how much had changed since Agas' day. The Dunwich river could now take only tiny craft; its function was to channel to the Blyth marsh water pumped out by windmills. Moreover, he relied on the evidence of his eyes rather than his ears. Major losses preceded his visit, and soon there were more. In 1729 a violent storm tore away the last of St Peter's cemetery; people gathered on walls and rooftops and "loudly cursed the sea". In November, 1739, according to an anonymous account in the museum, "a furious gale blowing hard for several days drove the sea with such force against the cliffs that they broke and crumbled and the sea roared in triumph as it surged like a victorious army across the town".

Thomas Gardner wrote of another storm the next year that a

wind blowing very hard from the north-east, with a continuance for several days, occasioned great seas doing much damage to the coast . . . by inundations, breaking down the banks and overflowing many marshes. The sad effects thereof were severely felt by Dunwich when a great deal of their cliffs were washed away, with the last remains of St Nicholas' churchyard and the road heretofore leading into the town from the Key, leaving several naked wells, tokens of ancient buildings. And from Maison-Dieu Lane northwards a continued scene of confusion. Part of the old Key, built with stone, lay bare, making canals across the beach, through which the river had connections with the sea, to the hindrance of the people on foot travelling that way, for some days. Kingsholme (alias Leonard's-Marsh) . . . laid under water, and much shingle and sand thrown thereon from off the beach, rendering it ever since of little worth, much of the pasture and other arable land destroyed. The sea raged with such fury that Cock and Hen Hills, which the preceding summer were upwards of 40ft high, and in the winter partly washed away, this year had their heads levelled with their bases, and the ground all about them rent and torn, that the foundations of St Francis' chapel, which had laid between the hills [and] the secret repositories of the dead were exposed to open view, several skeletons on the ouze, divested of their coverings, some keeping in pretty good order, others interrupted and scattered as the surges carried them.

The storms of 1739 and 1740 exposed a stone coffin broken in two by the waves, lead and earthenware aqueduct pipes near the site of St Francis', foundations of houses, the banks of Hummerson's Cut and the later New Cut, and tree roots north of Maison Dieu Lane. Later in 1740 men cutting a flood-relief channel on the course of the old haven—those "canals across the beach" came close to turning the clock back four centuries—found "a stone wall, cemented exceeding strong, which was part of their old key. And near that a well, both of which I saw as they were working. At which time several pieces of old coins and curiosities were found". One was a "9½in brass instrument" with the image of a rose, the motif IHS (Jesus) and the phrase "Ave Marie Gracia PLE" ("Hail Mary, full of grace"); it was speculated that it was the Emperor Constantine's standard. There was also a silver amulet inscribed "Jacpir, Melchior, Baltazar", the magi who followed the star to the baby Jesus.

The Dunwich story would be incomplete without Gardner's *A Historical Account of Dunwich, Anciently a City, now a Borough, Blythburgh, Formerly a Town of Note, now a Village, Southwold, once a village, now a Town Corporate, with Remarks on Some Places Contiguous Thereto*. Published by subscription in 1754 just as Miles Barne acquired the manor, the book attracted only three sponsors in Dunwich: Philip Howard, Edmund Leeds and John Payne (of the old family?). Gardner—antiquary, coin collector, salt officer and deputy borough comptroller of Southwold—had in 1745 presented to the Society of Antiquaries in London "A True and exact Platt, containing the boundaries and town of Dunwich, and the entries of certain records and evidences, and some things now in variance made the 14th of March 1589 by Ralph Agas." This was an update of Agas' map to show what had been lost since, with a border depicting the area's surviving ecclesiastical buildings and a prospect of Dunwich from the north.

Gardner's book dealt mainly with the decaying borough within a whisper of his home (by an atmospheric freak, a whisper in Dunwich can at times be heard in Southwold). In the preface he wrote:

I have presumed to publish this small tract of some places, especially the once famous city of Dunwich, which will afford speculation sufficient to remark on the vicissitude and instability of sublunary things. For whoever hath been informed of the antient State thereof, and beholds its present great and wonderful Decline, would be apt to conclude that they had never possessed the grandeur really enjoyed by them. The oldest inhabitants of this neighbourhood report that Dunwich (in antient time) was a city, surrounded with a stone wall and brazen gates; had 52 churches, chapels, religious houses and hospitals; a King's place, a bishop's seat, a mayor's mansion, and a mint; as many Top Ships as Churches etc. and not fewer windmills. Also a forest that extended from the town south-east 7 miles, now covered by the sea. And the Port converted to firm land.

These Relations excited my curiosity of visiting this place, where I beheld the remains of the Rampart, some tokens of Middlegate, the foundations of down-fallen Edificies, and tottering Fragments of noble structures, Remains of the Dead exposed, and naked wells divested of the Ground about them by the waves of the Sea, divers coins, several Mill-hills and part of the old key. These antique objects induced me to make a further search into the Reality of the town's original state; but to my surprise I found its Archives ransacked of all records, except the Common Court Books, and those too close confined for my inspection; notwithstanding to preserve the fame of that renowned City, now

A stone coffin uncovered by the waves during a great storm in 1739 or 1740.

almost swallowed up by the sea from Sinking into oblivion, I have endeavoured to collect such occurrences dependent thereon, which may perpetuate the Memorial of to Posterity.

He nonetheless managed to produce a definitive work; the more valuable because many of his own sources are now lost. If it has a weakness, it is that judgement is seldom passed on the theories of others. Gardner reckoned that Dunwich thrived under the Saxons, was oppressed by the Danes and not favoured by the Normans, reached its zenith under Henry II and declined thereafter, a victim of the sea and the "raging plague of fire, with which it has been visited at sundry times". He wrote:

> The freemen, for want of a sufficient number, are obliged to . . . hold more offices than one, and for the generality, upon account of the stagnation of trade, are poor and indigent. But the inhabitants, by their representatives erecting new edices and repairing others, entertain reviving hopes of becoming once more a flourishing town.

Its main business was fishing in the bay with seven small boats for herring.

Gardner died at almost 80 in 1769, and was buried in Southwold churchyard between his two wives, under the epitaph:

> Between Honor and Virtue, here doth lie
> The remains of Old Antiquity.

The gravestone of his first wife Rachel and their daughter of that name reads:

The interior of the abandoned All Saints' church, drawn by the Rev. John Pridden. Dunwich Museum

> Virtue crowned, during life,
> Both the daughter and the wife

and that of his second wife, Mary:

> Honour ever did attend
> Her just dealings to the end.

His mention of a new spirit at Dunwich must have seemed ill-timed, given the closure around 1760 of its last church. In 1725 the aisle of All Saints' had been demolished to finance repairs to the rest and the casting of a new bell, but its fabric was past saving and the shrinking congregation abandoned it, like St Nicholas' and St Peter's in earlier centuries. The Dunwich story seemed almost over.

At this nadir of its fortunes, Dunwich became a centre for smuggling. Skirmishes with revenue men in Sole Bay became commonplace as contraband, mainly spirits and tea, was run ashore; All Saints' tower was a landmark for the boats, lookouts watched at its top or on the cliff and there was a network of spies to signal whether the road inland was clear of riding officers. Not far from the cliff top were "holds"—some natural like a simple pit at Minsmere, others in the ruins of the old town, the rest specially made—where goods were stowed for removal under cover of dark. Some have been exposed by cliff falls; holds remaining include an old ice-house near the Barne manor and a strange structure known as The Vault, close to one of the smugglers' main escape routes on Westleton Walks behind Scotts Hall.

Plans were hatched and goods stored at the village inn, and the friary ruins concealed contraband and smugglers; a secret passage from a bricked-up doorway in the cellar of the inn is said to connect the two. The Dunwich river also played a part: Elijah Larter had a light boat that he carried to a point behind the strand near where contraband was to be landed, then punted back laden along the stream, evading revenue men lying in wait.

Smuggling in Suffolk went back centuries. In 1224 Orford was ordered to combat it; under Edward I wool was spirited out to Flanders and by 1592 butter and corn were being smuggled to Holland. Illicit imports grew from 1652 when heavy duties were imposed to finance the Dutch wars. By 1734 an MP could tell the Commons: "All the young, clever fellows in Suffolk are employed by the smugglers and have 2s 6d a day while waiting, and when on horseback going about the country to dispose of the goods they have a guinea a day and are well entertained." He spoke of gangs "40 to 50 strong and so well mounted the dragoons could not catch them", and up to three hundred farm workers, fishermen and others waiting for word that "the cow has calved". Smuggling reached its peak around 1745, when an estimated 4,500 horse-loads of contraband were run in Suffolk in just six months; in 1783 a parliamentary committee reported that the trade was conducted "with the most open and daring violence in every accessible part of the coast".

Two revenue cutters based at Harwich and one at Yarmouth could not properly patrol this coast, and revenue men were few and badly paid. With no disablement pension or compensation for their families for death on duty, they tended not to force the issue, even taking money to let captured vessels go instead of burning them as required by law. This applied less to the riding officers, deployed from 1698 to curb illegal wool exports and left to operate on their own, than to customs men, who often had to call in the troops. In 1779, for example, Lord Orford's Norfolk regiment was sent, making camp at Aldeburgh. In due course a cargo was landed at Dunwich and run inland: twenty mounted militiamen chased the smugglers for forty miles. They did not catch the smugglers or the goods, but one of the gang dropped his bundle, with a letter giving notice of their next exploit. The militia lay in wait, only to find that the clergy, lawyers and doctors of Aldeburgh were behind the run. Lord Orford recorded that the parson was the only one who had not taken an active part.

Many smugglers' tales concern Dunwich, where in 1726 John Pughe was commended as "a good officer, diligent in the prevention of smuggling". In one a ship's captain came ashore to report that a sailor had died of the plague, suggesting he be buried secretly by night. Needless to say, the entire law-abiding population turned out at All Saints' graveyard . . . while the cargo was landed and run through the village to Blyford. The only problem with the incident, said to have taken place around 1810, is that it is reported with equal conviction at Lowestoft.

One true story involves "preventives" led by Henry Walters, who were worsted by a gang led by the notorious Will Laud near Minsmere Haven and driven back toward Dunwich. Walters was grappling with Laud when a man on a white horse bore down on him; he shot the horse and escaped with his wounded brother Samuel. The smugglers found one officer hiding in a pigsty and only released him after making him say the Lord's Prayer backwards. It may have been in this skirmish that a man had his right hand cut off by a preventive's sword; thereafter he wore a hook, gaining the nickname "Hookey Miller".

The authorities scored a success in 1758 when exciseman Walker, with a party of dragoons camped at Southwold, "made seizure on the beach near Dunwich of 1,330 gallons of foreign brandy and genever, the same being run goods". However, the Southwold excisemen William Woodward and Benjamin Lowsey were thrown into the sea when they challenged men landing a cargo at Dunwich, and one smuggler was sentenced to transport-ation at Bury assizes for shooting a revenue man who intercepted a nocturnal run.

Early in the nineteenth century there was a large landing at

All Saints' from the north, circa 1915, then still a landmark for boats.

Dunwich, mostly of brandy. The gang loaded the kegs on to ponies and was about to move them to Dunwich Walks when its spies reported that revenue men were watching there. The ponies were led to the Queen's Head at Blyford, whose landlord, John Key, put some kegs in a cavity over the fireplace; more were hidden under the altar and pews of the church. The rest of the brandy was kept in the "valley" of the roof at Westhall Church until it could be sent on.

In the Napoleonic wars, smugglers were almost immune, as they could give the authorities "intelligency" about the enemy. But in 1811, as Britain gained the upper hand, the riding officer service was reorganized; Dunwich gained an "inferior riding officer", Edward Huntrod, paid £65 a year plus £30 for his horse. After Waterloo, the Navy imposed (on the Suffolk coast from 1818) the kind of blockade previously applied to the Continent; several Martello towers were pressed back into service. Smuggling declined fast, especially after 1822 when the coastguard, initially a joint naval and civilian force, was set up. The eight preventives stationed at Minsmere were moved to Dunwich and billeted in houses by Maison Dieu Lane; it was the 1920s before the last left.

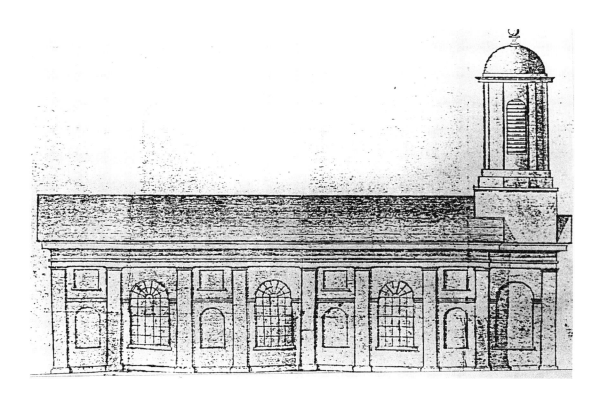

Revival and Reform   24

DUNWICH in the late eighteenth century still had its market (held on Mondays until at least 1813) and St James' Fair. Nothing of note had been eroded since the storms of the 1740s; All Saints' was well clear of the cliff edge, and burials continued in the churchyard. It also still had one, if not both, of its medieval hospitals; when in 1764 the parishes of Blything hundred combined to build a workhouse at Bulcamp, it opted out.

The patrons of the borough slipped easily into their role, the freemen sending them or their nominees to Parliament in return for lavish hospitality. Their appetite can be judged from bills totalling £29 4s 10d and £28 6s 8½d for food and drink sent to Miles Barne the younger and Lord Huntingfield in 1797 after the choosing and swearing of the burgesses. The freemen sank four dozen bottles of wine on the first occasion and three and a half on the second, and still needed "beer in the morning".

Miles Barne was already a Dunwich MP at the time of the patronage agreement; a Whig who once supported John Wilkes in the face of Tory indignation, he retired through sickness in 1777. His second son, Barne Barne, took his seat, supporting Pitt and Lord North and becoming a tax commissioner. The eldest, Miles, of Sotterly and May Place, Kent, replaced him in 1791 but had little interest in Dunwich. A third son, Snowdon, held the seat from 1796 to 1812, being a lord of the Treasury and later a commissioner for customs. The fifth, Thomas, became chaplain to George III, George IV and William IV. None left sons, so the estate passed to their half-brother Michael, commandant of the 7th (Queen's Own) Light Dragoons in the Netherlands campaign of 1793–94 and on the Helder in 1799.

The Vannecks kept their involvement to the minimum required by the patronage agreement; Dr Pickard found that the freemen once toyed with changing patrons. Sir Joshua nominated his son Gerald, the second baronet, to their Dunwich seat in 1768. He was followed in 1790 by his brother Joshua, the third baronet, who in 1796 became Baron Huntingfield—an Irish title, a technicality enabling him to stay in the Commons, as he did until 1816. His son Joshua, the second baron, spent three years as an MP, then leased the seat to others including Andrew Arcedeckne, a relative by marriage. By marrying a Blois, Joshua completed the family's assimilation into the Suffolk gentry; he was the last Vanneck to sit for Dunwich, though William Arcedeckne, fifth

Opposite page: St James' church with its original 'pepper pot' tower, as designed by Robert Appleton, 1830.
Dunwich Museum

baron and his great-grandson, was Conservative MP for the Eye division, which embraced it, in the 1920s, later serving as Governor of Victoria, Australia.

Despite a government committee's conclusion in 1785 that there was little local risk of invasion as ships had grown too large, Dunwich did play a part in the Napoleonic wars. In 1798 a signal station was built on a site still known as Beacon Hill; manned by "sea fencibles" and used until 1811, it was one of a chain of ten along this coast able to warn of enemy ships and send semaphore messages from Yarmouth to London. And in 1803 a seventy-three-man militia company was raised under Captain Robinson of Dunwich; it saw no service.

March, 1803, brought the mysterious "Battle of Dunwich". Villagers were woken at 2 am by gunfire, flashes of light offshore and the whistle of cannon balls. Word spread that the French were about to land, then the firing ceased. A large vessel was seen crowding on sail away from shore and a smaller one, like a fishing smack, creeping northward close to the beach. The "battle" could have been a figment of the imagination, save for one thirty-two-pound cannon ball: it furrowed the cliff top, passed through a stack of firewood, punched a hole in the Barnes' stable wall and there came to rest. The ball bore the naval broad-arrow marking, but the Admiralty denied any involvement. Some villagers suspected an encounter with smugglers; others felt that if a run had been planned, someone would have known. Maybe the Admiralty suspected the French; when two years later Martello towers were built on sensitive stretches of coast, the most northerly (save for one at Leith) was sited at Aldeburgh.

In 1821 the first Viscount Dunwich was created: the great-great-grandson of the Cavalier Dunwich MP, Sir John Rous. This Sir John, the sixth baronet, was created Baron Rous of Dennington in 1796 and when elevated further chose the titles Earl of Stradbroke and Viscount Dunwich; he himself had no known Dunwich connections. Since his death in 1827 the title has usually been borne by the earl's eldest son, if he has one. The second earl, who served with Wellington in Spain and at Waterloo, did not use it but his son George did. Succeeding as third earl in 1886, he became Lord Lieutenant of Suffolk, Governor of Victoria (before Lord Huntingfield) and a junior agriculture minister. The fourth earl, John Alexander Rous, Lord Lieutenant from 1948 to 1978 and a long-serving county councillor, demolished the house at Henham in 1953; having no sons, he kept the Dunwich title on assuming the earldom in 1947. When he died in 1983 the earldom passed to his elderly brother, who was farming in Australia. William Keith Rous died after five days as earl; his son Robert Keith Rous was thus Viscount Dunwich for five days before becoming the sixth earl, the viscountcy passing to his eldest son. In 1988 the sixth Earl, by now a father of thirteen, returned to Henham vowing, in the face of some scepticism, to build a new home for the Rouses.

Dunwich was by the Napoleonic wars staging a modest recovery, thanks both to the Barnes and a rise in the fortunes of rural East Anglia. After centuries of decline its population rose from around a hundred in 1754 to 184 in the first census of 1801, and 232 in 1831. The reviving community had an inn, the Barne Arms, and a town hall and schoolroom in houses in St James's Street, but no church in use, marriages of Dunwich folk being performed at Westleton. Michael Barne saw the need for one, and in 1826 a village meeting decided that it should be built beside the chapel ruins of St James' Hospital, where a few paupers still lived in squalor. It cost £1,600, towards which the stored bells and lead from All Saints' were sold for £195 3s 6d, two church societies paid £600 and villagers gave generously; Michael Barne found most of the remaining £800 odd. When work began, a mass grave was found; it was first thought to be of lepers, but the bones could have been of plague victims, buried outside the town to check the contagion. Had the bodies been brought for reburial from a grave-yard threatened by the sea, they would surely have been in coffins.

In August, 1832, the Bishop of Norwich consecrated the parish church of St James', Dunwich. Designed in simple classical style by Robert Appleton, its circular "pepperpot" tower displeased Frederick Barne, who inherited the estate in 1837 (Miles Barne was buried in the new family vault in the chapel ruins). He had St James' converted to the Gothic, its white brick clad with flint and given appropriate windows and a square tower concealing the "pepperpot". For years there was puzzlement as to why it was round inside, until a sketch showing the round tower was found; later the original architects' drawings came to light in Lambeth Palace library. St James' was better suited to a small village than All Saints' had been; as built it was even smaller than today, comprising only the nave, 62 feet 3 inches by 21 feet 10 inches, the diminutive porch and the tower, just 8 feet 6 inches wide. Until the chancel, 25 feet 9 inches by 17 feet 8 inches, was added in 1881 for almost £2,000, the gift of Frederick Barne, the altar stood where the chancel screen now is. The first curate was the Reverend Robert Howlett, and the living, worth £40, was in the gift of the patrons of the borough.

Dunwich Corporation had by now been embroiled in a ruinous lawsuit over the right of "wreck" granted by King John. On 26th October, 1827, the Leith smack *Queen Charlotte*, London-bound with seventy-six hundred-gallon puncheons of whisky, was sunk off Lowestoft by the Tyne collier *Silvia*; her crew and seventeen passengers were landed at Yarmouth. On 24th January, 1829, a

Walberswick man found a puncheon on the beach just south of the Blyth and notified Southwold Custom House, where James Sterrey, that town's water bailiff, had it taken. Dunwich sued Sterrey for £100, the value of the whisky, and at Bury assizes on 6th August was awarded 1s damages. The legality of Southwold's act was argued at Westminster in 1831, Dunwich again winning but emerging with lawyers' bills of £864 5s 6d. Sterrey—also deputy harbourmaster, marshal of Southwold's Admiralty Court and clerk of the market—turned out to be insolvent; his committal to a debtors' prison cost Dunwich £50 9s 8d. In all, the borough had to find £1,001 18s 4d (Southwold had to pay Sterrey's costs of £400); its annual income of £150 just covered outgoings, and it had to borrow the money.

At this point a royal commission on municipal corporations was set up to recommend which ancient boroughs should be retained, reformed or abolished. The evidence gathered at Dunwich around 1833 by its clerk, John Buckle, was both detailed and hilarious. He noted that "the town is considered to be rather improving, its buildings have increased, and a new church has recently been erected by subscription". But after listing the quirks of its worthies and the civic body's limited duties, he concluded: "Whether, in its present state, the town requires a distinct municipality may be inferred from the statistical facts."

The corporation had twenty-eight members, burgesses and other freemen, of whom nineteen lived in Dunwich. Each burgess was entitled to two "feeds" for his stock from the marshes and heath, for 2s 6d to 5s per beast. The two bailiffs were elected by the burgesses and "feoffees" from among the fourteen aldermen; they were then Colonel Michael Barne, aged 74, of Latterly Hall, occasionally resident", and 81-year-old Francis Robinson, a gentleman living in Dunwich, probably the son or grandson of the alderman who led the freemen against Sir Jacob Downing. They sat as magistrates and were responsible for the drainage of Minsmere Level; their only privilege was to graze more cattle on the common than the freemen.

The aldermen were chosen by the freemen. After the Reform Act of 1832, three of the seven "resident" aldermen gave up their normal property in Dunwich; those remaining included the landlord of the Barne Arms. The non-residents included Sir Charles Blois of Yoxford, the Reverend H. Unthoff of Huntingfield, Captain John Robinson of the East India Company, Henry Barne Sawbridge, with whom the town clerk had lost touch, and a farmer at Wingfield. Twelve common councilmen were chosen from the freemen, including Lord Huntingfield; the Hon. Thomson Vanneck of Cookley; the Reverend Thomas Barne of Crayford, Kent; two London merchants and William Sawbridge,

Corporation Farm (now Mount Pleasant Farm) built by the borough in 1824. The family home of Lucy Maud Montgomery, author of Anne of Green Gables. Dunwich Museum

address again unknown. Freemen were created by inheritance or by election at their annual meeting for a fee of 1s to 2s; among them were James Mure, borough recorder and a London gentleman; Captain Frederick Barne; the Reverend E. Norton of Southwold; a farmer from Westleton and a coachman.

Eleven civic offices were filled by the freemen. The recorder had until recently had four assistant justices, though his court sat only once a year. The coroner was a 79-year-old alderman of small means who doubled as water bailiff, collecting trifling fees for the custody of wrecks. The town clerk, paid £20 a year, was a Southwold lawyer, and the sergeant-at-mace—bearer of the bolt-shaped civic emblem, town crier and policeman—took the fees from newly admitted freemen. Among "non-charter" officials were an ale founder to check weights and measures, a fen reeve to keep the marshes stocked with game and a chamberlain (the publican), who kept the accounts.

Those accounts showed debts of £1,200: the loan taken out after the Sterrey case plus £200 outstanding on Corporation Farm (now Mount Pleasant Farm), built in 1824. This was let to Robert Woolner, who emigrated to Canada in 1836 with his wife and eight children; in 1911 his great-granddaughter Lucy Maud Montgomery visited Dunwich on her honeymoon—she went on to write *Anne of Green Gables*. The borough's income came mainly from rent on farms, arable land, marsh and heath, and from a toll of 3d recently imposed on each basket of coal landed. The money went mostly on repairs to sluices, piling and farm buildings. The borough's rateable value was £475, its estimated annual rental just over £700.

John Buckle noted:

> The Corporation have no concern with the management of the poor;
> but a privilege which they have allowed on their heath has attracted
> many paupers to the borough. Increased numbers led recently to an
> application by one of the bailiffs for their admission into a workhouse
> of the adjoining hundred of Blything . . . But the application was
> rejected by the directors on the ground that their Act of Incorporation
> would give no control over the Dunwich paupers, if they were admitted.

Poor relief was 3s a week, compared with the 10s farm wage on
which thirty-three Dunwich families were living. The corporation
allowed the poor cheap fuel and used this as a pretext for not
paying them their tiny share of the income from land at Carlton
Colville left by John Pye, or Baxter: of £75 a year from this, divided
with Laxfield, £2 was for the poor of Dunwich. The borough also
appointed the long-serving master of St James' Hospital.

Dunwich still boasted a panoply of courts. The court of record
had lapsed, but the recorder presided each October with a bailiff
and a magistrate over a court of sessions. Buckle wrote:

> It is many years since a felon has been tried, and there is only one
> instance of misdemeanour within the last five years. Since 1829 [the
> report was issued in 1835] no prisoner has been committed to the
> county jail for trial at the assizes.

Dunwich no longer had a prison, "and some inconvenience has
been felt by the lack of one". For the magistrates' court, the bailiffs
were joined by their predecessors, an 84-year-old farmer and Sir
Charles Blois. They also licensed the Barne Arms and appointed
two constables to assist the sergeant-at-mace. The bailiffs no longer
had a civil court, but sometimes convened a court of Admiralty,
when a proctor had to be paid to come from Yarmouth to
represent the parties.

Buckle's survey coincided with the end of Dunwich's representa-
tive in Parliament. Pressure for "rotten boroughs" to make way
for the new industrial cities had long been building. In 1782 the
Corporation refused to sign a petition for Parliamentory reform
from The County Association of York, "appearing to this Assembly
that every innovation to the Constitution may be dangerous"
Indeed it might, for when in 1784 Pitt the younger sought to
disenfranchise thirty-six boroughs; on his criterion of number of
houses, Dunwich would have been one. Luckily for the patrons, the
motion was lost by 248 votes to 174. The French Revolution turned
MPs against such initiatives, one in 1797 being lost by 256 to ninety-
one. The Society of Friends of the People stated in 1793 that one
hundred borough members were returned by 1,449 electors;
Dunwich had forty, Marlborough and Old Sarum just seven apiece.
Yet in a debate that May, R. B. Jenkinson, later Lord Liverpool,

argued that "the close boroughs . . . were absolutely necessary to the Constitution".

Toward the end Dunwich was represented by one Barne and one other, the Vannecks not always sitting themselves. MPs were elected in the Town Hall, then carried shoulder-high past it. At the 1831 general election, Frederick Barne and Charles Pratt, Earl of Brecknock, were returned; Pratt resigned and Viscount Lowther replaced him. As his co-patron was losing interest, Barne may have made the choice himself; both were racing men and Lowther's horse Spaniel had just won the Derby. Lowther, heir to the Earl of Lonsdale and an opponent of reform, had been ousted by Lord Brougham in Westmorland and hoped to sit for Dunwich until he got his revenge.

The Reform Bill introduced after the 1831 election was tougher than any since Pitt's, but enough MPs feared civil strife to give it a second reading by 367 votes to 251. The Dunwich members neither spoke nor voted, even when a new bill was promoted after the Lords rejected reform by a majority of forty-one. The Commons passed it by 324 to 162, and this time the Lords let it through by nine votes, the Duke of Wellington leading a body of abstainers. The Act disenfranchised the smallest boroughs, among them Dunwich, Aldeburgh and Orford; after it nearly five thousand East Suffolk electors returned two members.

The impact on Dunwich was immense, as its whole system was geared to parliamentary patronage. When Buckle asked why Colonel Barne and Lord Huntingfield had the right to nominate half the freemen, civic leaders would only cite "influence of property". He wrote: "Upon all other subjects information was freely given, upon this alone was it denied." Yet he was told how Lord Huntingfield sulked after the Reform Act:

> It has long been the custom of the borough to celebrate the election of municipal officers by an annual dinner given to the freemen. This dinner had for many years been provided by one of the aldermen, at the expense of . . . the patrons or their nominees. In the first year of the Reform Act, the dinner fund disappeared; and the burgesses are now left to pay for their own dinners. Under these circumstances they have had recourse to the corporate fund, and in the [account] for last year appears for the first time a charge for this annual feast.

There was a "farewell donation" from Colonel Barne, but "the other patron has taken leave without any donation".

> "The case", says a venerable magistrate, laying aside his official caution to account for the appearance of a new charge in the corporate expenditure, "stood thus: if I cannot pipe in St Stephen's chapel, you must excuse my declining the purveyorship of the feeding department at Dunwich".

St James's Hospital

St Peters Ch. Dunwich
From an old Etching

Flag

Sluice

uins

DUNWICH HAMLET

Victorian Reverie   25

A S ROMANTICISM blossomed Dunwich became fashionable as an inspiration to aesthetes. The artists came first, drawn by its ruins—notably All Saints', depicted from the 1780s in prints and, later, watercolours and oils. Some were true reproductions; others involved artistic licence. Turner moved the tower to seaward to dramatize a drawing of men launching boats in a fierce sea beneath a stormy sky, and Cornelius Varley, in *The Bishop's Palace, Dunwich*, which won the 1851 Royal Academy Gold Medal, showed a building that would have been opposite the friary ruins but was probably imaginary. Dunwich also attracted Edwin Edwards, a Halesworth-born lawyer who in the 1860s painted, sketched and etched from a cottage opposite the inn. A friend of Fantin-Latour and others of the French School, Edward Fitzgerald termed him a "brave boy but indifferent painter".

The *Punch* cartoonist Charles Keene visited Dunwich for almost thirty years from the early 1860s. Keene, who unnerved villagers by serenading the waves at 10 pm with his bagpipes, drew All Saints' and made an etching of Southwold harbour. Fitzgerald called him "one of our sort, very bookish and fond of art and delightful company". In 1864 Keene wrote: "I enjoy Dunwich so much I can't help talking of next year directly I leave it", and twelve years later: "I'd a very pleasant visit to Dunwich . This is a charming lonely place." The year before his death in 1891 he reminisced: "I pick up every book I can that treats of dear old Suffolk, you will find Dunwich a queer old place."

Local poets took the first literary interest. Henry Dell's musings on the fate of Dunwich and its "sacred dead" appeared in 1818. Next came the more boisterous "Dunwich", by Bernard Barton, a Quaker bank clerk from Woodbridge and a friend of Southey, Byron and Lamb. When Barton asked Lamb if he should become a full-time writer he was told: "Keep to your bank, and your bank will keep you." The reader can judge whether Lamb was right: the poem appears in Dr Pickard's Dunwich anthology. The anthology does not carry in full the next poem written about Dunwich, which is just as well, as it runs to 136 pages. The value of the heroic epic "Dunwich: A Tale of the Splendid City", written in

Opposite page: *St Peter's church; we only have Hamlet Watling's word that it actually looked like this.*
Dunwich Museum

181

1828 by James Bird, postmaster at Yoxford, lies in thirty-four pages of historical notes.

In 1848 the Reverend Alfred Suckling (formerly Inigo Fox) produced *The Antiquities of the County of Suffolk.* In it he wrote:

> Dunwich is so enveloped in the halo of traditionary splendour that he who ventures to elucidate its history by pursuing the path of topographical enquiry must exercise unusual caution, lest he be led by imaginary light. The steady ray which the truth might have shed over its earliest origin is almost wholly extinguished by the violent assaults of the ocean, for, unlike those ruined cities whose fragments attest their former grandeur, Dunwich is wasted, desolate and void. Its palaces and temples are no more, and its very environs presents an aspect lonely, stern and wild, assimilating well with the wreck of its former prosperity.

Agnes Strickland, author of *The Queens of England*, who lived at Reydon Hall, Southwold, also dwelt on past glories. She told Suckling of Sir John Rous's concealment in the oak, and wrote "Dunwich Fair" after reading in Southwold parish register of the seventeenth-century shipwreck. In the early 1820s she sat in All Saints' ruins and wrote:

> Oft gazing on thy craggy brow,
> We muse on glories o'er;
> Fair Dunwich; thou art lowly now,
> Renowned and sought no more.

And in 1849 she published a book of short stories with a Dunwich background.

In 1852 Hamlet Watling, who taught drawing at Dunwich school, published a *History of Dunwich Ancient and Modern*. He also drew the churches of bygone Dunwich, using his imagination where no description existed, and an equally fanciful map of the medieval town, adding to Agas' plan of what survived in late Tudor times. More valuably, Watling made an extensive record of what remained; important drawings of his found in a private collection went on show at the museum in 1988.

One more local author drawn to Dunwich was Edward Fitzgerald, who is best known for his translation of "The Rubaiyyat of Omar Khayamm". He came regularly between the early 1850s and 1878, staying with Joseph Dix, whose house he christened "Dix Hall". He would rise early, sit writing against one of the buttresses of All Saints' in a tall hat and later take a long walk, barefoot, wearing a red bandana and carrying his boots. When not staying in Dunwich, he would anchor offshore in his yacht, the *Scandal*, or drive over with a fellow-author. In 1855 he brought Thomas Carlyle and in 1877 he wrote: "I am starting today for Dunwich—Aldis Wright goes with me and Edwards, the artist, is at Dunwich so we propose to make merry together". The next July he noted: "I have just taken that rough little lodging at Dunwich for the next three months, and shall soon be under those priory walls again—but the poor little Dunwich Roses brought by those monks from the North Country will have passed." His stay was cut short; in October he wrote: "I got little more than a fortnight at old Dunwich, for my landlord took seriously ill and finally died."

Dunwich attracted many well-known writers and poets, who must at first have been surprised to meet each other there. Algernon Charles Swinburne brooded on the Dunwich clifftop during two summers at Wangford, 1875 and 1877, and "felt the fancies which come to those who muse over the relics of this tragic, historic spot". Best-known of his Dunwich poems is "By the North Sea", published in 1883 and dedicated to his companion T. Watts-Dunton, who shared his interest. It began:

> A land that is lonelier than ruin,
> A sea that is stranger than death.

Of All Saints' he wrote three years before:

> Here is the end of all his glory—
> Dust, and barren silent stones,
> Dead like him, one hollow tower and hoary
> Naked in the sea wind stands and moans.

Henry James acclaimed these verses for their "extraordinary poetic eloquence", giving his own view that "there is a presence in what is missing". The American expatriate, in an essay of 1897, declared that what was left of medieval Dunwich was:

> not even the ghost of its dead self; almost all you can say of it is that it consists of the mere letters of its old name. I defy any one, at desolate, exquisite Dunwich to be disappointed in anything. The minor key is struck here with a felicity that leaves no sigh to be breathed, no loss to be suffered; a month of the place is a real education to the patient, the inner vision.

M. R. James, director of Cambridge's Fitzwilliam Museum at the turn of the century and Provost first of King's College and then of Eton, was also a frequent visitor, though he wrote in 1930 that on his previous visit the shell of All Saints' had still been standing; it had evidently been some years before. His knowledge of local lore inspired "A Warning To The Curious", one of the renowned collection *Ghost Stories of An Antiquary*; here he set down the legend of the three crowns.

At the turn of the century Jerome K. Jerome and Sir Harry Rider Haggard were frequent visitors. Jerome took Fitzgerald's old room and easy-chair; he wrote of his visits in his last book, *From My Life and Times*, and was reputedly *en route* to Dunwich when struck down by his final illness. The Norfolk-born Haggard bought a summer home at Kessingland, letting it in 1914 to Rudyard Kipling. Famed for yarns like *King Solomon's Mines*, he forged a link with Dunwich in 1884 in *The Witch's Head*, set mainly in Africa. It reappeared in 1904 in *Stella Fregelius*, so obscure that Haggard's biographer does not mention it, and again in *Red Eve*, written in 1911 and judged among the best third of his output—maybe because Kipling helped him. Haggard was also a member of the Royal Commission on Coastal Erosion, co-opted after telling Lloyd George, then president of the Board of Trade, of his success in checking erosion at Kessingland with marram grass. "I do not suppose there is a groin or eroded beach on the shores of the United Kingdom that I have not seen and thoughtfully considered", he wrote.

Despite the pace of Victorian change, Dunwich remained a backwater. In an age when seaside resorts were springing up, it never became a magnet for holidaymakers (as, sedately, did Southwold); its visitors were either aesthetes or families from villages inland, whose excursions were vividly recalled by the local author Allan Jobson. Its seclusion was enhanced by its distance from a railway, the nearest stations being at Blythburgh on the short-lived narrow-gauge branch from Halesworth to Southwold, and at Darsham on the East Suffolk line. Dunwich's closest contact with the new technologies was a submarine cable to Holland laid in 1858, among the first telegraphic links with the Continent.

Dunwich's population peaked at 294 in 1851, then shrank as the end of "high farming" brought a drift from the land; by 1901 it

Dunwich in busy summer days at the turn of the century. The sea has advanced some way since.
Dunwich Museum

was back to 157. The new church was joined, briefly, by a tabernacle of the Plymouth Brethren, the first non-Anglican place of worship since Charles II's day. And Frederick Barne gave Dunwich a school for sixty pupils in 1853 and built brick cottages for the villagers with lattice windows, Elizabethan chimneys and the Barne crest of three leopards' heads, the assay mark for London. On his death at the age of over 80 in 1886, the estate passed to his son, Lieutenant-Colonel Frederick Barne, of Racecourse Farm, High Sheriff of Suffolk in 1892 and for nineteen years MP for East Suffolk. He died in 1898 leaving a widow, Lady Constance, and three sons; when the eldest, Captain Miles, returned from the Boer War in 1902 she donated the clock that adorns the church tower. The next war would treat her offspring less kindly.

During the nineteenth century the clifftop crept toward All Saints' until it was at imminent risk, and between 1826 and 1901 the parish shrank from 1,360 acres to 1,193. The loss included the last two acres of the Temple demesne, from which the lordship of the manor derived, but the title lived on. The Barnes converted Shrubbery Hall, a shooting-box south of the friary, into a mock Tudor mansion, renaming it Greyfriars; each May the household migrated from Sotterly with cart-loads of silver and impedimenta, staying till the chill September winds set in. Greyfriars, now divided into flats, had in its grounds a circular covered way for exercising bloodstock and a cemetery for the family's horses and dogs. It was reputedly haunted, though ghosts might have preferred the Barne vault in the ruin of St James' Chapel. The house once contained a family collection of relics of ancient Dunwich, but by Suckling's time it had been dispersed. There were two other Barne residences nearby: the Hollies and Racecourse Cottage, just over the parish boundary in Westleton.

The borough was legislated into oblivion in 1882; the last freeman, Mr R. G. Arnott, lived until 1936. In its final years it commuted the burgesses' rights to graze cattle after an outbreak of disease and had to send prisoners to Ipswich gaol for lack of a cell. In place of the borough, as at Orford, a town trust was formed, in 1886, taking on civic property and regalia and the assets of the two hospitals. St James' had survived into Victorian times, its master living in the farmhouse behind the church and the inmates in its outbuildings, but toward the end of the century it gave up the ghost, leaving a small amount of land and £93 9s in cash. What happened to the last inhabitants of the hospitals is unknown. But there is an intriguing reference in the town register of 1836 to the "emigration of paupers from Dunwich to America." Another casualty was St James' Fair, held near the church each 25th July. Most villagers did not mourn its passing; in 1836 the borough had to spend 10s replacing broken church windows, and the next year a bouncer was hired for 2s. There was little such trouble at the horse races held behind Dunwich each summer, apparently under Frederick Barne's patronage. They were very different from what he was used to; he has pride of place in Spy's *Vanity Fair* cartoon "The Jockey Club", printed in 1882.

Dunwich's links with its seagoing past weakened steadily. Once the coal trade ended, the shore was left to a few herring and spratting boats, the pleasure craft of those hardy enough to

'The Jockey Club'
—Col. Frederick Barne,
by Spy, 1882.

attempt a launch and, briefly, a lifeboat. The first move for one was made in 1797, but although the shore was undoubtedly dangerous —thirty ships had been driven on to it in a single storm in 1770—Dunwich was not "sufficiently inhabited by seamen". A distress mortar was installed around 1815, but it was 1873 before the Royal National Lifeboat Institution set up a station on the shingle.

The first boat was the *John Keble*, built with a legacy of £500 from the author of the *Christian Year* and maintained by his family. Of traditional local type with a belt of cork below the gunwale, it was self-righting and had a crew of fourteen; Edward Brown was coxswain and Isaac Dix second-in-command. On its wooden carriage with wheels for running into the sea, it was drawn to the church gate on 9th October, 1873, to be blessed and was then launched. On the way back to shore one of the crew, overcome by the occasion, jumped into the sea; the ebb tide swept him to a safe landfall toward Walberswick[39]. The *John Keble*, with Dix as coxswain from 1877, served almost fourteen years. Near the end, on the night of 20th December, 1886, it went to the aid of the *Day Star* of Ipswich in a violent sea, found the mate clinging to the rigging weak from exposure and got him to safety. Southwold lifeboat took off four more men but the ship's cook drowned; the Southwold coxswain was washed overboard but his mates managed to haul him back. The record states that the *John Keble* "behaved admirably, and the crew showed great pluck".

It was replaced by the larger *Ann Ferguson*, named after Mrs Fergus Fergussen of Bolton, who had left money to the RNLI. Launched in 1887, she was called out five times in seven years, saving twenty lives. On 3rd November, 1888, the barque *Flora* of Oland sank on Sizewell Bank in a gale; one crewman was washed overboard and rescued, and Dix had to beach the *Ann Ferguson* at Sizewell. The *Flora*'s nameboard was hung over the door of the Dunwich tearoom.

A third lifeboat, the *Lily Bird*, entered service in 1894 and was launched three times without saving any lives. In 1895 Dix retired after eighteen years' service; Lady Constance Barne presented him with a purse of gold from the RNLI at a village meeting. The boat was removed in 1903, for three reasons: lack of hands as the population fell, the proximity of Southwold lifeboat, which took over the *Lily Bird's* duties, and erosion of shingle from under the lifeboat hut.

In Living Memory 26

THE LOSS of All Saints' Church cast a long shadow over twentieth-century Dunwich. Its tower had outlived the medieval town, acting as a melancholy inspiration to artists and writers and a landmark for shipping. Yet the symbol was threatened by the decay it evoked; age and neglect caused the collapse of the east end by the 1870s, the crumbling of parts of the chancel walls and the fall of sections of the nave roof. Then the sea arrived to hasten the process. After a cliff fall in February, 1904, the chancel wall "seemed to hang over above, as though the hour had come"[40]. By 1906 the chancel and the east end of the nave had fallen to the shore; three of the nave's five bays had gone by 1912, and at the outbreak of war only the tower and one bay remained. In 1919 most of the tower crashed to the shore, the rest following in 1922. One buttress was rescued and re-erected in St James' churchyard. Erosion also tore bones from All Saints' graveyard, some seemingly from communal graves, dug hastily during the Black Death or when other churchyards were endangered.

The last of All Saints' was still standing when Suffolk regained its own diocese in 1914 after a thousand years: St Edmundsbury, carved from the bishopric of Norwich and including Dunwich deanery, which had continued even when the parish had no church. On 14th August, 1927, Dunwich at last became a place of pilgrimage when the Guild of St Felix and St Edmund held an open-air service in the village; on 8th March the next year the first mass for St Felix since the Reformation was said in a barn there. A "service of the waves" on the clifftop in late August or early September in memory of Felix and King Sigebert became customary; the pilgrimages, promoted by Roman Catholics from Southwold, lapsed in the late 1960s.

In 1934 East Suffolk was given a suffragan bishopric, nominally of Dunwich under an act passed in Henry VIII's reign. George V gave his assent, and the Right Reverend Maxwell Homfray Maxwell-Gumbleton was installed as the first bishop of Dunwich since the ninth century. It became the practice for the Bishop, who is based in Ipswich, to take a service in Dunwich on St James's Day; the present incumbent, the Right Reverend Eric Devenport, has held services on the beach and even conducted baptisms in the sea.

Interest now revived in Dunwich's great days, as opposed to fascination with its humbled state. It was sparked by Ernest Read

Opposite page: *The last buttress from All Saints'; re-erected in St James' churchyard, 1922.* Russell Edwards

189

Cooper, town clerk of Southwold, Suffolk secretary of the Society of Antiquaries of London and writer on local curiosities; his researches paved the way for work by Parker, Dr Pickard, Katharine Chant and others, and he was instrumental in founding the Dunwich Museum. In 1935, at Cooper's suggestion, Michael St John Barne provided a room for exhibits in the old coastguard rocket station; here the charter was brought in 1939 (it is now kept by the county council) to join a number of coins, medieval relics and the whistle Isaac Dix used as village constable. As a member of the Town Trust, Cooper also secured the erection of two almshouses as a memento of the Maison Dieu and recovered the charter of 1215. Missing by Gardner's time, it turned up in the 1920s in the papers of Sir Kenneth Kemp, a descendant of several Dunwich MPs. Sir Kenneth first refused to part with it, then insisted that it go to a museum at Ipswich; in 1939 the trust bought it from his estate.

Michael St John Barne became lord of the manor when only 12, through a double tragedy that Lady Constance thankfully did not live to see. Her youngest son, Seymour, was killed in action in France on 23rd April, 1917, and on 17th September, Miles, commissioned into the Scots Guards and awarded the DSO, died from wounds accidentally received at the front. The second son, Captain Michael Barne of The Hollies, survived, but the manor passed to Miles's son.

The Second World War turned Dunwich into a closed area bristling with fortifications. The marshes were sown with concrete tank traps and flooded, a secret radar station was set up at Minsmere and the ford at Deering Bridge was replaced by a concrete bridge. The old men of Dunwich, unable to fish once the beach was mined, took turns at a lookout post by the last stones of All Saints' graveyard. The friary grounds became home to an anti-aircraft battery; its guns were brought through the gates without a scratch, but after fixing sighting lamps to ancient walls and felling trees towards the clifftop, the unit found it could not track and fire on aircraft skimming the sea without breaching the perimeter wall. Once the threat from the Luftwaffe receded, the battery looked out for flying bombs. One German landmine did fall in the village, exploding near the buttress from All Saints' in St James' church yard; it did little damage. Captain Michael Barne, by then living in Colchester, wrote to Cooper in 1943 that he had heard Dunwich would be evacuated as part of a training area, and told him the next year: "I went as mate of a MFV for the month of June, and had an interesting time during the invasion, but the lack of sleep and hard work laid me up at the end of a month of it." Not surprising at 67.

Michael St John Barne, returning home a lieutenant-colonel in the Scots Guards, decided to concentrate on Sotterly and sever the

link with Dunwich. In 1947 he sold the estate to Commander F. O. G. Lloyd, RN, who gave All Saints' graveyard, the reading room, billiard room and museum to the Town Trust and put the rest of the village up for sale. The auction on 31st October in the ballroom at Greyfriars attracted six hundred people and raised just over £50,000. The big house was knocked down to the Westleton author Allan Jobson for £7,750. "No one was more surprised in this room than myself", he said. "I never came here intending to buy it." Cliff House, with fourteen rooms, went to Mr Spear of Wickham Market for £6,750, and the Barne Arms—soon to be renamed The Ship—was withdrawn at £7,000. Most tenants were able to buy their homes for between £380 and £500. Cooper noted that a local benefactor bought the friary ruins for £850 to "save them from desecration", Greyfriars field and, for £510, the village school, then with just twenty pupils. He concluded[41]:

Dunwich beach awaits the invader, World War II.
Dunwich Museum

> The final result was not so disastrous as was feared at first, but the quiet little old feudal hamlet, all that is left of the proud Saxon city, has alas gone for ever, and sooner or later the horror known as the sea coast developer will thrust in his cloven hoof.

191

Remarkably, this did not happen. Just as Dunwich had escaped the gentry in Regency times when Aldeburgh became fashionable and was passed over for Southwold by Victorian holidaymakers, it survived the motor age. Visitors did come, but not in ruinous numbers. And development was curbed by Dunwich's inclusion first in an Area of Outstanding National Beauty and, in 1973, in the Heritage Coast; the county council stipulated that "all new developments are so sited, and in the case of buildings, that the materials and design are such that no substantial injury to the view results". A café by the Maison Dieu car park and a small caravan site tucked away on the cliffs toward Minsmere are among the few concessions to the age.

Peace and isolation were also fostered by the Forestry Commission's planting of Dunwich Forest on the sandlings; begun in 1929, this accelerated after the war until two square miles of forest afforded a home to red deer. The creation from 1948 of the Royal Society for the Protection of Birds' major sanctuary at Minsmere ensured tranquillity to the south. The reedbeds of Westwood Marshes, providing a high-quality thatch, became a National Nature Reserve through the co-operation of their owner, Sir Charles Blois; efforts by the Countryside Commission to open a coastal footpath were frustrated by the lack of a continuous right of way. And to complete the benevolent regime of semi-public bodies, the National Trust acquired 240 acres of Dunwich Common, including much of the cliffs, from the Town Trust in 1968 with H. J. Heinz Ltd's contribution to Enterprise Neptune.

Some lovers of solitude retired to Dunwich and others bought holiday homes. But at first they were more than offset by an exodus of villagers in search of work; in a decade from 1961 the population fell from 157, the same as in 1901, to 115. Dunwich lost its school in 1964 on the retirement of Miss Laura Semmence, who had taught there for thirty-three years; a mere handful of pupils were left. St James' Church became part of a united benefice, the vicar living at Westleton. But when local government was re-organized in 1974 Dunwich itself rejected a similar merger with Westleton; it retains a parish meeting.

The population rose again toward the 150 mark, partly through Dingle's addition to the parish in 1982. All twelve electors at Little Dingle petitioned to be taken out of Westleton, noting that they had to go through Dunwich on their way to vote. Westleton as a whole voted to keep Dingle, but the Boundary Commission decided to respect the wishes of those most concerned. Tempers ran high, one woman visiting the Right Reverend Kenneth Riches, former Bishop of Lincoln, at his Little Dingle home pledged Westleton to resist the change "by all means short of war". An anomaly caused by erosion was also ended; this had left two detached fragments of Dunwich up the coast to the north. The annexation of Dingle reunited the nearer one with Dunwich. The more northerly one was joined to Walberswick; it had no inhabitants to be consulted.

During the twentieth century the sea has advanced at about a yard per year, not always because of great storms. In the cataclysmic storm of 1953 the tide rose eight feet above normal, the sea driving across the marshes to cut off Southwold and create appalling devastation—but little erosion, owing to the direction of the wind. The same was true of a storm in January, 1976, when a tide 6 feet 6 inches above normal lapped at the grass by St James' Church and the houses of Dingle. One tide that year did eat five feet into the cliff, however, and a storm in January, 1978, with a more northerly wind, made further inroads. The hurricane of 16th October, 1987, which devastated southern England, flattened much of Dunwich Forest but caused little erosion. From the late 1970s the rate slowed because a shingle bank was maintained in front of the cliffs, but it accelerated from the winter of 1987/88 when the shingle was bulldozed northward to protect the marshes. In February, 1989, the sea scoured away most of the shingle to leave a sandy beach, and six feet was eaten from the cliffs in places. On the initiative of Sir Russell Wood, chairman of the parish meeting and a former senior official of the Royal Household, the Anglian Water Authority hurriedly trucked in shingle, augmented by wartime tank traps, to prevent the inundation of the car park and the marshes beyond. Dr Pickard said he had "never seen a public authority move so fast".

Late the following year much of what remained of All Saints' graveyard suddenly collapsed to the shore, including the grave of John Brinkley Easey, an unofficial memorial to the old town, which the parish had been planning to move to St James' churchyard. Easey may not have been the last person buried at All Saint's; a village rumour persists that the remains of two nameless black sailors washed ashore in 1879 were interred there. The cliff fall, reckoned the worst since 1904, also left the seaside path dangerously near the edge, and it was soon diverted inside Greyfriars' seaward wall which itself began to tumble over in 1994.

After All Saints', several potential archaeological sites were lost, notably Temple Hill, after 1925, and the site of Middlegate, in 1968–69. Old Dunwich was now just fifty yards across at its widest near the site of Bridgegate, tapering along the cliffs. Their condition—two visitors were killed in 1959 and one in 1969—meant that only a small area could be safely examined. In 1970 the Ministry of Public Building and Works sponsored a dig in the last thirty yards of the filled-in Palesdyke ditch. It uncovered three pieces of Romano-British pottery, proving "some sort of occupation during that period, but nothing more", and pottery and other articles from the eleventh century onwards. Other relics came to light elsewhere, notably three skeletons under the Maison Dieu car park. A cliff fall in 1988 produced some nondescript pottery and a bunch of apparently medieval needles, and one the next year human bones that trippers insisted on taking home as souvenirs. There was nothing to compare with the freak tide in 1849 that washed up entire primeval trees, or that nearby in 1911 which yielded hundreds of gold, silver and bronze coins—some from early Saxon times—bronze rings, ornaments and an early thirteenth-century clasp.

In 1972 the Earl of Stradbroke opened a permanent museum in a house in St James' Street. The first had closed in 1966 on the death of its curator, Mr Edwin Clarke; the Town Trust, aided by the Museum Service for South-East England, provided a replacement that has attracted thousands of visitors. Its display puts Dunwich's former glories in the context of the area as it is today. In the main room is a model of the town in the late Middle Ages, based on research by Katharine Chant into the street pattern in the earliest parts to be lost. Close by is the town chest, now almost

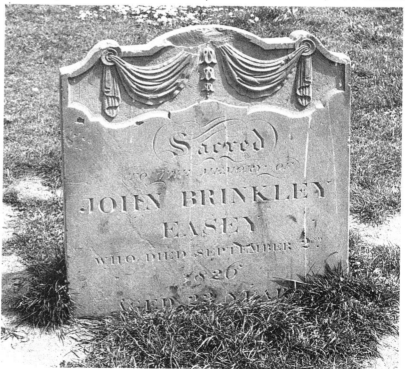

Tombstone of John Brinkley Easey.
Russell Edwards

empty. The civic regalia and relics from each period of the town's history are on show, and explanatory diagrams line the walls. Upstairs are a wildlife display and photographs of Victorian Dunwich onwards, notably a sequence showing the loss of All Saints', arch by arch. Outside stands a large anchor of wood and iron, said by the National Maritime Museum to be from a warship of Nelson's time, which was trawled up by fishermen four miles offshore and brought to the museum in 1989 through the good offices of Admiral of the Fleet Lord Lewin, who had moved to the area on his retirement. Beside it is the "Dunwich cannon", a small late seventeenth- or early eighteeenth-century iron ship's cannon which stood in the village until around 1940, when it was stolen. In 1976 it was mysteriously offered to Stuart Bacon and his divers, who restored it and presented it to the museum with a new carriage.

On 25th April, 1971, divers led by Mr Bacon began probing Dunwich's secrets, using a grid system to trace the extent of the old town; they came first from North-East Essex Sub Aqua Club, and later from his own Dunwich Underwater Expedition. Relics they have recovered are on show in the museum; a permanent Dunwich exhibition over Mr Bacon's craft shop at Orford includes a display of their work. Dispute continues over whether objects found on the seabed would have come from whatever building stood at that point; currents will have moved much of the debris, though the prevailing southward drag is offset off Dunwich by a pull in the other direction. Finding anything is hard enough: the water is usually very cold and visibility often down to inches, seldom extending to twenty feet. Conditions are worst in the area of the Daine, but everywhere divers have been handicapped by movement of the seabed sediments, which can obscure masonry discovered only days before. Below water the shingle slopes rapidly to a bed of mud and sand twenty to thirty-five feet down, running half a mile out to sea; beyond this trough a sandbank runs north and south only a few feet below the surface. Under this much of the debris of Old Dunwich could lie.

In the first month the divers found a sizable part of All Saints' tower lying across ruins that had fallen earlier. Their luck continued: on 12th September, 1971, a seventy-pound piece of carved stone was found nearby and on 27th November a 133-pound flagstone where the debris of the Temple was thought to lie. The next year they located timber and undergrowth a mile out, maybe from the Eastwood, slabby remnants of Second World War defences and an immovable handle—apparently of silver—protruding from stonework among the ruins of All Saints'. But the "find" of 1972 was a piece of gravestone half a mile out, close to where St Peter's would have stood. Brought ashore with difficulty and presented to the museum, it had carried a brass from the early fourteenth century. A larger piece of marble found nearer the All Saints' site in 1979 apparently came from a stone about nine feet long bearing a life-size brass of a knight, with lettering of the type used by London masons around 1320.

The search continued, interspersed by dives for relics of the Battle of Sole Bay and a Great War submarine. In 1972 a yacht was wrecked on the shore as divers watched. Unexploded bombs have come to light and once a large shark appeared. The divers often untangled fishing nets from objects on the seabed, one possibly a cannon. On 20th May , 1973, Mr Bacon found ruins he reckoned were from St Peter's, and a year later he found an octagonal stone object three feet across, apparently a font or its base, in sand near the site of the Temple. He tied a marker to it, but returned to find the marker fixed to a wartime obstacle. Around the same time the divers also saw a church window near where St Nicholas' would have stood. In 1981 they found just offshore a wealth of carved stone including two twelfth-century imposts, possibly from the Maison Dieu chapel. The expeditions grew and gained commercial sponsorship; that of 1983 housed equipment in marquees on the beach and attracted two American military divers. Its harvest was a master mason's plumb-bob, twelfth- and thirteenth-century stonework, the neck of a seventeenth-century bellarmine jug and an early seventeenth-century Nuremberg token. In April, 1987, the divers raised tracery, a mullion and a sill from a medieval church window. There could be more to come.

Opposite page:
Middlegate Street, now only a footpath, looking towards the sea. The last surviving rustic bridge is in the foreground; beyond it the makeshift fence marks the cliff edge after another winter of erosion, April 1991.
Russell Edwards

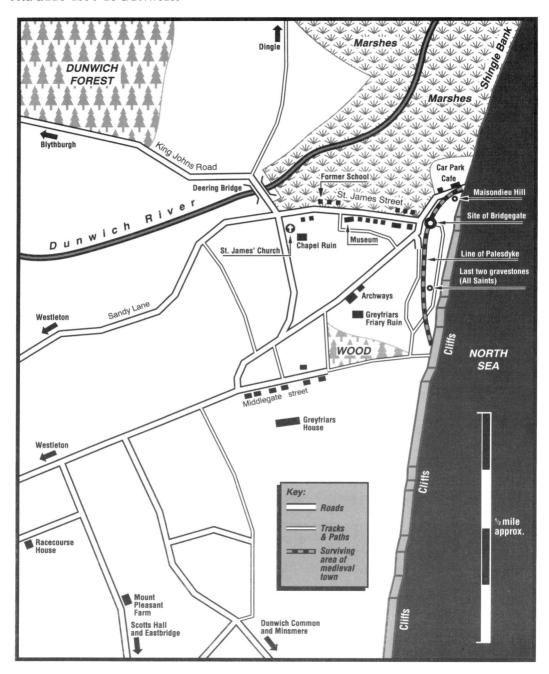

Dunwich Today— 27
and Tomorrow

DUNWICH today is a village of some 150 souls on perhaps the nearest long stretch of unspoiled coastline to London (provided the nuclear power stations at Sizewell are disregarded). Apart from roads to the towns of Southwold and Aldeburgh/ Thorpeness, minor roads reach the shore at only five points in eighteen miles. Dunwich is at one of these points, though it has turned its back to the sea. From the corner of St James' Street and the lane from Westleton, a track (once Bridge Street) leads over a rise to the shore, where a few fishing boats are beached. To the left is the car park on the site of the Maison Dieu, and beside it the café, replacing a less elegant one burned down on Easter Monday, 1988; fire engines called when a villager saw flames at 4 am were too late. To the north stretch the shore and shingle bank backed by marshes, round the bay toward Walberswick, the Blyth and Southwold; crumbling sandy cliffs stretch south toward Minsmere.

The village is in two parts. To the south, Middlegate Street begins on the cliff edge as an overgrown path and runs inland as a hollowed way through a wood with the friary wall to its right. There were three rustic bridges over it, but one fell to the beach between the wars and a second fell in 1969. Several houses, none of great age, line the paved section to the Westleton road; Greyfriars is set back to the left, with other large houses beyond. A walk round the perimeter of the friary grounds and ruin is well worth while. From the car park one reaches the clifftop by a path known as Lovers' Lane, the last remnant of St James' Street within the Palesdyke. The path has been diverted inside the friary walls away from the edge of the cliff, but walkers can still see a narrowing strip of scrub and the last of All Saints' graveyard, now owned by the parish church; just two gravestones now lie half-obscured by the bushes. It then turns inland into Middlegate, then right along a track by the friary's west wall, joining the lane from Westleton which descends by a series of twists and turns to pass the friary gateway, more imposing than the ruin in the field beyond.

The larger part of Dunwich starts at the foot of this lane and slants away from the sea, west-north-west along St James' Street. The first building to landward is the seventeenth-century Ship Inn, then there is a row of late medieval houses, in the middle the final Town Hall and at the end the museum. After an open space come more recent homes, set back from the road, then a crossroads. On

Opposite page:
Dunwich today. Only a sliver of the medieval city remains, and the village comprises two clusters, one on St James' Street and the other on Middlegate Street. The cliffs are still retreating, and the shingle bank to the north is in danger of being breached by the sea. Oliver Bradbury and Adam Green.

the left is St James' Church, with the ruined hospital chapel behind it, and beyond it a farm. Sandy Lane, the medieval route to Westleton and the south, lies ahead, and King John's Road bears right over the wartime Deering Bridge across the trickle of the Dunwich river, beyond which a track forks through a farmyard to Dingle. To seaward of the street are Victorian and older houses, some bearing the Barne arms; among them are the old school, the store and post office and the cottages where Fitzgerald and his fellow-aesthetes once stayed.

Visitors to Dunwich—and at summer weekends it is crowded —include "surf-canoeists", walkers in search of peace and nature and a steady trickle of searchers for the medieval city. Expectations vary; some peer hopefully out to sea and others are amazed at what has survived: the ruin, gate and walls of the friary, the ruin of St James' Chapel, the museum, St James' Street and Middlegate Street, and the last sliver of churchyard atop the cliff.

Most have two questions: what still awaits discovery, and will Dunwich eventually disappear? It is a safe bet that more relics lie buried. The friary grounds have been a fruitful source of coins and domestic articles from bygone ages. The Maison Dieu site has produced the odd skeleton and may yield more of interest, though work on the foundations of the new café revealed nothing. The site of Bridgegate, beneath the track leading shoreward from the corner of St James' Street, could also be of interest. Little came to light at Middlegate, but as Bridgegate was the main entrance to the town in its great days, the chances might be greater. The washing up of relics by the sea should continue, and there could be more bonuses like the finding in April, 1989, by metal detectors—fortunately responsible ones—of a hoard of 482 twelfth-century silver coins at Wicklewood, Norfolk, which included the first coins indisputably minted at Dunwich. An inquest at Dereham declared the hoard treasure trove, and after the British Museum had its pick 320 of the coins went on sale at Christie's in May, 1990; they raised £26,037, one Dunwich penny fetching £902.

Dunwich's future is hard to predict, as there is no guarantee that the rate of erosion will be constant. Moreover, two processes are at work that could in due course leave it on a headland. The cliffs continue to retreat; the seaward wall of the friary is going and the ruins could be threatened by 2150. The last of Maison Dieu Hill, just fourteen feet high, could before long be engulfed by shingle. The buildings that line St James' Street face no threat from erosion, but in 1989 the sea almost broke through to the car park and the meadows between it and the street. If the shingle bank of the bay cannot be maintained—or if the "greenhouse effect" takes hold—the freshwater reedbeds that were once part of the estuary will again become an inlet of the sea.

Opposite page:
Dunwich Museum with the Napoleonic ship's anchor by its door.
Russell Edwards

Further Reading

DOZENS of books touch on some aspect of Dunwich's history, but most confine themselves to a passing statement that a once great town has been lost to the sea. A number go into more detail, but just ten or so tell enough of the story to have been sources for this work and to offer something more.

The one recent full-length book on Dunwich is Rowland Parker's *Men of Dunwich*, published by Collins in 1978. It draws heavily on the author's study of medieval documents to paint a picture of life in Dunwich towards the end of its great days, laced with semi-fictional episodes. In conversation style, Parker, a former Cambridge schoolmaster who died in 1989, brought Dunwich's influential families to life, catalogued the town's disputes with its neighbours and corrected some errors of earlier historians.

The Elizabethan chronicler John Stow made two important contributions to the history of Dunwich, both of which are significant sources for this book. His *Visit to Dunwich*, of 1573 is in the British Library; it provides the finest eye-witness account of the death-throes of the medieval town. Stow's *Chronicles of England from Brute unto this Present Year of Christ 1580* is important as the source for dates of several of the storms that afflicted the town, both in medieval and in Tudor times. Though a fascinating read, it is not easily available.

Another useful source, and well worthwhile for further reading on a broader front, is Francis Blomefield's twelve-volume *History of Norfolk*, published at the turn of the eighteenth and nineteenth centuries. While its references to Dunwich are incidental, they give a clue to the wealth of material the work contains not just about Norfolk but the history of the whole of East Anglia.

Surprisingly many copies survive of Thomas Gardner's invaluable history of Dunwich and its neighbours, published in 1754. It has the daunting title *A Historical Account of Dunwich, Anciently a City, now a Borough, Blythburgh, Formerly a Town of Note, now a Village, Southwold, once a Village, now a Town Corporate, with Remarks on Some Places Contiguous Thereto*. This lively if unstructured work contains a wealth of information from sources since lost, with copious illustrations. Also useful on detail is the *Victoria County History of Suffolk*, first published in the nineteenth century, which places Dunwich in a wider perspective.

If you can find a copy, *Glorious Dunwich its story throughout the ages* by the Rev Norman Gay (Suffolk Press, Ipswich, 1947) is also valuable. The then vicar of St James' manages in 120 pages to give an accurate account of what was then known and quote at length from surviving borough registers. There is also a memorably snooty foreword from the Bishop of the day.

The Search for Dunwich, City Under the Sea, by Stuart Bacon and his late wife Jean, published by Segment in 1979, is a highly readable account of the divers' early operations. It captures the romance of the Dunwich story, giving legend the benefit of the doubt, and quotes Stow's letter of 1573 in full. *Dunwich, Suffolk*, from the same stable is shorter and brings the story further up to date.

Major Ernest Read Cooper's *Memories of Ancient Dunwich*, published by the Southwold Press in 1931 and updated since, is also valuable. It combines gleanings from medieval and later records with childhood memories of Victorian Dunwich.

Briefer but highly informative is *The History of Dunwich*, by Katharine Chant. Published by the museum in 1974 and updated in 1986, it is as clear and accurate a pocket guide as one could find.

Dr Ormonde Pickard's *Dunwich: Time, Wind and Sea—Poems 1173–1981*, published by the museum in 1983, brings together twenty-seven poems inspired by Dunwich, from Fantosme's account of the siege of 1173 to verses by Anthony Thwaite, with prose passages and historical notes. Dr Pickard has also written *Dunwich—the Rotten Borough*, an entertaining paper on the doings of "King John" Benefice, Sir George Downing, the Barnes and the Vannecks; it is on sale at the museum.

Finally, *The Parish Church of St James, Dunwich*, an eight-page booklet on sale at the church, tells its full story.

A number of books have more to tell about the surrounding area over the centuries. Daniel Defoe's account of his travels, Dowsing's diary, James Bird's epic poem, the Reverend Alfred Suckling's *Antiquities of the County of Suffolk* (John Weale, 1846–8, 2 vols) and Redstone's engaging *Memorials of Old Suffolk* are all of interest, but the following are more recent and easier to find:

Bates, Martin. *Regional Military Histories: East Anglia*. Osprey.
Jobson, Allan. *Suffolk Villages*. Robert Hale.
Jobson, Allan. *Victorian Suffolk*. Robert Hale.
Read Cooper, Ernest. *A Suffolk Coast Garland*. Heath Cranton.
Scarfe, Norman. *The Suffolk Landscape*. Alastair Press, 1987 (revised edition).
Strugnell, K. W. *Seagates to the Saxon Shore*. Terence Dalton, 1973.
Steers, J. A. *The Coastline of England and Wales*. Cambridge University Press, 1946.
Thompson, Leonard P. *Smugglers of the Suffolk Coast*. Boydell Press.

References

1. *The Guardian*, 20.5.1989.
2. *Daily Chronicle*, 8.4.1904.
3. Gay, *Glorious Dunwich*, p. 72.
4. *The Listener*, 22.7.1976.
5. Morris, *The Age of Arthur*. Weidenfeld, 1973, p. 562.
6. Butler, *Lives of the Saints*, 1956.
7. The Anglo-Saxon Chronicle says 636.
8. Bede, *Historia Novella*, ed. Plummer, 1896, vol. 2.
9. Pevsner, *The Buildings of England: Suffolk*. Penguin, 1961.
10. Leland, *De rebus Britannicis Collectanea*, vol. III, p. 24.
11. Blomefield, *History of Norfolk*, vol. III, p. 454.
12. *Journal of the British Archaeological Association*, XXIV (1961), pp. 55–9.
13. Matthew Paris, *English History 1235–73*, 3 vols., Henry G. Bohn, 1852–4.
14. Parker, *Men of Dunwich*, p. 53.
15. Ibid., p. 37.
16. Ibid., p. 26.
17. Ibid., p. 170.
18. Ibid., p. 210.
19. Read Cooper, *Memories of Bygone Dunwich*, p. 7.
20. From court document referred to by Allan Jobson, *Victorian Suffolk*.
21. Parker, p. 76.
22. Tobias Gentleman, *England's Way to Win Wealth*, 1614.
23. Quoted in H. Aitken Tripp, *Suffolk Sea Borders*.
24. Parker, pp. 250–3.
25. W. S. Bevan, unpublished study of the ecology of Dunwich, 1961.
26. Redstone, *Memorials of Old Suffolk*, 1908.
27. Read Cooper, pp. 14–15.
28. Ibid., pp. 4–5.
29. Monastic chronicle quoted by Stow.
30. Parker, pp. 150–1.
31. Ibid., p. 248.
32. Ibid., p. 206.
33. Ibid., p. 159.
34. Ibid., p. 243.
35. Holinshed.
36. Landsdowne MS, British Library, no. 213 of 315.
37. Dr O. G. Pickard, *Dunwich—the Rotten Borough*, p. 4.
38. Ibid., p. 7.
39. Read Cooper, p. 32.
40. *Daily Chronicle*, 8.4.1904.
41. Read Cooper, p. 41.

Index

illustrations in bold type

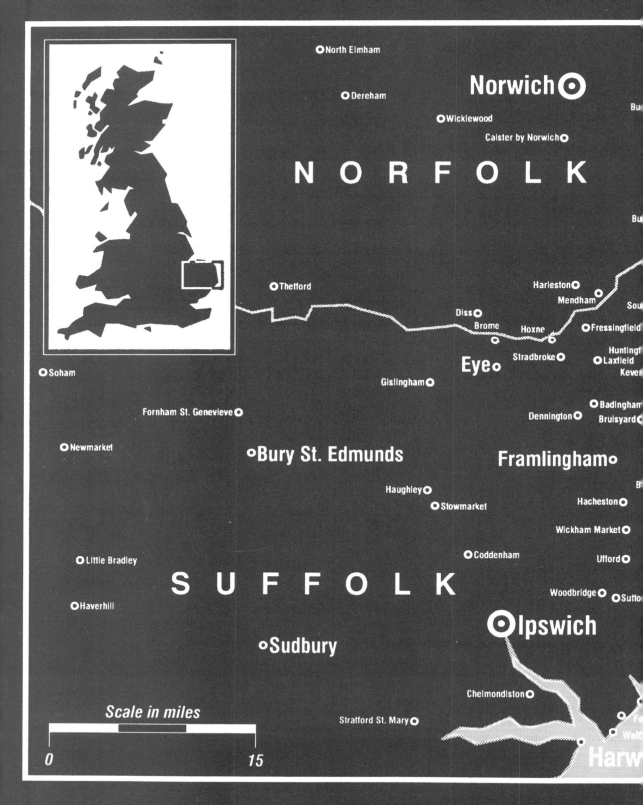